2 -
1/22

Camaraderie

Celebrating Faith, Learning and Living at Harding University

1987-2013

DAVID B. BURKS

COPYRIGHT

DEDICATION

The Harding family comprises many constituencies, all of whom are absolutely essential to its ongoing operation and success and – all of whom I appreciate more than I can ever express. But the bottom line for any educational institution, especially Harding University, is its students.

We have been blessed to have some of the brightest and best young people anywhere in the world in our student body. We have been given opportunities to develop amazing lifetime relationships with students for whom we have become friends, teachers and mentors. We have learned from and been inspired by our students' faith and their desire to share the love of God with people all over the world.

My greatest joy as president of this great institution has been interacting with students, and it is to them that I thankfully dedicate this book that chronicles our twenty-six years together.

"*The fountain in the plaza between the McInteer building and Benson auditorium is representative of the living water that Jesus provides. This fountain is my favorite spot on Harding's campus. Its design is patterned after a baptistery in Ephesus where many people have been baptized over the years. I provided a picture of the Ephesus fountain to the architect for our fountain, and he designed the steps and baptistery with the same dimensions as the one in Ephesus.*" – David B. Burks

ACKNOWLEDGMENTS

This book is my attempt to share part of the celebration of our mission at Harding over the twenty-six years that I was privileged to serve as president. I could not have completed the responsibilities connected with this job without the Harding family – trustees, faculty, staff, students, parents, donors and community members. Certainly, I could not have completed it without the help of my family.

I would first express appreciation to members of Harding Board of Trustees, who asked me to assume this position in 1986, uplifted me, encouraged me and empowered me to serve as president. I am grateful for their prayers, and I am grateful for the tough policy decisions they made that allowed Harding to prosper.

Second, I want to thank the faculty for their belief in the Harding mission and their willingness to express their faith in the teaching process as they interact with students. Harding has been blessed with great faculty members who steadfastly believe in the mission of Harding.

Third, I would express thanks to every member of the staff at Harding. Whatever your role, you have embraced the responsibility to implement Harding's programs. Harding has been blessed with a dedicated staff of individuals who serve our students in the cafeteria, clean the dorms, answer the phones, issue financial aid, admit students, answer their questions in the residence halls late at night and, in fact, act as parents away from home.

Fourth, I thank our student body – the best student body in the world. Our students come from the entire world, and they want to serve God and His fellowman. They have been an inspiration to me, and I have loved working with all of our students.

Fifth, I express thanks to parents, alumni and donors for their unwavering support of our mission at Harding. We could not exist without them. They have been a blessing to us in our work in every way. I am also grateful for members of the Searcy community who have supported us so beautifully.

I would particularly express thanks to members of my administrative cabinet, who have provided insight and leadership for me on a day-to-day basis. These men and women were invaluable partners as we made decisions relative to our work at Harding.

A very special thanks is extended to Claudette Bratcher and Cindy Hunter, who worked with me for the entire twenty-six years as administrative assistants. They were such a blessing to me as they served as the voice of Harding.

Words would fail me in expressing appropriate appreciation to members of my family for their support over this period of time. I especially thank Leah for supporting and encouraging me as this job kept me away from home a great deal of the time. She served well as first lady of Harding and represented Harding in a beautiful way. I also thank my sons, Bryan and Stephen, our grandchildren and all of our family for their support during this period of our lives.

Finally, with respect to this effort to compile some of the events and stories that made up my time as president, I express thanks to Will Waldron, my research assistant, for his hard work and insight into this project. I express thanks to Claudette Bratcher for typing the manuscript and making wonderful suggestions, to Debbie Berry for helping make last-minute corrections and to Tim Cox for formulating the index. I express thanks to Kay Gowen, who served as general editor and was responsible for laying out the book. She has been a blessing to me for many years. I also express thanks to the people who served as an advisory committee for this book, providing valuable insight – Bruce McLarty, David Collins, David Crouch, Greg Harnden, Jim Carr, Kay Gowen, Keith Cronk, Larry Long, Liz Howell, Mel Sansom, Mike Williams and Will Waldron.

❖ David B. Burks

FOREWORD

by Bruce McLarty

Last summer, I had the opportunity to attend a week-long seminar for new university presidents. There were fifty of us in the class, and all of us had recently stepped into a leadership role that was, to say the least, overwhelming in its scope and significance. The instruction we received that week was outstanding, but by far the greatest impact that the seminar had on me came from my interaction with my forty-nine classmates. Somewhere during the week, I became aware of how unique my situation at Harding University was. Almost all of the other presidents had little, if any, contact with their predecessors. For some, the previous president had been fired, and in most situations the president had left town. It seemed that more often than not, the presence of the former president was viewed as a source of embarrassment or potential conflict. Harding, I began to realize, is not the norm when it comes to presidential succession.

As I write this, Harding University is entering its 91st year. During that time, we have had only five presidents and five chief academic officers. I have yet to find anyone who knows of a university that has had such a record of stability and continuity in its leadership. More than that, every one of these leaders has stayed in the community and continued to teach, mentor, raise money and, often, even hold some other position within the University. This has given us an unbroken thread of continuity in our history and in the mission of this school. Dr. David Burks now takes his place in this amazing story of leadership succession at Harding University.

I am honored to have been invited to write an introduction for this important book, written by my friend and mentor, David Burks. For fourteen years, I was his preacher, and for much of that time, he was one of my elders at the College church. Then, in 2005, he hired me to work at Harding as the Vice President for Spiritual Life. Ann and I have been blessed by the friendship and encouragement of David and Leah. They are truly wonderful people and beloved Harding University icons.

Harding and how to survive the fishbowl of being a college president's family. At every opportunity, they have encouraged us, supported us, shared with us and, most importantly, loved us. Dr. Burks now serves as our University Chancellor and has an office near mine – across the lobby of the building that now bears his name, the David B. Burks American Heritage Building. He is continuing the rich tradition we have at Harding where former presidents stay around and, in so doing, bless both the next president and the entire University.

In this volume, Dr. Burks mentions the ceremony of the key exchange on May 31, 2013. It was the Friday before I would assume the presidency on Saturday morning, June 1. On that occasion, he expressed to the crowd his gratitude for the opportunity Harding had given him to serve as president for twenty-six years. It was a labor of love he had tirelessly given himself to from 1987 until that day in 2013. Then, after saying some kind and affirming things about the new president, he invited me to speak. For that occasion, I had chosen to read two scripture texts, one about him and the other about me. The first was from Paul's sermon to the church in Antioch of Pisidia. The apostle said about King David of Israel, "... he had served God's purpose in his own generation..." (Acts 13:36). I think it is always easier to see the hand of God in the lives of others than it is in our own life. Looking back over the twenty-six years of David Burks' presidency, it seems undeniable to me that he truly "served God's purpose in his own generation." His administration was a phenomenal success. Under his capable leadership, Harding University grew and developed in impressive ways. Most importantly, during the Burks tenure, the University remained faithful to the Christian mission on which it was founded.

The second text that I chose to read on that day contained the words of Solomon when he was asked what he would like the Lord to give him as he began his reign. Solomon answered,

> *... I am only a little child and do not know how to carry out my duties. Your servant is here among the people you have chosen, a great people, too numerous to count or number. So give your servant a discerning heart to govern your people and to distinguish between right and wrong. For who is able to govern this great people of yours? (1 Kings 3:7-9).*

This text, which has become my prayer each morning, expresses well the burden of leadership. I clearly remember the feelings I had at the key exchange – of walking into something that was more than I could do. That is why it is especially meaningful to me to read in this book that on the day Dr. Burks was invited to become the president of Harding, he, too, "was both honored with and terrified of the responsibility." There was no way he could know what lay ahead for him in the next twenty-six years. That is why this book is so important; it details the challenges that both he and Harding University faced during his tenure and the faithfulness of God in doing "immeasurably more" than all President Burks could have asked or imagined (Eph. 3:20).

Finally, I need to say something about Dr. Burks' favorite word. "Camaraderie" is not only the perfect name for this book; it is the only title that would have been appropriate. Initially the name of a newsletter he published when he was dean of the College of Business, it came to be the term that is most closely connected with the presidency of David Burks. Each year on the first day of chapel, he would call on some unsuspecting freshman to stand and spell "c-a-m-a-r-a-d-e-r-i-e." More often than not, the new student failed the test. Dr. Burks would then proceed to teach us not only how to spell the word but also that it meant "high-spirited fellowship." We could all see that, for David Burks, that is what the Harding experience is all about.

Last year, as I approached my first day of chapel as president of Harding, I was at a loss for what to do. The returning students had been conditioned by Dr. Burks to expect the traditional spelling of "camaraderie" to be a centerpiece of the morning. However, to me, "camaraderie" felt like his word, not mine. Eventually, I decided that I would take a hand-held microphone, walk back to the center of the auditorium where Dr. Burks was seated and ask him to spell the word. I took a video of the moment with my iPhone so that I could send it out as a tweet. Dr. Burks stood and spelled the word with gusto, and the students gave a thunderous ovation to this man they dearly love. Now, in this volume, he gives a special gift to the entire Harding family by describing his own remarkable Harding experience. I guess you could say he is still teaching us the importance of camaraderie!

Today's the Day to Pass the Key to the President's Office

CONTENTS

"Joseph and the Amazing Technicolor Dreamcoat"

PROLOGUE

One of my favorite experiences as president of Harding University occurred on the first day of chapel each semester. During the first few years at that time, I would ask several freshmen to spell "camaraderie" and define it. They generally were unable to spell it, but they seemed to get a lot better at it in the last few years. It was a way for me to make a point about high-spirited fellowship at Harding – and about family and what our work is all about. I had no idea that it would become the word people would use to describe my term as president.

Sometimes on this first day in chapel, I would ask students to greet a neighbor with an Italian kiss. I loved having students who had been to our program in Italy demonstrate how this should be done. Faculty helped as well but were not as good as the students. The true way to do an Italian kiss is to kiss the person on the right cheek first and then the left. You are not to touch the skin – just get close. That is the Harding way. Of course, if you forget the order and one goes left and the other goes right, you can have a problem. One of the great blessings at Harding is the close fellowship that develops over time in this intentional Christian community.

What is camaraderie? It is Saturday night at Spring Sing when they announce the winners at the end of the show. The stage is full of unbelievably excited people, and the audience is filled with excited visitors, parents and friends. While you may not be able to define it, you can feel camaraderie in the air. It is high-spirited fellowship where lasting relationships are created. I especially appreciated Spring Sing 2007, when "Camaraderie" was chosen as the theme.

I also see camaraderie in the Homecoming musicals, which I have loved all the time I have been at Harding. I am amazed at the work that is put into the musicals by those who perform, those in the orchestra, those behind the stage, and the faculty and staff who work with them. My all-time favorite musical was "Joseph and the Amazing Technicolor Dreamcoat."

Another great example of camaraderie is the Rhodes Rowdies, whose home is the Rhodes Field House. I enjoyed the gym full of students, faculty, staff and friends cheering on the Bisons. I liked the Harding band and the drums. I was thrilled at Harding being selected as the Best Road Trip in Basketball in 2012. That is high-spirited fellowship.

Camaraderie can take many forms. I recall beginning fall semesters for years with a gospel meeting that typically lasted one week, with speakers in chapel and at night as well. I remember Neale Pryor, Jimmy Allen and others speaking for these meetings when we would have 100 or more students respond either for prayer or to be baptized and hundreds of students coming forward to encourage those who had responded. This event often set the spiritual tone for our campus each year.

One of my favorite examples of camaraderie involved a week-long series in chapel, called "Struggles of the Faith." This special week showcased stories by people who had experienced difficult situations as they shared how God had led them through these tough times. It was a blessing to hear from these individuals. The Harding family continues to be blessed by these heartfelt testimonials.

Perhaps the very best example of camaraderie comes from singing in chapel – especially the days when the singing is just beyond description, and all are

singing their hearts out in praise to God. I particularly loved chapel singing when we were all in the Benson together with the balcony full, chairs along the side and students in the orchestra pit. What a sound and what a memory to have more than 4,000 people singing in one place! From my front row seat on these days, I believe I caught a glimpse of heaven.

Another example of camaraderie was shown to me by students who experienced our social club system. Students go through an induction week activity that is quite intense. The whole purpose is to draw students close to one another, to become brothers and sisters, and to develop lasting relationships that will last not only during this life but also in eternity.

Of course, camaraderie does not have to be something found in large crowds. It can be in a small home Bible study of students and faculty who study, pray and bond together. It can be in a small prayer group when people simply meet and share their needs, their love for each other and their concerns for the world. It can be found in mission

teams, perhaps just three or four people who go to Africa or Italy or anywhere in the world and form a bond that will last forever.

Camaraderie may also be experienced in an International Studies Program. It may involve a memorable devotional in Zambia, in Greece at the top of Mars Hill or in Italy at Cinque Terre overlooking the sea. For me, Gordon's Tomb in Israel, just outside the gates of Jerusalem, is a place I will always associate with the camaraderie of our group in focusing on the resurrection of our Lord.

For many students, camaraderie is rooted in memories they share from living in a residence hall for three or four years and the late-night times they shared together and learned from each other. This might be one of the best forms of camaraderie.

I particularly love the May graduation experience because it is such a happy occasion, not only for the students but for the parents, uncles, aunts and friends who are there to celebrate. It is a time for big smiles, tears, hugs and bittersweet memories. I can picture so many of these graduations as I associate camaraderie with completion and commencement.

Camaraderie reminds me of legacy as well. One of my fondest memories as president was the dedication of Legacy Park, our newest housing development. It is dedicated to men and women who loved Harding and gave their lives for it to progress. I hope we are always grateful for all of those people who have preceded us because we stand on their shoulders.

One of my favorite experiences was to observe baptisms at Uplift during the summer. I remember one night standing in the C.L. Kay Plaza in front of the McInteer Center and witnessing more than 100 students baptized into Christ. Most of the Harding family is gone during the summer and unable to witness this kind of event.

I have experienced it for years, and it is always a great encouragement to me.

What do all of these experiences have in common? Over my twenty-six years as president, I simply lump them all into a category I call "camaraderie." I used the concept to describe the sense of community, family and high-spirited fellowship I wanted everyone to experience as part of the Harding family. I defined it as a sense of connection and belonging. I called it a celebration of faith, learning and living.

I am amazed at how many students remembered the word "camaraderie." When I traveled to speak at various churches, I was never surprised when students asked me about Harding and spoke of camaraderie! On numerous occasions, I would speak at a church, and there would be Harding graduates seated on one row with a sign spelling out camaraderie, each person holding a different letter.

I considered a different title for this book, perhaps calling it "stories about celebrating life at Harding University 1987-2013," but as I talked with friends concerning this project, everyone encouraged me to use the word that best defined my presidency – "camaraderie."

As you read through this book, I hope you will see numerous examples of high-spirited fellowship and the development of lasting relationships as portrayed by the stories of faculty, students, administration and friends who make up the Harding family.

The beautiful campus quadrangle welcomes students each fall

PART ONE
Introduction

David Burks as a student in 1964-65

CHAPTER ONE
Preparation for Leadership

<u>Enrolling at Harding</u>

During my senior year in high school at Truth or Consequences, N.M., I decided to enroll at Harding. My only knowledge of Harding had come from our local minister, Brodie Crouch, who graduated from Harding in 1948. I had known Mr. Crouch for many years, and he had baptized me into Christ. I had always planned to go to New Mexico State University or the University of New Mexico, where my friends were going, but he suggested that it would be good for me to come to Harding for at least one year to study the Bible. My plan was to stay for one year and then transfer to a "good" university in New Mexico.

My father and mother were supportive of my coming to Harding, but they knew practically nothing about it. My dad had read about Dr. George Benson and his anti-communism fight, but he knew very little about Harding. Late in my senior year, I wrote to Harding and, through correspondence with Dr. Joe Pryor, obtained a scholarship in photography to work on the *Petit Jean* yearbook, which helped me make the decision from a financial perspective. I had no idea as to the influence Dr. Pryor would have on my life in the years to come.

I remember driving to Searcy for the first time by myself in 1961. I was driving the car of my dreams – a green 1949 Ford. I decided to go to Missouri on my way to Arkansas to visit relatives in the Springfield area. I then turned the car south toward Arkansas, drove through Harrison and came to Searcy County. I thought I was in Searcy, but I found out that Searcy was in White County, further south. I remember arriving in Searcy and parking behind Armstrong Hall. Despite the heat that August day, I stayed in the car for what seemed to be a long time before getting the courage to go to my room. I met Dot and Cecil Beck, who were managers of the dorm, and they were the first members of the Harding family to welcome me to campus.

Student Activities

One of the first people I met as I left the dorm was Dr. Pryor, dean of the college and an icon, but I didn't know him. I knew he was sponsor for the *Petit Jean*, on which I worked for four years, loving every minute of it. Like many other students, I was invited into the Pryors' home and took trips to Oklahoma City to "put the yearbook to bed," with Dr. Joe driving and talking all the way. His influence led me to stay at Harding a second year.

One memorable activity during my freshman year was my Speech 101 class. I had Dr. Jack Ryan for this class. At the time, they had a contest for students who were enrolled in speech, regardless of the teacher, to make a persuasive speech that the winners would give in chapel. I spoke on "The Abolishment of the Electoral College" and was strongly in favor of doing away with the Electoral College. I won the contest, but I now believe the Electoral College is a good process, and I am in favor of keeping it. Understanding does change over time.

I worked as a resident assistant during my junior and senior years. My most interesting experience was to be an R.A. in Graduate Dorm under Dr. Jerome Barnes. Harding had a policy at that time of putting students who smoked together in one wing of the dorm. This was the wing that I was given to serve under the excellent leadership of Dr. Barnes. He knew what I was getting into but I didn't. Little did I know that, at some point in my life, I would have something to say about the rules at Harding and how student life should be managed. My favorite part of this experience was to go to the Barnes' apartment on the first floor and listen to music with Dr. Barnes and eat Mrs. Barnes' wonderful food. That made it all worthwhile.

I came to Harding planning to major in math, study Bible and then transfer after my freshman year. I remember taking algebra that first year with Dr. Ken Perrin. I thought this would be easy because math was easy for me in high school. I learned quickly, however, that serious study was necessary.

I changed my major to accounting because I loved Principles of Accounting with Dr. James Hedrick, who became a good friend and mentor. I had many opportunities to be in his home. Dr. Hedrick was a quiet man whom I had for thirty-three hours of accounting before I graduated in 1965. By my senior year, I was pretty much aware of what he was going to say before he would ever say it.

I was a member of Beta Phi Kappa social club and served as president my senior year. Our club queen was Leah Gentry, from Alhambra, Ill. She had dated one of my best friends for two years, and I was sad because I really liked her but thought she was taken. However, during my senior year, she became available, and we started dating. Our first date was to a club function at Blanchard Springs.

I had been elected S.A. president, and I asked Leah to be in charge of advertising and other activities. She was well qualified because she was an art and English major, and she made wonderful desserts. I still have the letter I sent to her, asking her to assume these tasks. It was a formal, business-type letter, signed Respectfully, David B. Burks. It is a wonder she accepted this role.

I also remember trying to date her during the summer before my senior year, but I couldn't seem to find the door to the house where she was staying with her brother, Lloyd. He lived in the rock house on the corner of Grand and Center streets, and she lived on the second floor. It had a number of doors, and I was not certain which door led to her apartment, so I never dated her that summer. We did get together during the fall, were engaged in November and were married in August following our June graduation.

S.A. President

My year as S.A. president was a pivotal year in Harding's history because it was the last year of Dr. Benson's twenty-nine years as president. There was a lot of excitement on campus about the transition from Dr. Benson to Dr. Cliff Ganus Jr., the new president. Dr. Benson was a larger-than-life individual, very much in charge of what happened on campus, and most of the students were in awe of his travels, his fight against communism, his love for Harding and all of the good work he had done on behalf of the Lord's kingdom.

While I was intimated by him, I enjoyed the opportunity to meet with him on a one-on-one basis and work with him while I was S.A. president. One of our encounters resulted from the S.A. deciding to utilize the Green Room on the second floor of the Student Center, which now houses history and foreign languages. The Student Center was on the first floor, along with the post office and bookstore. The second floor had been used as a dining room for special events but was no longer used for this purpose. I talked with Dr. Benson about utilizing that room as an extension of the crowded Student Center, having it open in the evening for games and other activities for students. Dr. Benson agreed, and the S.A. set out to make arrangements to prepare the room. We decided it needed to be painted a different color because everything on campus seemed to be painted green. We thought it should have new curtains, new couches, new furniture and games available for students. We also felt that we should rename the room so that it would have a new identity, so we proposed to hold a contest to let the students decide the new name. I made a chapel announcement (in the Administration Auditorium at that time) concerning the name change and contest.

Suddenly, Dr. Benson had heard enough and asked me to stop. He said that I did not have the authority to change the name of that room because alumni all over the world knew it as the Green Room. He was not saying we could not utilize the room; he was simply saying we were not going to change the name or the color. Obviously, I was embarrassed about being called out in front of the student body, and that led to more conversations with Dr. Benson. As I reflect on this incident, I realize I learned a great deal from this experience – the most important lesson being that I had not clearly communicated what we were planning to do. We did end up changing the color of the room, but we did not change the name of the room.

In looking over my correspondence from my year as S.A. president, I ran across a letter from Dr. Benson, dated July 1, 1964, which authorized the S.A. to place a picture in the first floor of the Science Hall, honoring Mrs. Ruby Stapleton, a faculty member who had been killed during that year. I was instructed to consult Lott Tucker to determine the exact spot for the picture and the inscription to be printed on the plaque to hang beneath the picture.

I also discovered a letter I wrote to Dr. Benson, requesting an opportunity to speak at the Pre-Session Conference. His reponse to me, indicating that he would be glad for me to do that, was in my files, too.

Another letter I found from him authorized a $500 scholarship for the S.A. president for that school year.

I also discovered Dr. Benson's response following my recommendation that we attend a session with the presidents of other Christian colleges at Lubbock Christian to share information about Harding's leadership. He wrote, "I continue to stand by my decision that these meetings will not make any contribution, and all those represented at that meeting would discourage their continuation." Although I disagreed, I respected him a great deal.

Later, I had the opportunity as S.A. president to present a gift to Dr. Benson on the occasion of his retirement and to speak at his retirement dinner in May 1965, which was an honor for me. Of course, I had no idea that I would return to Harding to teach or that I would one day be president.

I treasure a letter from Dr. Benson, expressing thanks for the gift made by the S.A. We presented him the Encyclopedia Britannica, a 54-volume set of the Great Books of the Western World, a 10-volume set of Gateway to the Great Books, a 10-volume set of the Great Ideas Program and a World Atlas.

University of Texas at Austin

Even with these wonderful experiences, I was excited to graduate in 1965. Leah and I were planning to get married in August. I had accepted a job with Arthur Anderson & Co. in Dallas, Texas, and Leah had accepted a teaching job there. We thought we had our game plan all set, but then I received a fellowship from the University of Texas at Austin. It intrigued me as I thought this was the best time for me to get a master's degree, so we changed plans in the middle of the summer just prior to our marriage and went to Austin for me to get an M.B.A. degree and for Leah to look for a job. It was difficult for her to get a teaching job in Austin, so she accepted a job as a proof reader at the University of Texas Press.

My experience at Austin was a major change that I did not expect. Because they were short on teachers for Principles of Accounting, the chairman of the department, Dr. John Zlokovich, asked if I would teach two classes in Principles of Accounting, which was unusual because you were not expected to teach if you had a fellowship. Because we needed the money, I agreed to teach these classes. Of course, the last thing I wanted to do in life was to be a teacher like my dad.

The best part about teaching was that I was able to share an office with another teaching assistant right next to the chairman's office at U.T. Austin. I thought this was a great opportunity to get to know my professors. I never expected that I would love teaching. I was later asked to write an evaluation system for all students teaching in Principles of Accounting, and I even wrote the syllabus for the Principles of Accounting class at U.T. that was used for the next several years.

One of the events that occurred while I was at U.T. was the shooting from the University of Texas tower in January 1966. The shooter was Charles Joseph Whitman. This was the first major college event of this kind in America. Armed heavily, Whitman went to the top of the University of Texas tower and began shooting just before noon. The plaza was full of people. Using various weapons, he attacked people from long range, killing seventeen people and injuring more than thirty others. I was inside the business building at the time. I was concerned about Leah because she was coming to pick me up for lunch at noon, but she was not able to get to the building because police had stopped everyone outside the campus area. Unfortunately, this first major mass killing on a university campus was not the last.[1]

Working for Exxon

I graduated with an M.B.A. from Texas in August 1966. I debated whether to go with an accounting firm such as Arthur Anderson or take a job with Exxon, but finally decided on the job with Exxon because I thought it would involve far less travel. Leah was pregnant with Bryan so we took the job in Houston. On my first day on the job, I was informed that I would be sent for at least nine months on an audit at the Baton Rouge Chemical Plant in Baton Rouge, La. We had just moved into our apartment, so this was a big surprise. It turned out to be a wonderful turn of events as we moved to Baton Rouge immediately and found a lot of Harding graduates who attended the Student Center Church in Baton Rouge. We have wonderful memories of the nine months we spent there. I even had a visit from Jimmy Allen – requesting a gift for Harding – during this time.

While I was working at Exxon in Baton Rouge, I received a call from Dr. Hedrick. He offered me a job teaching accounting at Harding and asked if I would accept the position. I was stunned by the invitation and yet flattered to be asked to return to Harding to teach. I was interested in teaching only because of the experience I had had at the University of Texas. After some consideration, Leah and I decided we would accept the Harding position. We loved the idea of living in this community where our children could attend Harding Academy.

Teaching at Harding

I began my career as an instructor in accounting on the faculty at Harding in August 1967. I loved teaching and working with the faculty and students in the Department of Business.

After my first year of teaching, I was asked to be the director of placement for Harding, in addition to my teaching responsibilities. I loved this challenge, which also required a move to the American Studies Building. I continued in that position for ten years. After teaching at Harding for five years, I decided I wanted to go on to get a doctoral degree. Dr. Jimmy Carr was instrumental in piquing my interest in Florida State University, which had a highly ranked higher education program at the time. Dr. Carr put me in contact with Dr. Maurice Litton, who would become my major advisor for the program. I will always be indebted to Dr. Jimmy and Stephanie Carr for their help in this very important time in my life.

Florida State University

Prior to making the trip to Florida State, Leah gave birth to our second son, Stephen. He was born ten days before our move to Florida. I will never forget the move as we pulled a trailer, shared the front seat with our dog, and Leah – holding Stephen – rode on the passenger side. Bryan was in the back seat, along with many things we had packed. It was a stressful trip, to say the least, but a memorable trip as we began the Florida State experience.

I attended Florida State University from 1971 to 1972. This was an interesting time in higher education. We had just completed the tumultuous 60s when there was enormous campus unrest all across universities in our nation. I had not experienced any of that at Harding because we had dealt with it in a very different way. At Florida State, I saw a different picture – where an active number of "Students for a Democratic Society" attracted a great deal of attention on the Florida State campus during 1969 and 1970 and were still being talked about when I became a student in 1971.[2]

As a student, I had the privilege of meeting on several occasions with Dr. J. Stanley Marshall, the president of Florida State University. Dr. Marshall later agreed to become a member of the American Studies Institute Board at Harding and has been a great friend to Harding and higher education.

I experienced things at Florida State that changed my life in significant ways. We attended the Call Street Church of Christ, and they had an active student center church. Many university students who had not grown up in the church and had many questions with regard to their faith were converted to Christ.

I learned quickly that I needed to play a leadership role in this church because there were few adults working with these young people. I also learned that I did not have the answers to all the questions they were asking. I found myself often calling Dr. Neale Pryor, Dr. J. D. Bales and Jimmy Allen for answers to very tough questions they were asking. This experience inspired me to later start a Bible class at Harding, called "Facing the Issues," to help deal with students' questions as they went through their Harding experience.

Back at Harding

After my Florida State experience, I returned to Harding to write my dissertation, and I finished my Ph.D. degree in 1974. After returning, I helped initiate new majors in management, marketing and finance.

I also worked with Dr. Billy Ray Cox in sponsoring business teams that competed at Michigan State University and Emory University. These business teams were highly successful in competing against Notre Dame, University of Michigan, Emory and other major universities. Harding won seven national championships in intercollegiate business gaming during this time. I was privileged to work with a number of very talented students on these teams.

Business Team with Gov. Dale Bumpers and Dr. Billy Ray Cox with Dr. Benson.

Out of this intercollegiate experience came the establishment of a business policy class for all students at Harding. I wrote a business simulation game exclusively for Harding students. Today, most universities have a required capstone course in business policy, but this was the first such experience at Harding back in 1973.

I later developed this simulation experience for executives and conducted numerous simulation business policy seminars for executives in Detroit, Mich., and other cities. The focus was top executives, but it provided a valuable leadership experience for me as well.

Another course developed specifically for Harding students was Christian Business Ethics. This course was offered for the first time in 1974, and I published a book, *The Christian Alternative for Business*, as a text for this class.[3] This class is still required for business majors. It was one of the first classes in Christian Business Ethics to be offered at any business university.

The Christian Alternative for Business

BY DAVID B. BURKS

As an offshoot of this work, I developed a one-day seminar in business ethics for businessmen. I was fortunate to present this one-day seminar to a number of business executives. From 1980 to 1986, George Oliver and Don Beck were associates who worked with me, both with the simulation seminar and the Christian business ethics seminar.

I also was privileged to conduct church leadership seminars. I had never thought I would do something like this, but Alan Bryan came to visit me one day when he was here to see his oldest son, Brant. Alan suggested that the church had a great need for leadership seminars that would combine business leadership management principles and the Bible as it related to elders, deacons and other church leaders. I remember telling him that I thought his idea was a good one, but I was the wrong person to do it. Alan was quite a salesman, and he convinced me to give it a try. Dr. Bobby Coker worked with me, and Alan set up our first seminar. We ended up doing more than forty of these seminars in different cities in the United States before 1987.

Another powerful influence for me in terms of leadership came from the invitation to work with the University of Arkansas Extension Service in providing supervisory seminars. I did this work for eight years and conducted leadership seminars for supervisors in businesses throughout the state of Arkansas. I conducted about twenty of these each year on Principles of Leadership, Time Management and Conflict Resolution.

In 1982, Dr. Ganus gave me the opportunity to work directly with the American Studies Program in addition to my duties as dean of the College of Business and teaching courses in business policy and Christian business ethics. Notable speakers I remember during this time frame were Zig Zigler, Alex Haley and Sen. Dale Bumpers, but my favorite was Tom Peters, the author of *A Search for Excellence,* who was considered the guru on management and leadership at that time in America. More than 2,000 people attended his one-day seminar in the Benson Auditorium.

While I was dean of the College of Business, I decided to partner with my friends, Jim Henderson and Hugh Groover, to build a racquetball center in Searcy. I loved racquetball and was excited to play – it was pretty much the rage at the time. We planned to build only two courts on Race Street so that, if it didn't work out according to our plans, we could use the property for some other purpose. However, the three of us decided we should dream bigger, so we built an elaborate four-court system on the west side of town and invested a great deal more money that we had first planned.

We loved this project, and we hired students to help manage it. It was a huge success the first year, but raquetball turned out to be a passing fad as people turned to tennis and other summer sports, leaving us with deficit winter months. We ended up closing the building and paying off our loans.

This failure in business was a great learning experience for me. I was embarrassed to be in a leadership position at Harding, especially in the College of

Business, and to be a failure at this business venture. I took it very personally at the time, but the experience turned out to be a blessing as I learned that one failure does not have to keep you from moving forward in life.

Another one of my memories of this time was my involvement in the con-

struction of the Mabee Business Building, which provided a separate home for the College of Business for the first time. We had been sharing the American Studies Building with education, history and other departments. Our new building involved moving Harding Academy to a new location so the Mabee Business Building could be erected on that location. I remember working with the Mabee Foundation relative to their gift and with a number of other businesses that made gifts to the building. I particularly recall working with the architects, Yearwood and Johnson, as the building was designed. With the help of other business faculty members, we drew up the basic design for the building.

Once, I met with Dr. Ganus and the architects about the building. Dr. Ganus felt the proposed building was too big and would be too costly. He said we needed to remove about one third of its proposed size. I was dismayed and couldn't imagine why a president would make such a decision, but I would understand when I later found myself in his position regarding reducing the size of projects. We did remove about one third of the building and were tickled to death with what was built, as it served our needs well for many years.

One of my initiatives that is not familiar to most people is a publication that was designed in 1977 to draw together alumni, friends, students and faculty of the School of Business. The name of this publication was "Camaraderie," a word that has obviously long been a favorite of mine.

Selection As President

At age 65, Dr. Ganus announced his plan to retire in May 1987. The board had been aware of his intentions and had begun to search for a successor in 1985. I loved my position as dean of the School of Business, and I loved teaching classes. I was not seeking this position but, like most people at Harding, was curious as to who would be selected.

Several people asked me about my interest in being considered for the position. I did not feel prepared or worthy of the position. I was not a preacher, not well known in our brotherhood and not an expert in higher education. Nonetheless, I ultimately agreed to allow my name to be submitted, thinking my experience in church and business leadership could possibly help me in this position. If I were selected, I also knew my degree in the Administration of Higher Education would be

helpful. I was especially committed to the unique mission of Harding and thought I could help promote it.

When I interviewed with the Board Selection Committee in Little Rock, Ark., I outlined a five-year plan for their consideration that came from my experience in leadership and teaching business policy. I believe this discussion was critical to my being selected as the next president of Harding. I still have the red notebook with the notes I prepared for that meeting.

I well remember the emotional meeting I had with the Search Committee and later with the entire board when the invitation was extended. I was both honored and terrified of the responsibility. I could hardly imagine agreeing to follow Dr. Ganus. My life and that of my family was about to change.

I was selected one year prior to Dr. Ganus' retirement, which would bring about a year of major transition. I will always be grateful to Dr. Ganus, Lott Tucker and numerous others who helped me during that pivotal year. I am so grateful to my family for their support throughout this entire process, and I am particularly grateful to my wife, Leah, who played a key supporting role.

During this transition year before I became president, Dr. Ganus allowed me to work with key leaders in a strategic planning process for the new year. We began in the spring of that year with this Strategic Planning Committee, which was an essential part of plans for Harding's future.

Also during this first year, I was involved with my first building project – our own personal residence on the west end of Harding Park. Leah and I worked with architect Fred Moseley in design-

ing this house, which was to provide a place for entertaining guests who visited the University. The board selected the site on the east side of the campus.

The second building project, although minor in nature, also appeared during this transition year. It was the selection of an office space for the president. The decision was made that Dr. Ganus would remain in his existing office in the Administration Building. I selected a place in the American Heritage Building just off the lobby as a place for my office suite. It was designed and ready for us to move into in May.

Conclusion

As I think back on this turning point in my life, I can hardly believe the changes that had occurred in my life to that point. Why was I offered this position? What factors led the board to consider me? Who had played a pivotal role in my life? How did my experiences in conducting leadership seminars play into my preparation? What about my student days at Harding, the University of Texas and Florida State University? I don't know the answers to these questions, but I do know that God works through imperfect people to accomplish His plans. I am grateful for the wonderful support of my family and the Board of Trustees.

Passing the gavel from Dr. Ganus to Dr. Burks in 1987

CHAPTER TWO
My First Year as President

<u>Inauguration Activities</u>

My Inauguration on September 18, 1987, was a larger-than-life event for me. While I became president at commencement on May 13, the Inauguration marked my official induction as president of Harding University. I was nervous, excited, fearful and hopeful. I was intimidated by some of the speakers who were on the Inauguration program – Gov. Bill Clinton; Jim Bill McInteer, one of the best-known evangelists of our time; Dr. Ray Thornton, president of the University of Arkansas and a Harding alumnus; David Glass, president of Walmart; and Board Chairman, James Cone.

The Harding University Band, under the direction of Warren Casey, opened the ceremony with a fanfare. The processional and recessional were premiere performances written especially for the occasion by Dr. William W. Hollaway, chairman of the Department of Music. The last piece was named "Bryan's March" in honor of my oldest son who was a member of T.N.T. social club, which Dr. Hollaway sponsored.

The music program also included a mass chorus that combined the Academy Chorus, the A Cappella Chorus, and the University Chorale. I remember their presentation of "Glory Be to God," directed by Dr. Cliff Ganus III and Dr. Kenneth Davis Jr. The chorus ended its performance by singing "America, the Beautiful."

I will never forget some of the comments made that day by Gov. Clinton and Jim Bill. It was because of the influence of James Cone that Gov. Clinton came to speak at the Inauguration. He told me as we shared some moments before the Inauguration that he really did not care for inaugurations and found them to be formal, stiff and boring. He wasn't being critical; he was simply stating his feelings. I didn't know quite how to respond, but when we had occasion to visit after the Inauguration, he told me it was the best one he had ever attended. He loved Jim Bill as the emcee, especially his jokes. In fact, they would communicate later about sharing jokes.

During the Inauguration, I sat beside Gov. Clinton and watched him write his speech on the back of a small piece of paper as he awaited his turn to speak. He obviously did not have anything prepared, but his remarks were outstanding because he was a gifted speaker and was encouraged by the comments that had already been made by Jim Bill and others.

Dr. Joel Anderson, now chancellor of the University of Arkansas at Little Rock but then vice chancellor and provost, wrote after the Inauguration that he was pleased to be a Harding alumnus and a part of the Inauguration. He indicated that it was the best he had ever attended, and he was very proud that it took place at Harding.

Just prior to my presentation, Chairman James Cone reviewed the process the trustees had used in the presidential selection. He concluded with the following

statement,

> *Therefore, as chairman of the Board of Trustees of Harding University, and on behalf of all the trustees, I formally and officially charge you with this position of leadership and invest upon you the title of president of Harding University, this 18th day of September, 1987. May God bless you in this good work.*

The exchange of the seal of Harding University then took place between former president, Clifton L. Ganus Jr., and me.

By this time, I was fairly well scared to death, given the fact that Jim Bill had told numerous jokes and was warmly received by the audience, and Gov. Clinton had responded by telling additional jokes and laughing heartily at Jim Bill's jokes. Nonetheless, it was my turn to make the presentation I had prepared.

The title of my presentation was "Integrating Faith and Learning into the 21st Century."[1] I borrowed this phrase, I think with permission, from Dr. Don England, a professor of chemistry at Harding. I had heard Dr. England speak on this topic as he addressed his science students, and I thought it was a neat way to express my goals for the University. I was not aware at the time, but it is the oldest mission statement to be found anywhere for colleges and universities in America. I found out later that it was the original mission statement for Harvard University, although they have since changed their mission. I was also unaware at that time that it would become the key theme of my administration.

I began by relating the history of Harding from its inception until 1987. I reiterated that the original purpose was not just to teach professional preachers but rather to integrate faith and learning for every student, regardless of their major. I paid particular attention to James A. Harding and David Lipscomb, who had profoundly influenced Christian education as we know it. I believe Bro. J.N. Armstrong, Harding's first president from 1924 until 1936, provided the soul for the University that continues even to this day.

I particularly emphasized a reaffirmation of mission, which was to become a key theme for me in my presidency. I noted that many undergraduate colleges and universities had lost their sense of mission and were confused about how to impart shared values on which the vitality of higher education and society depend. I made reference to our theme of integrating faith and living and the six-point reaffirmation of this statement that had emerged from a year-long study prior to my taking office. During that time, we changed the language to integrating faith, learning and living.

I closed my presentation by sharing my dream for Christian higher education at Harding –

It involves a strong, deliberate effort by all of us to build a great Christian university in the foothills of the Ozarks, one with students who have a sharpened understanding of their ministry, regardless of their choice of a major; a university that stresses Christian scholarship and excellence with regular study, with superb teaching and with caring faculty members who shower students with attention and service beyond their wildest expectations; a university that provides the best student services in the country, that promotes Christian ethics that foster lasting relationships and teaches liberty and freedom. In short, I dream of an absolutely premiere Christian university.

I made reference in the conclusion of the presentation to *A Passion for Excellence*[2] by Tom Peters, in which he stated that for any organization to truly succeed, it must put the customer first, constantly champion innovation and believe in people who make it happen. It calls for teamwork, coaching, enthusiasm, prayer, bone-deep beliefs, ownership and commitment. I still believe these principles are true. I believe we must have this kind of passion for Christian education at Harding if we are to truly succeed.

I believe our founding fathers had this kind of faith, and I believe Jesus demonstrated this kind of leadership. I concluded by stating that I did not make plans for this position, but I promised, by God's grace, to make every effort to perform the responsibilities of this office to the best of my ability. I then asked for prayers for us to work together to integrate faith, learning and living at Harding University.

The Inauguration proceedings were concluded by the singing of Harding's alma mater, directed by my friend and neighbor for many years, Dr. Dean Priest. Dr. Jimmy Allen led the closing prayer, and the Harding University Band performed "Bryan's March."

After twenty-six years as president, I reflect on the comments in my inaugural speech, and I am surprised at how much they represented the emphasis of the next twenty-six years. If I were to make the speech again, I would attempt to say essentially the same thing.

The Inauguration was preceded by a number of activities during the week leading up to it. These included a performance by the Memphis Symphony Orchestra, a luncheon for community leaders and civic clubs with Ray Thornton, and an

American Studies presentation by Dr. Paul Faulkner, director of the American Family Institute at Abilene Christian University. The week's activities concluded with a luncheon and reception in the Ganus Athletic Center following the Inauguration.

I will always treasure a hand-written letter from James Cone, chairman of the Board, when he summarized comments of the Search Committee. In his writing, he stated that the Search Committee had invested eighteen months, including many hours and much prayer, in searching for the person to serve as Harding's fourth president. He quoted their conclusion – "We believe we found the right man, with God's help, in David Burks. The Search Committee was unanimous in its vote for David, as was the full Board." I was impressed with his candid statement, which encouraged me for many years to come.

I felt empowered by the Board, and I believe the Harding family was empowered because of the approach they took. Bro. Cone concluded his note by quoting the challenge he made to the rest of the Board –

> Dr. Burks will be different from Dr. Ganus and Dr. Benson. However, it is essential that we rally around and give our support, prayers and encouragement to David. With our help and backing, I fully expect David and his team to carry Harding to higher ground, just as each of his predecessors did. Private education in general and Harding specifically face many challenges, such as declining enrollment, increased competition for gift income and low endowment. I am grateful for the men who have led us in the past. As this Board gets behind Dr. Burks – as it has for past presidents – I believe Harding will meet every challenge successfully. May God bless us to this end.

Family Support

I want to acknowledge the important role of my wife, Leah, whose input was essential to my decision to accept the invitation extended by the Board, and she was an extremely important support in my decision to accept this responsibility.

In an interview that was printed in the Harding Bulletin in October 1987, Leah said that her role as first lady was not exactly what she had in mind for her life.[3]

"I married an accountant and assumed I would move to a city somewhere, probably Dallas," she said. "I never envisioned myself in Searcy, Ark., and certainly never dreamed that David would be president." But she accepted her role and lived it extremely well.

Letters of Encouragement

After the announcement was made, I received a number of congratulatory letters, three of which were particularly important to me. The first was written May 12, 1986, by Jim Bill McInteer. He was on the Search Committee, but I did not know him well at the time. In his letter, he congratulated me and made wonderful comments about Leah that would become providential because of her bout with cancer later. Then he wrote that he wanted to "kid" me about something. He said that I might have thought the questions he asked during the interview process were too personal, but he wanted to make sure that we understood each other. His question was, "What do you read, and how do you keep up with brotherhood affairs?" I answered that I often read the *Spiritual Sword* and the *Gospel Advocate*, among other publications. He wrote that, in my absence at the Board meeting, he reported this response to the full Board and stated, "I am going to vote against that guy, because not one time did he mention the *20th Century Christian*." He added that he wanted to enlarge my reading program and, as a first gesture of kindness, purchased a year's subscription to the *20th Century Christian* for me. I have read it carefully ever since.

A second letter that I have treasured since my selection was dated June 19, 1986, from Ralph Edwards in Hollywood, Calif. Most people would not be familiar with the relationship of Ralph Edwards to our family, but he was the creator of the "Truth or Consequences" radio program and later the "This is Your Life" television program. He knew our family because he came to Truth or Consequences every year for a week-long celebration and rodeo, with numerous other Hollywood stars, to conduct the radio and television programs utilizing the Hot Springs High School auditorium. My dad was superintendent of schools, and Edwards worked with my dad for years in this connection. Dad would later be inducted into the "This is Your Life" program.

A third meaningful response came to me from Dr. Russell P. Kropp, vice president for academic affairs and provost at Florida State University. Dr. Kropp was my major professor for my doctoral program at Florida State. The letter reads,

> *I read in the Chronicle – that is the plain ordinary worldly Chronicle*
> *of Higher Education, not the longer standing and more notable*
> *1 and 2 Chronicles in the Bible – that you have been named president*
> *of Harding University. I realize now that my earlier congratulations,*
> *no matter how sincere, were quite premature having been based on*
> *the inevitability that had not yet come to pass. So it is my distinct*
> *pleasure to congratulate you for a second time.*[4]

While I was a student at F.S.U., Dr. Kropp often said he thought I would be president of Harding some day.

Enrollment

One of my first priorities was to increase enrollment, and my first administrative hire was the selection of Dr. Jim Carr from Tallahassee, Fla., to lead our total enrollment management program. Dr. Carr brought many years of experience in enrollment management from working with American College Testing on a national level. In my judgment, he was one of the most qualified professionals in higher education, and I was delighted that he joined me as I began my presidency.

We moved the admissions office from the Ganus Building, where people had to come to the campus by way of the railroad tracks, the boiler room and the laundry for their first view of the campus. Some people never got past that view. We moved the offices to the American Heritage Building and began making changes that would create an aggressive student-oriented admissions program for Harding.

Enrollment increased the first year and then continued to increase each year thereafter, with the help of Jim Carr, wonderful admissions directors – Mike Williams and Glenn Dillard – and a host of admissions advisors who really believed in the mission of Harding. It was a goal I had mentioned to the Board in my interview with them before being asked to serve as president. After six years of enrollment decline, our enrollment increased, providing a much needed boost to the budget for our tuition-driven income. However, our most important purpose in working to increase enrollment was to be able to influence as many people as possible with our Christian perspective.

Food Service

Closely connected with changes in admissions was a decision to turn our food service over to an outside party. I well remember talking to Lott Tucker, our vice president for finance, about taking bids to see if we could contract with a major company to manage the Pattie Cobb Cafeteria and the American Heritage Cafeteria. We both thought it would be difficult to make the change within a six-week period before school started in August. Mr. Tucker agreed to look into the possibilities. I was pleased with the bids that came in and the willingness of the companies to make the turnaround in such a short period of time. Aramark was eventually selected and has continued to work with us ever since.

Registration

Another change during this first year was to shorten registration to only one day. Registration was consolidated into one location and moved to the Ganus Athletic Center, which required adding numerous computer terminals for the day. All workers wore yellow caps pinned with a "It's Great to be at Harding" button, an expression coined by the late Dr. Jimmy Carr.

Convocation

Also in the first year, we initiated a convocation ceremony for Harding University. While convocations were commonplace at many colleges and universities across the nation, Harding had never utilized this activity at the beginning of the academic year. Dr. Jimmy Carr was helpful in orga-  nizing that first convocation. The faculty marched in academic regalia and a mace was created for Harding by Mr. Bill Rushton, a member of our biology faculty. Each convocation utilizes students carrying flags that represent all of the states and nations represented in our student body. This impressive ceremony, which involves singing and speeches that are shared with community leaders, students and parents, marks the beginning of each year. The convocation continues today, although it is now done only for freshmen, transfers and parents during our student orientation.

Receptions

The new year in 1988 was marked with twenty presidential receptions for alumni, prospective students, parents and others in the Harding family. The first was in Dallas on October 27. A twenty-minute video about Harding was shown at each event, and Harding University and Christian education were celebrated on each occasion. These receptions served to provide opportunity for these individuals to meet me and hear my vision for Harding's future. These wonderful events helped me understand what members of the Harding family thought about things that should be done in the future.

I was still trying to establish myself as the new leader at Harding and dealing with the fact that people who did not know me were concerned about how I would address the spiritual mission of the University. Some people seemed to think my business background would lead me to promote the business affairs of the college at the expense of the spiritual needs of the University. These receptions gave me the opportunity to explain my spiritual mission for Harding.

I will always be grateful for a letter that was published by George Tipps, a well-known preacher in the Dallas area who has become a dear friend. It said, "We need to give David Burks a chance. I believe he will provide the spiritual leadership for Harding University in the future." [5]

Snow

We made Harding history at the beginning of the spring semester my first year as president. Students and faculty were greeted with fourteen inches of snow and fourteen-degree weather for the first day of classes. Given this record snowfall, we canceled classes for the very first time because of weather. Students loved this opportunity to enjoy Harding's beautiful snow-covered campus.

Utilities

An unexpected challenge that summer involved our cogeneration plant. The nature of the challenge and the difficulty of it were surprising, although the experience of pipes bursting was known to the entire campus. Fountains were popping up all over campus – never at a good time. We had converted to a cogeneration plant and had used both hot water and cold water from a central plant to cool and heat most of the buildings on campus. A number of lines had begun breaking when the change was made from cold to hot water. The plastic pipes simply couldn't take the change in temperature without serious breaks, causing several buildings to be without air conditioning or heat, sometimes for a day or two, while the pipe was being repaired.

This was an unusually difficult challenge because of the complex nature of cogeneration. I didn't know anything about cogeneration, and it reminded me of the time I took a job with Exxon to do an audit of the Baton Rouge Chemical and Refinery plant. My first assignment was to audit their catalytic cracking unit process. I could hardly spell "catalytic" and didn't understand its function. I felt the same way about Harding's cogeneration plant because I didn't understand very much about it. I simply knew the pipes were breaking.

As I studied the matter, I found that there were clearly two sides of thought on this issue. Many people on campus thought that cogeneration was the way to go since money had been invested in this process. These people also believed we would save money if we kept the plant. I learned that cogeneration uses stored heat and/or cold water to take care of the needs of the campus. Pipes had been put into the ground to take care of this purpose for the past several years.

Other people were convinced that cogeneration would not work because the change in temperature broke the pipes, and we were either going to have to

 put in steel pipes, which cost a lot of money, or change to a decentralized system. I didn't know which option to take, and the issue was quite controversial.

With the advice of our chairman of the Board, I hired an engineering firm out of Kansas City, Mo., to study the matter. They were experts in the area of cogeneration heating and cooling, and I thought it would be good to have an external recommendation. They did make a recommendation that included all of the positives and negatives surrounding both sides of the issue, but they recommended no solution.

I finally made the decision that we would phase out the cogeneration plant and build a decentralized system so we could have both heating and cooling at the same time when needed. Naturally, this decision cost some money to put the system in place, and most people were not aware of all of the work that went into this process. Toward the end of the summer, I asked Dr. Bill Ryan to reorganize, coordinate and direct the physical plant and the mechanical, electrical and construction services. Ryan was a mechanical engineer who had been teaching in the School of Business since 1983.

Strategic Planning

Perhaps the biggest change during the first year involved strategic planning. Actually beginning before I became president, Dr. Ganus allowed me to create a Strategic Planning Committee for long-term planning purposes. Much work was done by the entire campus relative to this project, and it continued during the first year, culminating in a report that was formally accepted by the Board of Trustees in November 1987.[6]

The overriding theme that emerged from the planning process was a reaffirmation of our historic mission of integrating faith, learning and living. The new words that came out of this study were enrichment, quality, service, ministry and involvement. All undergraduate programs were examined. A program was launched to increase the number of faculty with terminal degrees.

The establishment of a College of Religion on the Searcy campus was one of the first steps of the implementation of the new goals. Academic and faculty enrichment programs were outlined, along with an honors program for students. The plans included renovating some existing buildings, including Pattie Cobb Hall, and adding to the American Heritage Cafeteria during the summer after that first year. The plan outlined in this year-long study represented the blueprint from which Harding operated for the next five years.

One major decision during this first year addressed the operation of the Harding Graduate School of Religion in Memphis. There was a major question as to the ownership of the property where our graduate facility was located. A great deal of legal work led to the separation of property for Harding Academy of Memphis and the Harding Graduate Program there. This separation was necessary if we were to

37

proceed with expansions or renovations on the Memphis campus on Cherry Road. At the end of this study, the Harding Graduate School in Memphis was reaffirmed as a vital, integral and important part of our program of studies. A strategy was put in place to build the enrollment and raise money specifically for the graduate program and to develop an integrated working relationship between the Searcy and Memphis campuses.

At the close of my first year, the Board of Trustees approved a record $29.3 million proposed budget for 1988-89. They also approved an $860,000 budget for equipment and remodeling. A capital expansion budget of $1.2 million was approved to complete the American Heritage Cafeteria and Pattie Cobb renovations.

Conclusion

At the end of my first year, I was much more comfortable with the responsibilities and duties associated with being president. However, I knew it had been a year of change, which is never easily accepted. The *Petit Jean* staff dedicated the yearbook to me that year, which I appreciated, but they included this statement in the dedication, which is true – "This year has been difficult for all of us, and it simply takes time to see the result of changes made."

With all of the decisions of the first year, I was strengthened by my relationship with the Board of Trustees as they reached out to me, encouraged me and empowered me in my new position. I loved the opportunity to get to know these men and women, and I knew they carried a heavy load in regard to setting the policies to guide Harding University. I loved working with the faculty and students. We now had a plan in place, approved by the Board and developed by the faculty, for how we would proceed in the future. I felt good about the first year.

Students referred fondly to the president's office as "Camp David" and to the president's home as "Burkingham Palace."

The official seal and mace of Harding University

PART TWO
Faith

Banners on light poles promote Harding's mission

CHAPTER THREE

Harding's Distinctive Mission

Introduction

My understanding of the mission of Harding was vague when I came to Harding as a freshman in 1961. During my four years as a student, I listened to Dr. George Benson speak about the purpose of Harding, but my main memories of Dr. Benson were the messages he delivered about Zambia, China and the fight against communism.

I was invited to Dr. Joe Pryor's home, and Dr. James Hedrick became a substitute father to me. Ermal Tucker taught business communications. She was tough and demanding but kind in her demeanor. I was influenced by Neale Pryor as he taught Bible and by Jimmy Allen and his preaching; he had a passion for Harding, but he had a greater passion for the Lord's church.

I came to Harding because I needed to learn more about God and the Bible. I learned more about God and the Bible through the people I met who were all about the Christian mission.

Understanding Harding's Mission

After returning to Harding in 1967 to be an instructor in accounting, I carefully read what was stated in the catalog about the purpose of Harding. For many years, the Harding College Bulletin used the following language as a statement of purpose for Harding University:

Harding is a Christian college of arts and sciences. Its purpose
is to give students an education of high quality that will lead to

an understanding and philosophy of life consistent with Christian ideals. It aims to develop a solid foundation of intellectual, physical and spiritual values upon which students may build useful and happy lives.[1]

I was impressed with this language. I used it in teaching all of my classes but really did not understand the impact this language would have on my life.

After teaching for five years at Harding, I took a leave of absence to pursue a doctorate in higher education at Florida State University. During that time, I learned more about the purpose and mission statements of other universities. I realized that Harding was truly unique in its mission because universities that teach absolute truth, abiding faith in God, integrity, the importance of a strong family, the limitation of expression with explicit rules of conduct and serving are very much in the minority among more than 4,000 accredited public and private two- and four-year institutions in our nation.

As I said in a book written for our 75th anniversary, *Against the Grain,* character education was assumed to be a prominent reason for existence as colleges

began in America. Harvard University was established by Puritans at Cambridge in 1636, and its seal displayed twin Latin mottos – "Christ and the church" and "in Christ, we glory." The motto also carried a quotation from John 8:31-32, "And Jesus said, 'If you hold to my teaching, you will know the truth and the truth will make you free.'" This motto was typical of colleges at that time, as religion was the emphasis behind the founding of those early institutions. But the emphasis has changed so much in America today that we seldom find colleges that have an explicit spiritual mission as their purpose and way of life. Instead, concepts like diversity, political correctness, relativism and academic freedom dominate the curriculum of many universities, both public and private, today. The emphasis on the the Judeo-Christian heritage is all but gone for most colleges.

Upon my return to Harding after graduate study, I was given the book written in 1969 by Brother L.C. Sears, *For Freedom.* It was about the life of John Nelson

Armstrong, Harding's first president.[3] Dr. Billy Ray Cox gave me the book, and it made a great impression on me. It has continued to be a book to which I refer often. Although the book is out of print, Harding has reprinted it so that it can be given to every new faculty member to give them greater understanding of the unique mission of Harding and the people who sacrificed so much to make its work possible.

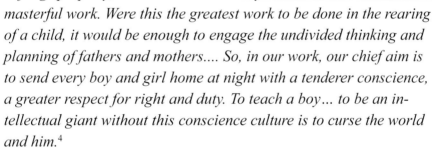

Bro. Armstrong had a clear understanding of Harding's unique mission. To this very day, Harding owes its moral compass and spiritual underpinning to the work of this man and the small faculty who worked with him during the early years of 1924 to 1936.

As cited in *For Freedom*, Armstrong wrote,

> *To guide a mind to think truly and wisely, to judge properly, and to reason correctly is a masterful work. Were this the greatest work to be done in the rearing of a child, it would be enough to engage the undivided thinking and planning of fathers and mothers.... So, in our work, our chief aim is to send every boy and girl home at night with a tenderer conscience, a greater respect for right and duty. To teach a boy... to be an intellectual giant without this conscience culture is to curse the world and him.*[4]

In the context of this statement, Bro. Armstrong was talking about the purpose of Harding and the ideal that he had for every student. He believed it should be the objective of every teacher to obtain the highest possible perfection in the material he or she taught. He stated,

> *Don't cry out that perfection is impossible. We have been attempting perfect spelling, perfect writing. We shall not make any worse mistake in attempting the perfect men and women. What kind of man or woman ought we to try to train our child to be? One whose body is sound, the ready servant of His will, doing with ease and pleasure all the work it is capable of; one whose intellect is a clear, logical force, dependable for thinking and expressing; one whose memory is stored with a reasonable amount of the great and*

fundamental truth of nature and the laws of her operation, of the important accomplishments of mankind; one who is alert, lively, cheerful, hopeful, with passions trained to heal; one who is the servant of a tender conscience, who has learned to love beauty, whether of nature or of art, to hate all vileness, to respect, to assist and to work with his fellowman – this is the sort of profit we teachers are expected to work for.[5]

To this day, I am still impressed with this statement, as I think Bro. Armstrong was ahead of many educators of his time in recognizing the importance of individual differences and the need to ask people to attain perfection in every way possible.

We owe a great deal to Bro. Armstrong for establishing the moral and spiritual compass for Harding during these early years. In the 1925 *Petit Jean*, the first yearbook published under the name, Harding, he addressed the students as follows –

You have been a great factor in whatever success has attended Harding College in her first year. You and your family have passed through the experiences, born the burdens, and made the sacrifice incidental to the beginning of a great and important work.... From this day on, wherever you may go... remember that Harding College lives as a result of keen sacrifice; that every brick in her walls, every book in her library, and every piece of equipment in her laboratories is a result of the influence of Christ upon hearts. Remember that we who man the institution would betray the most sacred trust did we not make first the instilling of the principles of Christianity in the hearts of her students.[6]

Wow! While we would use different language today, I think all of us connected with Christian higher education would applaud the words used by Bro. Armstrong. What a noble purpose for all of us to pursue.

Integrating Faith, Learning and Living

When I became president, as part of our planning process, a committee chaired by Dr. Larry Long reexamined Harding's purpose statement. The result of that study led to a reaffirmation of Harding's mission under the heading of "The Integration of Faith, Learning and Living." This slogan involves developing the whole person through a commitment to Christ and to the Bible as the word of God, an emphasis on life-long intellectual growth, and the encouragement of Christian service and world missions through a servant leadership lifestyle. I love the way this wording expressed Harding's spiritual mission. We then broke down this purpose statement into sub-points that I talked about on a regular basis.[7]

The first point was the development of Christian scholarship, which is what makes Harding so special to me. It is a commitment to Christian scholarship that acknowledges dependence on God while stressing commitment to intellectual excellence. It addresses and salutes true academic freedom by saying that it cannot be separated from Christianity. This purpose also suggests that caring teachers who integrate Christian values into their professional fields of scholarship allow for the exploration of truth in every discipline.

The second point was the promotion of Christian ethics, which involves a strong commitment to developing a unique community for learning and self-expression. It involves integrity and purity of thought and action. It recognizes that the real war in our world today is between the world value system that is often promoted by secular universities and the Christian value system taught by Jesus.

The third point in this mission statement had to do with lasting relationships, with Jesus as our model. We know from reading the Bible that Jesus had significant and frequent contact with His disciples. We know that He developed a loving and reciprocal relationship with His disciples, and we know that the disciples were exposed to His emotions. Our purpose at Harding is to do exactly the same thing.

The fourth statement, the promotion of wellness, is based on the fact that the body is the temple of the Holy Spirit. It encompasses the idea that life-long health habits contribute to a better quality of life.

The final point of the mission statement had to do with the promotion of citizenship within a global perspective. This principle embraces an effort to develop a Christian understanding of and respect for other cultures through an emphasis on liberty and justice. Our International Studies Program is a prime example of our

effort to realize this part of the mission statement.

A motto at Harding during this time was "developing Christian servants," which grew out of the mission statement's emphasis on faith, learning and living. Students were encouraged to live lives of service to Christ and His church and, in doing so, to bless the lives of others. This motto represents the heart of the matter.

Michael Crouch was S.A. president in 2008-09. He made the following remarks about Harding's mission –

We went on mission trips to every inhabited continent, competed against the best universities in the country, actively sought change in the student government, reached out to the community in service, invited world leaders to campus through the American Studies Institute and left to better the world through the church, enterprise and public policy. But the stories I remember most usually involved lifting a song of praise or sharing an early morning meal or a late-night milkshake. "Faith, Learning and Living" is a way of life at Harding, or as another person put it, "Our faith is not a slice of the pie; it is the flavor of the pie."

In speaking on this mission statement, I have referred to Deuteronomy 6:5-9 as a basis for Christian education. There we are taught to love God with all of our heart and with all of our soul and with all of our strength. The reference says it is our responsibility as parents and grandparents to impress these commandments on our children and talk about them when we sit at home, when we walk along the road, when we lie down and when we get up. I have always been impressed with the seriousness of this language.

I also referred to Matthew 6:33, "But seek first His kingdom and His righteousness, and all these things will be given to you as well." I believe that seeking His kingdom and righteousness are essential to a unique Christian education.

Focusing on Things that Count

I often had the opportunity to speak about the mission of Harding. In an address at the 1988 Lectureship, entitled "Focusing on Things that Count," I stressed the sovereignty of God. I stated that the focus of our lives must begin with God – the unchanging God in a changing world. Our temptation is always to focus on the world and its culture, but God calls us to focus on Him and the blessings that come from a relationship with Him. As Father of us all, He is not watching from a distance but is intimately involved in our lives, so much so that He would give His own child for us. He knew the essential bliss of the creature is to behold the face of the Creator. We must never trivialize the holy because, in doing so, we lose sight of the very thing that counts the most.

The second focus of that presentation was Jesus Christ as Lord. Our faith in Jesus makes us distinctive in the world and calls into account every thought we have and every action we take. I love Paul's statement to the Corinthians that is engraved on the front of the Ezell Building on our campus because it beautifully points to Jesus Christ as the true foundation – "No one can lay any foundation other than the one already laid, which is Jesus Christ" (1 Cor. 3:11).

The third focus of that presentation was a belief in the Bible as the inspired word of God. That belief is at the core of our reason for existence at Harding.

The fourth focus was the importance of the Lord's church. I emphasized that the underlying premise on which our distinctiveness is built is our identity as Christ's bride. Jesus has always called people in the community to communion with Him, His father, His spirit and God's other children. He warned the Corinthian church not to be yoked together with unbelievers (2 Cor. 6:14). The New Testament affirms everywhere that Jesus is the one head of the body, which is His church (Eph. 1:22 ff; Col. 1:18).

I challenged all of us to true worship; to love, the highest moral code God left us (1 Cor. 13); and to servanthood, the way we can change the world one person at a time.

Against the Grain

The most significant effort I was a part of during my presidency relative to Harding's mission statement was writing the book, *Against the Grain*, published in 1998.[8] Kay Gowen served as the general editor, and twenty-four faculty members assisted in writing the book. A part of the 75th anniversary celebration of Harding, the book was an effort to spell out the mission of Harding and how efforts are made to incorporate that mission statement into every aspect of life at Harding. It was a treatise on Harding's commitment to provide quality academic preparation for careers without abandoning its overall purpose of educating for eternity, as stated in the preface by the editorial committee.

The book was not really a history of Harding as much as it was a story of the effort of the University to be true to its mission. That commitment to its mission goes against the grain of society to present students with the opportunity to be educated in an atmosphere permeated by an eternal worldview.

Jim Bill McInteer's forward to the book addressed "Fulfillment of Purpose in Our Life." He recounted some of his great experiences while a student at Harding and as a member of the Board of Trustees for more than half a century. Dr. Cliff Ganus Jr. provided a brief history of Harding up to that time. Considerable attention was given to spelling out the mission of Harding and sharing the efforts to put the mission in place in all academic disciplines.

Reaffirmation of Mission

In the *Harding* magazine in 2000, my column was dedicated to a recommitment to our eternal purposes.[9] I began by saying that our building plans and endowment goals are essential, but our spiritual mission is the only thing that will survive in the future. I listed a number of spiritual doctrines, which included belief in the sovereignty of God, Jesus Christ as the heart of our curriculum, a belief in the Bible as the inspired, inherent word of God, and that Christ's church is distinctive as the one church Paul speaks of in Ephesians 4:4.

I emphasized that this strong sense of identity spurs us to truthfully claim all aspects of Christ's church – including a cappella music in worship, autonomy of the local congregation, weekly observance of the Lord's supper and the role of men and women in and out of the worship assembly. This listing of ministry principles also included the statement that baptism is essential, that servant leaders will change the world, that families must be nurtured and that the harvest is plentiful but the workers are few.

I concluded by stating that Christians are truth seekers, and God gives us the courage to seek to teach, even in the light of opposition. My goals and dreams for Harding cannot simply be presented in a report of numbers and building plans but must be the heart of what has sustained us thus far – our desire to follow God and humbly seek His guidance.

The response from this publication in the *Harding* magazine was overwhelming. I received hundreds of letters from alumni stating their support for Harding's mission and purpose. I was encouraged by the response from members of the Harding family to this recommitment to our mission.

The next major effort at stating the mission of Harding in a public way came with the strategic planning process in 2007-2008.[10] As a preface to the Strategic Planning Report, which involved a study with board members and faculty for about a year, a statement spelling out our mission was approved by the faculty in the College of Bible and Religion, the faculty of Harding and the Board of Trustees. This statement was later reaffirmed by the Board in May 2011, and has been distributed widely to the Harding family.

This restatement of our mission was the result of much work on the part of board members at a retreat in Branson, Mo., as well as faculty members and administrators. The statement was written by a host of people, but I believe it is a beautiful outline of our purpose. It begins with the wording,

Harding University was founded in 1924 upon spiritual convictions. We are, at our core, a Christian university. The character,

51

example and concerns of Jesus Christ are the standards that shape us and chart the course of our future. Because of this, an all-encompassing love for God and a corresponding love for people are at the heart of who we are.

This statement emphasizes that the Christian worldview is to be at the core of every academic discipline and every extracurricular activity on campus. It also emphasizes that we are to strive for both grace and truth because both were perfectly blended in Jesus – as He always spoke truth in a gracious way.

The statement also emphasizes the fact that our institutional identity is rooted in our belief that the Bible is the fully inspired and authoritative word of God. We hold it to be the God-breathed basis of our teaching and life. Reference is also made to Harding being a leader in world missions.

The statement finally makes reference to the fact that Harding has always been deeply connected with churches of Christ, and we reaffirm this connection. Our goal will be to continue to hire only members of churches of Christ as faculty and administrators. Though we live in a time of significant confusion over our brotherhood's identity, we are determined that Harding University be captive to neither a rigid legalism on the right nor a formless liberalism on the left. "With gentleness and respect" (1 Peter 3:16), we affirm such distinctive convictions of the mainstream churches of Christ as baptism for the remission of sins, a cappella music in worship and male spiritual leadership. [Complete mission statement is in Appendix B.]

Again, the response to this statement, both in 2008 and 2011, has been overwhelmingly positive. It has been beneficial in helping people understand the mission of Harding and our commitment to basic core values. This has been particularly important in times of great transition within the church and within our culture.

Embracing the Mission

Flowing out of this effort to clarify and state as clearly as possible the Harding mission was an effort by Dr. Bruce Mc-Larty in his doctoral dissertation to develop a training manual for all new faculty members. His work led to the publication of the booklet, "Embracing the Mission,"[11] which is used in a

52

required training session for all new faculty members to give them a better understanding of the goals of Harding. Dr. McLarty's booklet is a wonderful addition to the literature about Harding's mission. The material has been developed for online training as well as face-to-face training so that all full-time and part-time faculty are oriented to our mission as they begin their work at Harding.

Maintaining Our Distinctive Mission

Maintaining Harding's distinctive mission has been a challenge since we began in 1924. The issues are simply different today. No doubt, adherence to the mission will always be a significant challenge for us as we continue going against the grain of America's culture and the standard of the higher education community. As culture becomes more and more secular and demands for national accreditation increase, there is a growing sense that inclusiveness is the model that should be used within churches of Christ as they deal with other religious groups.

Unfortunately, movies, books and the media all attempt to make it look as though anyone who believes in God and the Bible and still holds traditional views toward the family and morality is a far-right fanatic. This battle is certainly not new in our country, but it is growing more serious all the time. The fragmentation of the family, the waning influence of the church in general and the refusal of the secular university to teach traditional religious values are realities we face today. Christian colleges face significant challenges to maintain their distinctive mission. However, this challenge also presents a marvelous opportunity for Christian education to stand in the gap and present an alternative to the secular value system taught in so many places. The contrast between the two will become even greater in the future.

One example of the shift in cultural values today has to do with the movement by the gay rights community to insist that Christian academies and Christian colleges and universities include the gay rights agenda as part of their mission statement. In 2011, a small group of students on the Harding campus organized a Web site, entitled "The State of the Gay at Harding University." As a result of this group's public effort, I issued a statement announcing Harding's position.

In that statement, I repeated the text in our handbook that says, "Harding University holds to the biblical principle that sexual relationships are unacceptable to God outside the context of marriage. Sexual immorality in any form will result in suspension from the University." I also reaffirmed that I believe the Bible teaches that homosexual behavior is sinful (Romans 1 and I Corinthians 6). What is acceptable and holy in the sight of God is not determined by societal norms or democratic compulsion. Plenty of recent writers use the words of the Bible as the bigoted writings of ancient men who were seeking to usurp power over others for their own advantage. I completely disagree with this notion. We believe the Bible is "God breathed" and is the revelation of our holy God to his beloved creation. Consequently, we believe that we are to live humbly with the prayer of Jesus on the cross in our hearts, "Father, your will, not mine be done."

I closed the statement by saying that I believe Harding is the most special place on earth, and that we have the most incredible student body anywhere.[12]

The response from the Harding constituency was overwhelmingly positive. As could be predicted, the response from some people was negative. I received thousands of letters relative to this issue, which confirm that a distinctively Christian university will continue to face challenges in the years to come.

A second challenge that Harding and other Christian, faith-based colleges will face to a greater degree in the future will involve accreditation issues. The national government is pursuing accreditation from a national curriculum point of view and is insisting that regional accrediting bodies, like the Higher Learning Commission that accredits Harding, enforce their policies and procedures. I have been a part of the Higher Learning Commission for the last twenty-seven years, and I see the directions in the past decade to be very alarming. The Higher Learning Commission, along with other regional accrediting bodies, used to be peer driven and, in my judgment, represented the best accrediting procedure to be found anywhere in the world. In fact, universities from other countries regularly seek accreditation from American colleges and universities because of the prestige of these organizations.

However, in recent years, the trend has been for the Federal Government to insist that regional accrediting bodies be the watchdog for various issues, such as price control. My major concern is that a national curriculum, which by definition would mean a uniformity of classes taught at every university in our country, would greatly inhibit Harding's distinctive mission of teaching Bible truths as the center of our curriculum. While I think this will not happen quickly, much attention is being given to this issue by many people at the national level. It is simply getting harder to be distinctive because of Federal control.

Another major challenge that Harding and other Christian colleges face involves the wave of inclusiveness versus exclusiveness with respect to churches of Christ and their relationship with each other and other religious groups. The current trend toward inclusiveness seems to be growing and seems to make the exclusive nature of the Lord's church less attractive to some people. Harding has always maintained an exclusive position relative to certain principles taught in the Bible. The current mission statement refers to baptism as a requirement for salvation, the differences in the roles of women and men in the church, and singing as cappella in nature. One of the great challenges that Harding will continue to face involves maintaining its exclusive doctrinal position while proclaiming the gospel invitation that is inclusive and open to everyone.

Harding is Mission

As I close this chapter, I am back to where I began. I have written a great deal about the distinctive mission of Harding, but I am still thinking about today's students and how they will learn about this mission. I suspect they will learn about it in a similar way that I learned about it when I came as a freshman in 1961. I think they will see it in the lives of their fellow students, and I think they will see it in the lives of their faculty members who are committed to this unique mission and live it out every day. By being in faculty homes, in prayer sessions with others and going on campaigns, these students will come to embrace the Harding mission and be influenced by it for the rest of their lives.

Harding University at Tahkodah (HUT) has built a series of villages representing various countries around the world, particularly some of the poorer nations. Students who study missions and/or are preparing to do mission work in these countries go through intense training with seasoned missionaries to learn how to live as the natives do in various cultures.

CHAPTER FOUR
The Aroma of Christ

Introduction

Paul stated in 2 Corinthians 2:15, "For we are to God the aroma of Christ among those who are being saved and those who are perishing." In chapel, I have probably quoted from Paul's address on being ministers of the New Covenant more than any other passage as I have attempted to explain the evangelistic mission of Harding. To me, Harding is all about being the aroma of Christ to the world. Paul's charge to all Christians to be ministers of the New Covenant begins in verse 14, "But thanks be to God who always leads us in triumphal procession in Christ and through us spreads everywhere the fragrance of the knowledge of Him."[1]

In chapter 3:1-11, Paul tells us that the confidence to be ministers of the New Covenant will come through Christ because we are not competent in and of ourselves. He talks about our being changed into His likeness and that, with unveiled faces, we reflect the Lord's glory and are being transformed into His likeness with ever-increasing glory.

In chapter 4, he talks about our having this ministry by the mercy of God; therefore, we should never lose heart. He states that we should never preach ourselves but Jesus Christ as Lord. Then He tells us that we should always fix our eyes not on what is seen but on what is unseen.

In chapter 5, Paul talks about knowing ourselves, knowing the Lord and knowing the lost. The grand conclusion of this dissertation on evangelism comes when he calls on all ministers of the New Covenant to be ambassadors for Jesus Christ as though God were making His appeal through us. He implores all of us to be reconciled to God. He urges all of us to make sure we have not received God's grace in vain.

These passages were first brought to life for me in a year-long series of lessons by Jim Woodroof when he preached for the College church in Searcy. I later used this message in all of my classes in Christian Business Ethics.

When I think of the purpose of Harding University, I think of it in light of Paul's admonition for all of us to be ministers of the New Covenant. I think the opportunity to study the Bible, be a part of world missions, go on spring break campaigns, be a part of global missions experiences, major in leadership and ministry or participate in home Bible studies makes the Harding experience real.

Jimmy Huff was S.A. president in 2004-2005. He understood this mission and helped make it real for many students. Here is part of his story –

> Toward the end of my senior year, I went to hear an evening
> message in the Benson auditorium by Don McLaughlin. He issued
> a response to the invitation, and I was at the front helping with
> response cards. I was surprised to see a large group of men come
> forward, requesting prayers for deep spiritual transformation in
> their lives. I knew these men, or so I thought. I hardly spoke to any
> of them, but I had labeled them as "good ol' boys," guys who gave
> a wink to a sinful lifestyle while playing up their charm to adults.
> My bias was not particularly conscious, but I would certainly avoid
> and dismiss anyone that I judged to be in this group, surmising that
> we had nothing in common. But the downtrodden faces that I saw
> in these men completely abolished a stereotype that I had so blind-
> ly employed. After everyone had left, I continued to talk with these
> men and saw their ardent desire to be ambassadors for Christ. They
> invited me to come to Waffle House to continue the conversation,
> and I remember talking well past midnight over waffles, syrup and
> coffee. In the wee hours of the morning, we circled in Waffle House
> and offered a collective prayer to God, thanking Him for His Spir-
> it that united us in spite of our presuppositions that went against
> one another. We continued to meet weekly and pray, and these men
> whom I once avoided became some of my closest friends in the final
> months of my senior year.

Steve Cloer, from the class of 2001-2002, also understood this special mission in the Harding community. He said,

> *Harding was the village in which I was raised. From kindergarten to graduate school, I was affirmed, encouraged and prodded by the teachers, coaches, administrators and staff members that make up Harding University. It was from this faith-building environment that God launched me into ministry. During my college years, I met my wife and partner in the gospel, Lindsay Snow. I developed deep, spiritual friendships that continue to this day. Plus, God used this time as a training ground to shape and grow my faith.*

College of Bible & Ministry

The training of preachers, youth ministers and missionaries is very much a part of the work of the College of Bible and Ministry. Dr. Monte Cox has served as dean since 2009, and we have thirty-two talented full-time Bible faculty members. In the spring of 2013, 274 students majored in Bible, which constituted 7.4 percent of the undergraduate enrollment.

Taylor Payne, a graduate in 2012, described his experience at Harding –

> *My life and ministry would be drastically different without the influence of Harding's Bible faculty. Every future minister should be blessed to sit at the feet of men such as Monte Cox, Kevin Youngblood, Scott Adair, Randy Willingham and countless others. It was at Harding that I was able to observe and develop friendships with men having a zeal for biblical truth, along with an equal zeal for that truth to permeate the most basic areas of life. Dr. Cox mentored me and showed me how to love God fully and to allow that love to trickle down in selfless love for other people.*

Dr. Willingham had an "open door" policy with me and was intimately involved and helpful in theological and personal struggles that I experienced. These men and others were pivotal in helping me develop a precision for biblical understanding, as well as a capacity for not only my head but my heart to treasure God. I do not think there will ever be a day in my future when I am surrounded by so many godly mentors in one place.

In keeping with the original purpose of Harding, the College of Bible and Ministry is also dedicated to providing courses and experiences for all Harding students, regardless of their major, as all students have the responsibility of sharing the good news of Jesus Christ through their life's work. Integrating faith and work has always been an important part of our mission at Harding.

Ryan Rummage, a graduate in 2012 and now a law student at Emory University, formed this goal –

My story at Harding is one filled with a desire to fuse two very different things. On one hand, Harding taught me to put Christ first in all that I do. From the teachers and administration to my close friends, I was surrounded by people who encouraged me to put Christ above all else in my life, and I am ever grateful for the talks I had and lessons I learned from these people. On the other hand, I had wanted to be an attorney since high school, a profession that doesn't always have the best reputation. I am currently in the middle of my time in law school, and I couldn't be more thankful for the experience I had at Harding, an experience that taught me to fuse my Christian values with the seemingly contradictory world in which I now live and study. I came to Harding wanting to be an attorney, and I left Harding wanting to be a Christian attorney.

In light of the importance of the Bible program to the mission of the University, one of the first things I pursued in 1987 was the change of the Bible Department from being a part of the College of Arts and Sciences to being a separate School of Religion with Neale Pryor as the acting dean. Dr. Philip Slate was then selected in 1988 as dean. Other individuals prior to Dr. Cox

who served in this key leadership position were Carl Mitchell, Tom Alexander and Bruce McLarty.

Harding University Lectureships

The annual Bible Lectureship has been a major event for Harding since its founding. I very much appreciate the leadership provided by Don Shackelford, Howard Norton and Bruce McLarty in directing these lectures for many years.

One of my earliest Lectureship memories as president occurred when Dr. Jack Evans from Southwest Christian College was the keynote speaker for the Lectureship. He was given a particular topic as was customary, and I expected him to walk in just prior to the evening lecture. When he wasn't there when it was time to begin, I started calling to see if something had happened. What I determined was that he was still in Terrill, Texas, and had Lectureship on his calendar for the next week. At the last minute, I remember asking Dr. Neale Pryor to substitute for him. He did speak on the very topic that had been assigned to Dr. Evans. We are so blessed at Harding to have people on the faculty who can step in and hit a homerun at a moment's notice.

One of my favorite times occurs on Monday of each Lectureship when we host a celebration ministry dinner, which was earlier called a Preacher/Elder Dinner. We celebrate those preachers who have been preaching for twenty-five, thirty or even fifty years. This is always a highlight of that dinner. One of the keynote speakers in recent years was Dr. Prentice Meador, who talked about his granddaughter's leukemia.[2] It was a masterpiece.

Center for World Missions

The purpose of the Center for World Missions is to recruit, train and mentor teams and individuals to intentionally spend their lives in holistic, cross-cultural ministry to all parts of the world.

While the Center for World Missions began in 2000, it certainly was not Harding's first effort at emphasizing evangelistic efforts on the part of our students and graduates. Most publications indicate that one-third of the missionaries of the churches of Christ are alumni of Harding. We have had a long-standing commitment to encouraging students and graduates to become missionaries.

One focus for the Center for World Missions is to send out one or two new teams each year. It is important to get students on the mission field, as one out of every three students who actively participate in training and the Global Outreach internships eventually make the decision to serve as long-term foreign missionaries.

Robert Meyer, from the class of 2004, was one student who had a great interest in missions. Here is part of his story –

When the semester began, I wasted no time in signing up for a study abroad program in Greece, and I joined the African mission's summer internship program. I wanted to see the world. At the time, I had no intention of becoming a missionary in Africa, but I spent my first summer break as an intern in Tabligbo, Togo, with a mission team working in one of the world's least developed nations. God opened my eyes to new realities and questions that I had never before considered. I ate corn meal mush in a spicy sauce made with fish heads. I experienced the heat of the tropics. I formed friendships with Togolese Christians with whom I could hardly communicate but who welcomed me as a brother in Christ and gladly shared the little they had with a wide-eyed college freshman from America. My intent in serving cross-culturally led me to Angola, where I have been with my wife for three years.

The Center for World Missions also sponsors a program at Camp Tahko-dah, near Searcy, where Harding offers training and experience in development of medical and church-planting ministry through its Global Village. Students are enrolled in weekend retreats for the development ministry intersession course and are assigned to live as families in one of the villages intended to simulate life in an area of the world such as Asia, Latin America, Africa or Appalachia. Teams of missionaries from Harding and other Christian schools use this facility for real-world experiential training. About twenty to thirty churches and/or youth groups use this facility every year. The two-week course in May generally has an enrollment of about forty-five students.

Global Outreach programs are also an important way to encourage young people to consider going to the mission field. These programs were previously called International Campaigns. Currently, about 200 students and faculty members go to thirty countries every summer. Students can choose from three levels of increasingly engaging short-term mission experiences, campaigns, internships and survey research trips. Students in campaigns travel in groups of six to twelve and participate in evangelism and service projects for up to six weeks. Interns are placed in groups of two to four for eight weeks with missionary families, shadowing the workers on their daily church planning work.

During 2013, 166 students and thirty-two faculty members participated in summer mission trips. This number included forty-four interns, three Let's Start Talking groups and one research trip to Peru and Bolivia led by Dr. Bill Richardson, which included sixteen student researchers. This means nearly 200 faculty and staff served in thirty-one mission sites around the globe during the summer of 2012. In addition, faculty and staff

PHOTO PERMISSION BY HEATHER GOULD

63

from the Center for World Missions are currently mentoring three foreign mission teams that have been formed – one team of three couples that departed for Tanzania, another team of four couples preparing for a church-planting ministry in Peru and one couple who are committed for long-time service in Thailand.[3]

Justin Sims, of the class of 2013, represents one student who experienced this exposure and decided to serve God in South America. He wrote –

By the time my junior year rolled around, I remained on track to earn a missions and Spanish degree but lacked any significant experience in Latin American missions. Ideally, I wanted a full summer internship that would expose me to multiple peoples, places and church planting models in order to at least partially confirm my life's trajectory. But that type of trip did not yet exist. So, we created it. With Dr. Bill Richardson at the helm, a Bible professor and former missionary to Latin America, we gradually assembled a team of students interested in a traveling missions internship across Bolivia and Peru. By the time summer arrived, we had assembled seventeen students representing ten majors from four countries to visit churches and missionaries in seven major cities during ten weeks. Through this internship, I finally found that my "place" was serving God somewhere south of America.

64

Global Missions Experience

The Center for World Missions also hosts the Global Missions Experience every third year. In the most recent experience in 2012, more than 1,000 participants and volunteers gathered over a weekend at Camp Tahkodah. Universities represented were Lipscomb, Freed Hardeman, Faulkner, Ohio Valley, Harding, Abilene, Lubbock and Oklahoma Christian, as well as several other churches and campus ministries. Keynote presenters spoke passionately about their areas of the world and shared stories from their countries of origin. Each evening closed with campfires and storytelling and, even though the days were full, the campfires representing different areas around the world were well attended.

On Friday evening, the Tanzania team, which departed for the field in January 2013, interviewed the Eldoret, Kenya, team on the thirty-year anniversary of the beginning of their work. The event culminated on Saturday evening when 200 young people made their commitment to become full-time, long-term foreign or domestic missionaries. This is what Harding University is all about – and perhaps one of the best definitions of camaraderie.

One of the first experiences I remember involving mission teams had to do with the Uganda team that formed in 1994. This team included Brent and Heather Armstrong Abney, John and Sara Gaston Barton, Mark and Marnie Rozell Moore, Deron and Becca Johnson Smith and Greg and Jill Smiley Taylor. These students

 were all leaders on the Harding campus, and it was really a neat experience to watch them develop their plans to go as a group to Uganda and to see their excitement as they talked to people about taking on this work.

These families made their decision to move to Jinja, the second largest city in Uganda, a country in East Africa about the size of Oregon and thousands of miles from the Harding campus. They left in March 1994, not only to fulfill a dream but a five-year commitment of living and sharing Christ with the people of Africa. An article about their work was in the *Harding* magazine in the fall of 1995, written by Alice Ann Kellar.[4]

Spring Break Campaigns

I have always been encouraged by our students going on evangelistic campaigns during their week off for spring break. Many college students go to the beach during this week, but at Harding, many students opt to go on an evangelistic or service-related campaign effort. These campaigns are student-led and organized. They even raise the money necessary for these trips. In 2013, 265 students went to fifteen places, including six foreign countries.[5]

For many years, spring break campaigns were organized out of my office and directed by Rich Little, Daniel Cherry and Nate Copeland. Cindy Hunter was the administrative assistant for the program for more than twenty years, but the Mitchell Center assumed the leadership in 2011.

One of the results of these campaigns was reported in a letter written to Daniel Cherry, who directed the campaigns in 2006. In the following excerpt, Thelma Annaloro tells how the students gave her hope and reaffirmed her faith in God –

> *This week, God sent me seventeen angels from Harding University spring break campaigns. In two and one-half days, they completely gutted and cleaned my home of all the debris. They sang, prayed, laughed and made me happy with their enthusiasm for just helping someone in need. They never once complained of the stench or piles of sewage they shoveled from my home. I will forever remember these young adults who gave of themselves, guided by the hand of God.[6]*

The Carl Mitchell Center

The Mitchell Center, named in honor of Carl and Frankie Mitchell, is directed

by Dr. Andrew Baker. One of the major activities of the Mitchell Center is the development of the leadership and ministry second major, which encourages students to prepare for service in the Lord's church upon graduation, regardless of their first major. Many students in business, education, nursing and other disciplines choose this as a second major, which gives them a far better preparation for service in the Lord's kingdom. For the 2012-13 year,

105 students were pursuing a second major in leadership and ministry.

The Mitchell Center is also involved in directing Uplift, a Bible camp in the summer for junior high and high school students. Uplift attracted 2,488 students in 2013. Campers often enroll as students at Harding when they graduate.

Many students in the last few years have participated in a trip called "The Experience" during the summer, which involves ministry opportunities in New York, Miami, Nicaragua and at Uplift.

Center for Spiritual Leadership

The Center for Spiritual Leadership is led by Dr. Randy Willingham, who in 2012-13 partnered with the Center for Christian Broadcasting to produce a thirteen-lesson series on Archeology in the Bible with Dr. Dale Manor. Dr. Willingham distributed workshop materials for the Mouse Trap Series on pornography for use in local churches. The Center provides conflict mediation for churches and parachurch organizations. It also provides minister transition resources that are available on their Web site. In 2012-13, they piloted a workshop in Oklahoma City, entitled "Care for the Caregiver: Inside Stories of Deep Grace," to equip churches to minister to people with chemical or other addictive behaviors. These "silent partner ministries" allow alumni to listen in on live church consultations and coaching sessions.

Other Programs

Harding also maintains the Center for Advanced Ministry Training, formerly known as Harding School of Biblical Studies, which is led by Dr. Bill Richardson. A number of students have scholarships to participate in this undergraduate degree program that currently has twenty-nine students enrolled. The Master of Ministry program is now in its tenth year and serves fifty-eight continuing students, with a fall enrollment of twenty-five students. Fifty-seven students have completed the Master of Ministry degree program.

Harding also offers Distance Education courses. In 2012-13, 351 students took online courses.

In the Marriage and Family Therapy program, thirteen students completed degree requirements for the Master of Science degree, and through their clinical services, provided more than 8,200 hours of face-to-face therapy for individuals, couples and families of White County.

Under the direction of Dr. Phil Thompson and Devin Swindle, the Center for Preaching hosted its first Kerusso Experience, a preaching camp for high school young men in the summer of 2013. Thirty students from four states and one foreign country participated in studying, preparing and delivering lessons from the book of James. The Center for Preaching also conducted a Preachers' Workshop during the Harding Lectureship.

Harding School of Theology

A very important part of the Bible program at Harding is the School of Theology in Memphis, Tenn., led by Dr. Evertt Huffard. Our oldest graduate program, H.S.T. provides advanced training for ministry. When I became president, the dean was Dr. Phil Slate. He was followed by Dr. Bill Flatt. Dr. Huffard accepted this responsibility in 1999 and was both dean and vice president through the 2012-13 academic year.

I have always been impressed with the School of Theology's commitment to rigorous scholarship and service to the Lord's kingdom. They have blended this together in a beautiful way and, in so doing, have been a great asset to the advancement of the Lord's church.

At the end of May 2013, the number of graduates had increased to 1,597. They now have graduates ministering in forty-six states, in addition to those who are missionaries in numerous countries around the world. Articles by H.S.T. students and faculty have been published in almost every possible magazine over the years. Dr. Huffard has done a masterful job in leading this program.

Home Bible Studies

Home Bible studies on Wednesday nights have become a favorite of the spiritual programs at Harding for many years. This is a strictly voluntary program where faculty and staff members invite students into their homes on Wednesday evenings for Bible study. More than 1,000 students typically attend Wednesday night small groups. Students repeatedly report the value of this experience as they have gotten to know fellow students and faculty members in a personal way.

Leah and I began a home Bible study in 1988, and I remember Terry Davis being very helpful as he led singing for the group for several years. I will always be grateful to him for getting us started in this experience. Our dear friends, Wilt and Judy Martin, assisted us in this endeavor, which we continued for twenty-five years. This allowed us to get to know a number of students on a personal basis that I would simply not have known otherwise. Students helped teach the lessons in many cases, and I learned a great deal from them.

Elizabeth Strate Kellett, who graduated in 2009, was in our home Bible study. Here is a part of her story –

> *The best friends I made were quite adventurous like me. We went on several road trips, including weekend trips to Niagara Falls, Canada and Mount Rushmore, S.D. We also went on a spring break trip that took us to the Grand Can-*  *yon, Las Vegas, Los Angeles, San Diego, Tijuana, Mexico, Carlsbad Caverns, Truth or Consequences, N.M., Lubbock and a campout in Dr. Burks' back yard. Dr. Burks was always supportive of our plans. From Wednesday night Bible studies at his house and Sonic happy hours in his convertible*

*to birthday parties in his office and a trip to the education building
with me to make a special valentine for his wife, he always wanted
to be a part of whatever we had going on.*

*Dr. Andrew Baker led some of the most real and significant
projects, including the National Day of Encouragement, Uplift
summer camp and the cardboard testimonies chapel that have influenced me to continue living in a way that touches people through my
words and actions.*

As we talk about the aroma of Christ, I can't help but wonder how important
dorm devotionals, all-school devotionals, one-on-one studies between students,
club devotionals and so many other activities are to the development of students'
spiritual lives. I believe these are some of the most important things that take place
on and off the Harding campus. No one other than God will ever know the impact
of these activities.

The Great Commission

The Great Commission has always been a guiding principle for faculty and
students at Harding. As Christians, we are the aroma of Christ, and we are called
to be ministers of the New Covenant – ambassadors for Jesus Christ as God makes
His presence known through us.

When you walk on the Harding campus, you will sense the urgency of this
message. In the American Heritage Center, you will see a globe of the world with
the Great Commission shown prominently. When you visit the McInteer Center,
you will read the words of the Great Commission in big letters around the depiction
of the world in the rotunda. When you meet the faculty and students, you will often
be talking with people who have been on the mission field.

Multipurpose Fountain

At a Christian university, the fountains provide excellent venues to baptize
people while also enhancing campus décor. Harding's fountains also serve other
functions. The primary unintended use of the Harding fountain follows a ring cere-

mony. While the surrounding women admire the ring, the friends of the guy attack from a nearby corner to throw their newly engaged friend into the nearest fountain, no matter the weather or temperature.

Global Domination in the McInteer

One less known Harding tradition involves the world map on the McInteer rotunda floor. According to those who tell, it is possible to tape off the floor of the McInteer to match the territories of a Risk game board. By doing so, students can play a life-sized edition of the global domination board game.

Harding is Evangelism

We are serious about sharing the good news of Jesus Christ with people everywhere. Our students come from all fifty states and fifty other nations. We want all to know about God and His son, and we want them to share this good news with others. Talk with Monte Cox about missions and be moved to action. Talk with recent graduates like Taylor Payne, Justin Sims, Robert Meyer and Steve Cloer, and you will be amazed at their commitment to sharing the good news.

Learn about spring break mission trips, summer global mission opportunities, our leadership and ministry double major, our Center for Spiritual Leadership and the School of Theology at Memphis. Harding students truly are the aroma of Christ, regardless of their major and regardless of where they live.

Camp Tahkodah, a Christian youth camp owned by Harding, is the site of numerous baptisms each summer. My sons, Stephen (left), and Bryan baptized their children, Kaley and Weston, there last summer.

CHAPTER FIVE
Favorite Chapel Memories

"Good morning to each and every one of you!" was my typical greeting every day in chapel. Delivered in a bass voice, this phrase was about as common for the student body as were my references to camaraderie. I had a front row seat for chapel and will always be grateful for the opportunity to be involved in daily chapel.

Chapel is one of the very special privileges at Harding University, where the entire student body and faculty meet together every week day to worship God. Every day, stu-

dents at Harding are given the unique opportunity to praise God for who He is and what He has done.

I often emphasized at the beginning of each semester in chapel how fortunate we were to be a part of a university where God is glorified every day. I often made reference to the fact that, in chapel, we learn about reverence. The world has taught us to be irreverent about almost everything. The world can be irreverent about anything that can be mocked if it gets a laugh – even scripture, even hymns, even God. But we unapologetically confess that we expect everyone to learn reverence as we come together in a worship experience in chapel. We realize that chapel may well be the most radically counter-cultural portion of a student's day because, in chapel, we practice reverence in the presence of the King of kings and the Lord of lords.

In chapel, we are also able to learn about community and family. We are unique in higher education in emphasizing chapel in this spiritual way. As we sit together, sing together, pray together, learn together and share together, we form a sense of community that is indeed very special. I remember, on many occasions, asking the student body to join with me and be committed to being a genuine community – one where we make time to be together, have fellowship with one another and join together in a cause greater than ourselves.

Of course, chapel involves more than just the devotional nature. After our devotional period, we often have programs that help us understand the total community at Harding. Musical programs are sometimes presented, and announcements provide a better understanding by the entire community about what is going on at Harding.

It was my privilege to preside over chapel and serve as chairman or vice chairman of the Chapel Program Committee during my twenty-six years as president. I have calculated that a total of 4,650 chapels were conducted during this time, counting dual chapels in the fall since 2002 and some dual chapels in the spring as well. I further estimate that I was out of town about ten percent of the time, and my guess is that I was on campus and able to preside for more than 4,000 chapel experiences. What a blessing to be able to listen to the singing and be a part of this activity!

One of my favorite memories of making announcements was when I introduced a new grandchild to the student body. On one occasion, Carter, only a month old, spit up on me while I was holding him for all to see. The *Bison* ran a cartoon about the event a few days later.

At Harding We Sing

The kind of program that received the strongest response from the student body typically involved music. We were privileged to hear from the University Chorus, the Concert Choir or A Cappella chorus over the years almost every semes-

ter. We were also able to hear from the Good News Singers and the Belles and Beaux. We heard music programs presented from outside groups, such as the Metropolitan Detroit Chorus in April of 1990.

Ray Walker of the Jordanaires came and led singing for three days in chapel. What a special time that was. Dean

Priest led us in very meaningful song services on several occasions, as did Mike Wood and Al Frazier. David Henry, a student from Jamaica, led us in song services while he was a student at Harding, and Terry Davis, Nathan Jordanson, Pat Bills and Botham Jean were among the favorite song leaders. For many years, Friday was designated as a singing day in chapel, and I always looked forward to this day, especially when students led us.

In recent years, I recall days devoted to singing favorite songs selected by students or faculty members, accompanied by reasons that the song was so meaningful to them. Dr. Michael Claxton led in the development of several of these chapel experiences.

Another favorite memory involved those occasions in the spring when the  Harding Academy kindergarten would present a program for the student body. It was always well done and well received by the student body. In fact, they would more often get a standing ovation than any other group in chapel.

One of my favorite memories of singing in chapel occurred on the last day of each semester when we would sing "The Lord Bless You and Keep You" to the graduating seniors – always an emotional time for all involved. At Harding, students express their deepest feelings through songs.

Another music highlight each year came in December when the holiday band appeared in chapel. Their traditional "Sleigh Ride" performance brought out song books and key rings to add to the festive spirit of the day, and I even played the tympani in chapel on one occasion.

Theme Chapels

During the last few years of my tenure as president, the Chapel Program Committee selected a theme, and a number of speakers, including students and off-campus guests, would speak to that theme. The first theme we used was "The Aroma of Christ." Other themes included, "I am a Christian Because...," "Life at the Foot of the Cross," "The Restoration Plea," "Take up Your Cross" and "Facing the Issues."

For many years, gospel meetings were conducted during the first week of the fall and spring semesters. We supported this meeting effort with evangelistic preaching in chapel. At the end of the sermons, an invitation to accept Christ was always extended. Unfortunately, gospel meetings have ceased for the most part, and we have not found anything to take their place that is as effective as those meetings were. I have great memories of the positive impact those weeks in chapel had on the entire campus.

Perhaps the most memorable series occurred in the spring and was called "Struggles of the Faith." In this series, presenters were asked to speak about their faith struggles. Some had to do with an illness in the family, the loss of a loved one or a personal problem to work through. These testimonials were well received by the student body. I especially remember presentations by Jerry "Bo" Mitchell about uncovering fraudulent practices in race relations in Mississippi; Chris Dell talking about the loss of his wife; and Paula Barbieri talking about her relationship with O.J. Simpson and about her coming to faith, which changed her life completely. The series continues to be popular today.

One of my favorite weeks was what we called Mission Awareness Week. Until the last few years, this was typically five days in a row during which mission opportunities around the world were presented to the student body. Different missionaries and/or faculty members who represented that part of the work would speak. Generally, they had worked in the country where they were asking students to consider some kind of short-term or long-term relationship in the future. Numerous students responded and went on these mission experiences because of these chapels. Closely connected with this kind of experience were those chapels when we had a mission send-off either for Spring Break Missions or summer long-term missions. This was a wonderful way to encourage students to do mission work.

My all-time favorite week in chapel during these twenty-six years was the week when Bruce McLarty had a live interview with Jim Bill McInteer. Bro. McInteer was well along in years and was clearly an icon for our brotherhood. He had been on our Board of Trustees for fifty-three years. As Dr. McLarty interviewed him, he responded to personal questions about his family, his relationship with his wife and his service in the Lord's church. He concluded the week by speaking to the student body on Friday of that week.

Another series that was conducted for many years by the Social Work Club was called Resident of the Month. My favorite recipient of that honor was Ida May Horton on the occasion of her 100th birthday. This presentation took place Sept. 23, 1998. After the presentation, she was asked to make a few comments, and she proceeded to cite a beautiful poem for the student body.

I also loved the Homecoming musical previews because so much work had gone into preparation for the musical, but the preview was always preceded by a devotional that related to the musical being presented that year. I remember some beautiful devotional presentations concerning "Fiddler on the Roof," "My Fair Lady" and "The Sound of Music." Robin Miller coordinated these programs and also directed the musicals.

A highlight during the first fifteen years of my presidency was the year-end slide show presented by Dr. Jerome Barnes during the final chapel. This became a day that students didn't miss chapel. Dr. Barnes put in an enormous amount of work in selecting hundreds of slides to represent the activities of the entire year.

Each year, we would have some chapels devoted entirely to prayer. I partic-ularly like those chapels that were led by student prayer groups, as they called all of us into accountability in our prayer life with God.

Finally, I want to recall the muffin chapel we had at least once each semester after our devotional. I always looked forward to this time of fellowship with the student body as we reassembled in the plaza to eat together. Later, we had gelato chapels, chicken biscuit chapels, etc.

Memorable Individual Presentations

Any list of memorable events risks leaving out some important presentations, but the following especially stood out in my memory –

Dr. Neale Pryor spoke one day about the essentials of be-coming a Christian.[1] He presented this lesson as if he had only one opportunity to talk with a lost person about their relationship with God. It was one of the most impressive lessons I have ever heard in my life. Dr. Pryor spoke on numerous occasions in chapel and in gospel meetings. In my judgment, this was one of his finest presentations.

Jimmy Allen was another of my favorite presenters in chap-el. He was very effective in presenting evangelistic messages.

On the basis of content and style, one of the most memorable presentations made in chapel during this period was given by Dr. Howard Wright. The first black student admitted to Harding who graduated, Wright, who preaches for a church in Atlanta, talked to the student body about his experiences at Harding since graduating. He described feeling like "the invisible man" while a student, dropping out of school at the end of his first semester but coming back later to finish. Special phrases from his lesson stand out to me – "shining shoes somewhere someday" and "Don't let anything take your snap away." This man's life

has been one of great service to others. Dr. Wright was later awarded the Harding Distinguished Alumnus Award, and I was privileged to present him with an honorary Doctorate of Laws degree on behalf of Harding and our Board of Trustees. His presentation in chapel outlined some of his impressions of Harding and the civil rights movement of the 60s.[2]

Another memorable presentation was one made by then Gov. Mike Huckabee on Sept. 13, 2001, just two days after the attack of 9/11 in New York City.[3] We de-

bated as to whether to go ahead with his scheduled presentation, but Gov. Huckabee agreed to come even with our nation in such stress. He spoke about the challenges that we faced after 9/11. He encouraged our students not to respond to the events of 9/11 with fear and bigotry but with God's spirit of power, love and sound mind. He said that if we respond with the former, the terrorists will have won a greater victory than destroying the Twin Towers, but if we respond with the latter, the act that was meant for our detriment would become our victory. He did a masterful job, and it is one of those presentations that I will always remember.

One of my all-time favorite speakers was Gene Stallings, the former football coach at Alabama. Most people would know of him because of his relationship

with his son who had Downs Syndrome and has since passed away. I had the honor of presenting the honorary Doctorate of Laws degree to Coach Stallings and introducing him on several occasions.

My favorite memory of Gene came the last time he spoke in chapel on March 19, 2012, as part of Struggles of the Faith week. He talked about his son's struggle, but the part I remember most is that, in typical Gene Stallings style, he began talking to the student body about respect for God. He addressed a few students who were wearing caps and asked them to remove them, explaining that out of reverence for God, they should not wear them in chapel. You could have heard a pin drop in chapel that day, and I assure you that the hats were removed.

This list of memorable presentations could not be complete without reference

to Dr. Ganus, former president and chancellor of Harding. On several occasions, he shared the history of Harding, but a presentation I well remember was on integrity. Dr. Ganus stands for integrity, and he described it as the key principle that one should live by.

I loved hearing from students in chapel as well. Many students were given opportunity to speak. One of my favorite student speakers was B. Chris Simpson, probably best known for a chapel presentation entitled, "Chicken Biscuits." I asked B. Chris to explain this presentation. Here is his story –

I was eighteen years old when I first reached Harding, sight unseen. My early years were defined by a dichotomy of wins and losses. I won because I was blessed with a strong Christian family who loved me and a church family that was determined to raise me "in the way that I should go." Both of these families triple-dared me to "depart from it when I was old!" Conversely, it often seemed that I lost out because I was a lonely "class-clown-rebel" without a cause, without many friends and without direction. However, as young as six years old, I remember a small voice speaking above the dichotomy telling me that I had something inside to help people and that I served a God who could turn my losses into wins. This voice led me to leave the hustle and bustle of my inner-city neighborhood and trade it for the sticks of Searcy. I am so glad I did.

While working in Chick-Fil-A as a poor freshman, I remember that even frying chicken was fun! I was on a high from all the relationships I had built, how awesome my teachers were, how living in Harbin Hall was like the most humorous episode of Survivor, and how for the first time in my life I felt the presence of God in almost everything I experienced. As I fried chicken with a co-worker, I realized that the chicken was really a metaphor for how God can transform us. We are all raw chicken, potentially harmful if eaten before He fries us to a golden crisp, thereby purifying all our imperfections. Having come from a past with so many losses and living in a new place where everyone could find wins, I was living out that metaphor. That small voice inside of me said, "If ever you speak in chapel, you should talk about this."

Being involved in the Multi-Cultural Student Action Committee at the University led me to our sponsor's office, where he and I discussed my signing up to lead singing in chapel for a special program recognizing Black History month. While talking with him, he explained that he had a speaker for that program who had cancelled and he was desperate to find another. He told me, "If you know of someone, let me know." As I heard his words, the small voice told me, "You know someone...." I thought to myself, "I could do it." I volunteered – and that day, by a fluke, I was switched from leading singing in chapel to speaking.

Five days later, feeling as nervous as humanly possible, I stepped onto the Benson stage with a chicken biscuit in hand about to deliver a message that described how trials can bring people closer to God, as did the trials that African Americans faced in our country's history. I taught that trials in general were like hot grease used to purify chicken so that it may be enjoyed and how the "grease" of trials is used by God to purify all of us according to 1 Peter 1:6-7. The official title of that message was "Fried to Perfection," but is remembered to this day as the "Chicken Biscuit Chapel!" The affirmation I got from my fellow students, the administration and my Bible professors left a lasting impression on me. For the first time in so bold a way, I was speaking on behalf of that small voice inside me. As my Bible professors and mentors taught me more about God's word and lived out an example of selfless service, that small voice grew louder and demanded that I change my major from education to Bible. At that moment, sitting in the Bible office in the McInteer building, God had completed my "call" to full-time ministry.

This metaphor has served my ministry to this day. Through so many great experiences and through so much "grease," God has proven to me that he can turn our losses into wins. It was his voice that led me to leave the hustle and bustle of my inner-city neighborhood and trade it for the sticks of Searcy, Ark. I am so glad I did.

B. Chris continued to be a very popular student speaker after that address.

Another student that I loved to have speak in chapel the last few years was Clay Smith.

Perhaps my favorite chapel presentation during my twenty-six years was another by Jim Bill McInteer. On Feb. 22, 2008, he spoke about his love for Harding and his love for his wife, Betty. They were engaged at Harding and he tells their special love story.

A very different kind of presentation was made at the beginning of the fall semester in 2008. It was presented by Andrew Baker, although he didn't do any speaking. It was something he had organized, and it was entitled "Cardboard Testimonies." He simply put up different cards for the audience to read. Then individuals who had testimonies to share regarding things they had to deal with in their own lives wore these cards. Both students and faculty members participated in this event, which was very powerful.

In my last year, the most popular speaker in chapel was Willie Robertson. The Duck Commander and his wife, Korie, attended Harding, and they had returned to make a presentation to the student body. Willie presented a marvelous message in chapel, and the two of them spoke to a packed house that night.

One of my favorite speakers in chapel, regardless of the topic, was Dr. Monte Cox, who was requested by the students on a regular basis and often spoke on the Christian worldview and missions.

Another memorable speaker for the Harding student body was Don McLaughlin from Atlanta, Ga. Don often came and spoke two or three days each year on different topics. I particularly remember when he was asked to speak on sexual awareness, and he dealt with this topic in a very strong but sensitive way. I have always appreciated his willingness to address critical topics.

I spoke on some occasions in chapel about my favorite song, "Because He Lives." I talked about the fact that God sent His Son, they called Him Jesus, and His resurrection gives all of us hope for life. Among my favorite chapels were those when I would hear a student sing "Because He Lives." One of my favorite renditions was by Rebecca DeRamus. I loved having this song sung by a soprano voice. I love the message of the song, and it is one of my favorite memories of chapel.

Humorous Chapel Experiences

When I think of humor in chapel, my first thought is of the Grumpy Old Men. The Grumpy Old Men were two students, Pete Vann and Marcus Neely, who were asked often to make announcements. They dressed as old men, sounded like old men and blamed everything on President David B. Burks. They were always a hit!

Here is an example of one announcement they made about an upcoming one-act play –

Final Chapel Announcement for Grumpy Old Men
And Highly Enthusiastic, Poorly Scripted Ben & Henry
"Hey, come see the play
It starts today, the first of May
The Real Inspector Hound, and we are sure it will astound
The stage is square; it is not round
and very soon we will expound."
Ben – "Man, those guys don't know how to do a chapel announcement."

Henry – "Yeah, they don't know how to get the important information in."

Ben – "Yeah, information like – the one-act plays are tonight and tomorrow night."

Henry – "At 7 p.m. in the little theater. Admission is only $3 per person or $5 per couple."

Enter the Grumpy Old Men

Grumpy Old Men – "Wait a minute, you guys! You don't know what you're talking about."

Pete – "Yeah, back in my day, we didn't have any plays or theater. Our only means of entertainment was getting jiggy with it."

Marcus – "Of course it was a 10-foot bear.

Pete – "And we didn't have any pansy musical instruments. We only used the instruments that God gave us."

Marcus – "And we liked it – lay down a groove, Ned."

Grumpy Old men –

"We're the grumpy old men and we're here to stay.

We love chapel announcements in a major way.

Gonna kick those dirty rotten scoundrels off the stage.

We're grumpy, we're old and we're minimum wage.

So come see the play, come see the play.

Ya better see the play 'cause we're not play–in."

"Oh, who are we kidding? Nobody can bust a groove like Dr. David Funky Motown. You bring the funky beat, and I'll bring the rhymes and the doritos, Burks.

Dr. Burks – "Lay down a beat, boys."

"So come see the play tonight and tomorrow night
at 7 p.m. in the little theater. Thank you. You are dismissed."

One of the popular humorists in chapel often was Craig Jones from Harding Academy. Craig can impersonate many people. Although he has never learned to impersonate me, he thinks he has. The students love hearing him impersonate people, and he always is well received.

In recent years, my attention would go to Dr. Cliff Ganus III and Dr. Michael Claxton as they made announcements on Thursdays under the heading of Cliff and Clax. This combo was a huge favorite of the student body and even became the face on tee shirts students wore around campus.

Of course, I occasionally made mistakes in chapel when I read announcements. At times, I intentionally made statements while reading the announcements just to keep everyone's attention, but sometimes I just made mistakes and got a lot of attention. For example, I made an announcement concerning Regina social club, and I mispronounced the name of the club. The mistake made it to YouTube in our wonderful world of technology. It has produced more laughs than you could possibly imagine at my expense.

Celebrating Special Events

One of the things that chapel allows is a time for the entire student body and faculty to join together to recognize special events. For example, we were able on Sept. 26, 1991, to have a chapel celebrating Dr. Benson's birthday. Dr. John Stephens, former president of Abilene Christian, came and spoke on that occasion.

Chapel also provides opportunity to have memorial services to honor students or faculty members who have died. I remember well the memorial service for Suzanne Spurrier, director of library services for Harding and a dear friend. She was called home on Dec. 23, 1998.

I also remember the chapel to honor Jim Bill McInteer after his death on March 8, 2010. In a similar way, I remember the memorial service in honor of Paul

Carter after he died on Oct. 31, 2009. Perhaps the memorial that will be remembered by many recent students is that of a Harding student who was killed in an accident after leaving here for spring break. Ty Osman was from Nashville, Tenn., and had just finished one semester at Harding. This gave the student body an opportunity to come together in support of him and his family.

One of the last special events I had a part in was a tribute to Dr. and Mrs.

Ganus as he retired as chancellor, having served as both president for twenty-two years and chancellor for twenty-six years. Dr. Ganus began his experience at Harding as a student in 1939. He became president in 1965. As I stated in chapel that day, "Facts seldom tell the real story. Harding is not about buildings or budgets or enrollment; rather it is about students, faculty, people and transformed lives." Dr. Ganus was a preacher and elder at heart, and he was able to represent Harding at its highest level.

Harding is Chapel

The experience of having 4,000 students come together to sing praises to God every day of the school year was awesome for me. Chapel was where the Harding community, faculty and students came together as family in one place. I can't imagine Harding without daily chapel – a place where we form our identity as an intentionally Christian university.

It was tradition for me to dismiss chapel each day by saying, "You are dismissed." People somehow believed they could not leave until they heard this expression. My last time dismissing them was very emotional for me.

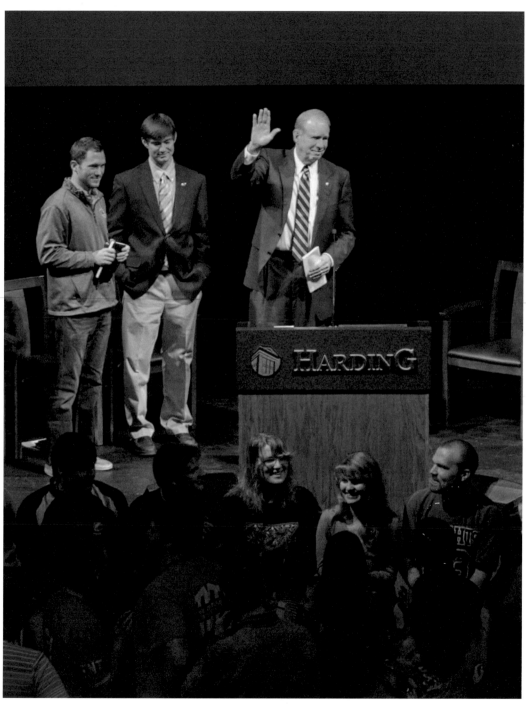

Dr. Burks' last formal chapel farewell – "You are dismissed!"

Brackett Library offers numerous channels of information

PART THREE

Learning

Dr. Dee Carson was all over campus interacting with students every day

CHAPTER SIX
Colleagues Who Care

While there are many definitions for the word, "colleague," I see faculty and staff members, administrators and board members alike as my colleagues at Harding. The comment I hear from students most is that they love the faculty and staff at Harding. This love is shown by caring faculty and staff colleagues who genuinely want to help students grow in their Christian walk with God. We are blessed with a caring staff and caring, genuine members of our Board of Trustees.

Faculty Recruitment

When I went back to Florida State to work on my doctorate, I selected as my dissertation topic, "The Development of Model Faculty Recruitment and Retention Programs for Selected Senior Colleges Supported by Churches of Christ." [1] In the study, I interviewed former and current faculty members to identify ways to better recruit and retain qualified faculty. It is amazing how important that study was to my time as president.

My study showed that the major factor influencing the decision of faculty members to come to Harding, or one of our sister colleges, was the mission of the university. Obviously, salary was an important consideration. Insurance benefits were also a factor, not only with coming but with staying. Perhaps because of my time as a faculty member prior to becoming president, I was concerned about what we might be able to do to increase faculty salaries.

With the help of Dr. Neale Pryor and Dr. Dean Priest, I began to develop new methods for determining faculty compensation. A Faculty Compensation Committee was formed, consisting of Dr. Bobby Coker, Dr. Larry Long, Dr. Paul Pollard,

Dr. Dean Priest, Dr. Neale Pryor and Dr. Cathleen Shultz. This committee met and reported to me in 1989, preceding the beginning of the salary matrix system that we use at Harding today. It takes into consideration years of service, degrees held and market factors – and it has served Harding well.

One of the changes that was made at that time moved faculty members from a twelve-month to a nine-month contract, with additional compensation paid to individuals who taught in summer school. Most faculty members had been on a twelve-month contract. The pay schedule for summer teaching represented an increase for faculty needed to teach those classes. It gave time off to others who were not needed for summer classes. We were then able to compare ourselves with national and regional averages and set goals for improvement.

Another major consideration was the matter of retirement. Harding had a good five percent matching program in place with TIAA-CREF when I became president. However, a number of faculty members were not utilizing this retirement planning provision and were accruing very little retirement, which left them dependent on social security benefits.

As part of this effort, a decision was made in 1989 to begin increasing the matching part of the retirement benefit from five to ten percent, with one percent added each year if the employee would also match the amount. Thus, beginning in 1994, faculty members who elected to participate in this program could put ten percent of their gross salary into their retirement, and Harding matched it dollar for dollar. This twenty percent of their gross salary going into their retirement fund gave faculty members adequate resources for retirement. To my knowledge, Harding has one of the most generous retirement packages available at any university.

1987-1988 Year	2012-2013 Year
161 Faculty	**328 Faculty**
44% Doctorate	**69% Doctorate**
153 Full-Time Equivalent	**264 Full-Time Equivalent**
15 Adjuncts	**150 Adjuncts**
5 New Faculty	**28 New Faculty**
600 Staff	**1,001 Staff**

*HU President's Report – Working with Colleagues

We were able to increase salaries every year. My intent was to increase to one percent above the Consumer Price Index inflation rate posted nationally. We did not announce an increase in 2009 because of the significant recession, but we were able to give a bonus that year so that, even in that year, faculty members had an increase. These increases were in sharp contrast to many colleges and universities that did not receive any increases at all.

Working with Cabinet Officers

I was privileged to work with many talented people in positions of responsibility for various programs. The executive officers when I became president were Neale Pryor, academic affairs; Lott Tucker, finance; Ted Altman, student affairs; Jim Carr, senior vice president; Floyd Daniel, development; and Philip Slate, dean of the graduate school. Dr. Ganus was chancellor.

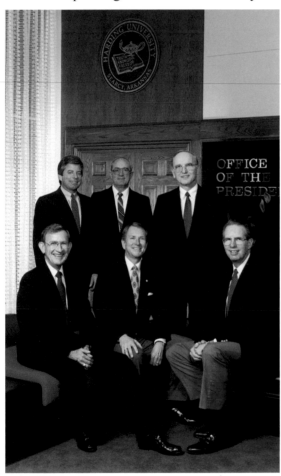

Cabinet officers in 1987

Naturally, a number of changes occurred during the next twenty-six years. In the area of finance, Buddy Rowan became vice president, followed by Mel Sansom. Jerome Barnes, Butch Gardner, Dee Carson and David Collins served in student affairs. Slate was followed at the graduate school by Bill Flatt and Evertt Huffard. Key administrators who were added to the Cabinet during my tenure were Greg Harnden, athletic director; Keith Cronk, chief information officer; Mike Williams, director of advancement; James Simmons, superintendent of the Academy; and Bruce McLarty, vice president for spiritual life. It is interesting to note that Jim Carr, Floyd Daniel and Dr. Ganus served during all of my twenty-six years.

The purpose of the weekly Cabinet meeting was to discuss matters pertaining to the University using a team approach. These meetings allowed all of us to know what was going on in every area of the University and to share the responsibility of decision-making when such decisions affected the entire University. As each came at issues from a different perspective, I knew everyone in the room was there because they loved the Lord and would put Harding's interests ahead of their own. What a blessing to work with these key leaders!

Working with Colleagues

I loved interviewing each full-time faculty member who was being considered for a position at Harding. This was the beginning of a possible long-term relationship with individuals who would be the future leaders at Harding. My focus in these interviews was not their academic preparation, which I left up to the department chairs, deans and provost, but their passion for Christian education. I enjoyed hearing from them about how they could integrate their faith with their discipline, and I met some wonderful people. I think I interviewed 920 people for new positions.

Leah and I later enjoyed having new faculty in our home for dinner at the beginning of each new year. I always asked them to share why they made the decision to join the faculty, and rich discussion followed.

In an effort to continually get to know faculty members better, I tried to have a faculty lunch each month with randomly selected faculty from different departments. It started as a box lunch but later became a served meal. The group was small, generally ten to twelve people, to allow time for discussion. We never had a set agenda, and some wonderful ideas came out of those meetings.

One of my favorite memories of fellowship with colleagues took place every day after chapel in the student center at Java City, where we would gather for coffee and conversation. I think Dr. Carl Mitchell called this a "coffee klatch." We had a round table and a lot of fun. Dr. Howard Norton was part of this gathering whenever he was in town, (which was generally just before pay day), and he made the following observation –

> If you stop by Java City in the Student Center, you'll find a
> table in the corner where a great deal of laughter takes place. Those
> around the table may include anyone from the chairman of the
> Board and the president of the University, to professors and staff
> members, to alumni and students, to retirees and visitors on campus.
> I love that experience and have enjoyed it for many years. Nobody
> checks the roll, but everyone who stops by is welcome. The spirit of
> camaraderie is contagious.[2]

Another important interaction with the academic mission of Harding and our nation involved our relationship with the Higher Learning Commission in Chicago, Ill. I was able to be a consultant/evaluator for the H.L.C. for twenty-five years, thanks to a recommendation made to them by Dr. Joe Pryor, who had worked with them for his entire career. As an evaluator, I was able to travel to more than fifty colleges to learn more about how others pursue higher education. It was a rich learning experience. I especially loved going to private, Christian colleges and universities. I was privileged to serve on the H.L.C. Board for six years and as chair of that Board in 2001-2002 when Dr. Steve Crow was president.

We always met in Chicago for the annual meeting. I loved getting together with faculty members who were in attendance and with faculty and administrators from other Christian colleges. We always had a communion service together on Sunday evening, often in my hotel room. Obviously, accreditation is very important for Harding, and I treasure the opportunities I had to work with these professionals.

Another opportunity to interact with administrators at the national level was the NAICU meeting held annually in Washington, D.C. Presidents from many private and independent colleges are members. This is the most effective organization in America that promotes and protects the agenda of private higher education. I was elected to represent our eight-state region on the board in 2006 and served as chair of the National Committee on Taxation.

Traveling with faculty members and students to Harding receptions also provided an opportunity to build relationships. We would generally leave in the early afternoon on the Harding "jet" (which was actually a King Air turbo-prop), with a reception later that evening and a late return trip home.

Some trips were more exciting than others. For example, lightning hit the plane, taking out an engine, on at least four of these trips. That's when you really get to know people.

I remember one trip to Chicago when David Ridings was our pilot. It was snowing, and the plane was de-iced in the hanger. We followed a snow plow and then picked up speed and flew over the plow. We had blue sky in just a few minutes. What fun!

Faculty members and students who attended these receptions were the stars. They shared their Harding experience with prospective students and donors. We always returned exhausted but richer because of the experience.

One of the highlights each year for me was the Faculty-Staff Dinner in April. For years, Harding has presented service pins to colleagues who have completed ten or more years of service to Harding in five-year increments. It is always exciting to see so many people receive these pins. The truth of the matter is that people come to Harding and often stay for their entire career. Retention is unbelievably high.

In the 2012-2013 year, ninety-six pins were presented, representing 1,855 years of combined service to Harding. What an accomplishment! We have had one colleague receive a sixty-five-year pin – Dr. Ganus. This dinner is also a time to recognize outstanding faculty and staff members, who receive monetary awards along with this recognition.

Retention of Faculty Members

Why do our colleagues choose to come and then decide to stay for a lifetime? I asked a few colleagues to share their stories.

The first response comes from Dr. Don England, who won the Distinguished Teacher Award on three occasions and was named a Distinguished Professor. He influenced many people for good because of his love for God and his love for chemistry. He said,

We never see providence working in the here and now. We al-

ways see providence in retrospect and, in retrospect, I see that it was providence that brought me to Harding. Not being a product of Christian education myself and having completed a master's degree in chemistry at the University of Arkansas in the summer of 1960, I was discouraged. I began contemplating attending one of our Christian colleges to better prepare for ministry since I was preaching at the time. A fellow graduate student who had been a chemistry major at Harding, Boyce Helms recommended that I write Dr. Joe Pryor, chairman of the Department of Physical Science at

Harding, to inquire as to whether I might teach labs at Harding while enrolled in Bible courses to prepare for ministry.

A letter to Dr. Pryor revealed that he had just become dean of the college, and Harding was in need of a full-time chemistry professor. Consequently, without even applying for the job, I became an assistant professor of chemistry because of a visit with Dr. Pryor. I soon became associated with the College Church of Christ and was invited to teach a Sunday morning Bible class for college students.

I felt that providence had been involved in my decision to come to this place – and meeting Lynn Alexander of Delight, Ark., who would become my soul mate for life, confirmed this conclusion.

I left Harding to earn a doctorate in chemistry. Soon after I returned, Dr. Pryor asked me to present a message on "Integrating Faith and Learning" to the faculty at our Camp Tahkodah pre-session conference. I immersed myself in early literature written by pioneers in Christian education, such as David Lipscomb and James A. Harding, and I interviewed Dr. Benson, Dr. Sears, Dr. Ed Sewell and Dr. Jack Wood Sears – whose lives were deeply imbedded in Christian education. The more I learned of the concept, the more I fell in love with it.

What has kept me at Harding is a conviction that I providentially discovered a hidden treasure and a pearl of great price here. "Going to work" each day has been an exercise in Christian ministry, and I have no regrets for the turn of events that led me here. It has been a pleasure beyond description to have served under Harding presidents, Dr. George Benson, Dr. Clifton L. Ganus Jr., Dr. David Burks, and to now be a personal friend of President Bruce McLarty. I have immense respect for all of these men, and I would have enjoyed knowing J. N. Armstrong.

My greatest joy was helping the struggling student to grasp essential concepts in an atmosphere that was conducive to their faith development. I told them frequently that chemical bonding is a study in how the word of God holds all things together" (Col. 1:17).

Another distinguished professor that had a great influence on students was Dr. Dean Priest, whose love for mathematics is inspirational. He uses math as a tool that allows people to investigate God's universe, an art form in and of itself. He shared,

In 1957, I was graduating from high school in Columbia, Tenn., and making plans to attend the University of Tennessee to study engineering. I believe that, at this point, the hand of God intervened in my life and redirected my plans.

In the summer of 1957, I met Wayne Ball, who took a keen interest in helping young people direct their lives toward God. Wayne had observed my singing in a gospel quartet, the Mid-Landers, which on one occasion had sung on stage with Jerry Lee Lewis. Wayne encouraged me to change the direction of my musical talents and use them instead in the Lord's church. He secured opportunities for me to lead singing in gospel meetings in the area. In one of these meetings, I met Carolyn Pogue, now my wife, who was attending Harding College at the time. She had a record of the Harding a cappella chorus, which she had been singing in, and she insisted I hear it. I was amazed at the sound. She began to tell about Harding, and other Christians in Columbia encouraged me to go to Harding.

Music played a primary role in my life at Harding. Though I decided against a music major in favor of mathematics, I enjoyed many of the amenities the music department offered. I sang in the Harding Chorale, the a cappella chorus, Belles & Beaux and the men's quartet. We traveled widely, singing in many churches in the United States and abroad. My trip to the Far East with the Belles and Beaux opened my eyes to the need for mission work and was the incentive that led me, many years later, to keep a Korean man in my home who was training at Harding to return as a missionary to his own country.

My background in Bible knowledge was weak when I came to Harding, but there were many opportunities to grow spiritually. The Monday night devotionals, led by Andy T. Ritchie, were inspirational, making a huge impact on my life and giving me an increased depth and direction in leading worship in song.

The educational environment at Harding has always been outstanding. During my day, many teachers were intellectual giants who set high standards, which to this day I attempt to emulate. Dr. Joe Pryor took special interest in me, encouraging me to go to graduate school and return to Harding to teach.

Working with colleagues who are dedicated to God, with students who have come from all over the world filled with a quest for knowledge and for God, and rearing my children in a Christian community where they met and married God-seeking mates have given me a life filled with blessings more abundant than I could have dreamed possible.

Dr. Wilt Martin, chairman of our Kinesiology Department, said,

My interest in Harding began in the spring of 1962 while listening to the Harding chorus sing in chapel at Freed-Hardeman. The

chorus, directed by Dr. Ken Davis, presented a selection of songs that were the most beautiful and most professional I had ever heard. After that experience, I began thinking about where I would attend college, and I talked to other students who I thought would like to travel to Searcy for a visit. Seven of us decided to make the trip and then decided to enroll. We began recruiting other students to go with us to Harding. About thirty more students chose Harding for the fall of 1962. This may have been a record number transferring to Harding from Freed-Hardeman.

Dr. Betty Watson was a distinguished professor of education. Here is part of her story –

> *I clearly remember praying one afternoon in Michigan where I was teaching first grade, "Lord, I do not know the path you would have me take, but please open the door where you would like for me to be."*
>
> *It never entered my mind that I might ever return to Arkansas. However, it was only a few days later that I heard from Dr. Ed Sewell... that he needed a teacher with an emphasis in language arts to come to Harding that fall.*

> *Over the years, the joy of getting to know the students has been my greatest pleasure and treasure! I have loved them all! I want to say "Thank you, Lord... for answering my prayer offered so long ago... in ways far more than I could have ever asked or imagined. Thank you that I have been able for all these years... to share in the lives of well over 2,500 students... to teach at Harding... where a large part of my heart will always be."*

Dr. Paul Pollard has been a Bible professor, teaching Greek and New Testament, for forty years. He did his graduate study at Oxford (England) and preached there for a time. He considered a career in the Air Force as a chaplain but decided to join the Harding faculty, partly as a result of an international campaign group, led by Dr. Michael Justus, to England. After deciding to retire in 2014, Dr. Pollard made these remarks,

> *Now, at the end of my teaching career at Harding, God has blessed me more richly than I have ever deserved. What I have learned is that no matter what our plans are, God – by his providential hand –*

guides, overrules, shapes and places us where we can do our best
service for the church and His people. For me, that place has been
Harding.

Staff and Administration

It is also a privilege to work with a talented group of staff and administrative staff members who contribute so much to the mission of Harding University. Their work is critical to the success of the mission of Harding. I have asked a few individuals to comment on why Harding is so important to them.

Dr. Larry Long serves as Provost and leads the faculty. He shared his story –

When I was offered the position at Harding College, I was

thrilled. I had enjoyed my
visit, I knew the mission of
the school and I was im-
pressed with the folks I met.
In just a couple of days, the
faculty in the English De-
partment had impressed me
with their friendliness, their
commitment to the school's
mission and their dedication
to the church. They also
invited me to a strawber-
ry-themed departmental
gathering that won my heart
and my stomach. After I
accepted the offer from
Harding, two individuals
well versed in higher educa-
tion who didn't know each

other – when they heard I had taken a job at Harding – responded in
nearly identical words – "That will be a good first job. After you've

been there a couple of years, you'll find a better job." Thirty-seven and one-half years later, I'm still looking for the better job to turn up. I tell prospective faculty members that I knew the mission when I came, and I committed to it. Since the mission hasn't changed, then I don't have a reason to leave.

I continue to work with great colleagues whom I respect, love and value. In fact, one of the great joys of my current position as Provost is to stand on the stage at Commencement watching the faculty march into the auditorium. They are good people who serve unselfishly, have a passion for teaching and mentoring to help students develop as scholars, professionals and Christians, and support and love their colleagues, including me. It is hard to believe that so many genuinely good people can be assembled in one place at one time.

Pat Rice began her career at Harding as a faculty member for the newly created nursing program and later served for twenty-three years as our school nurse. I had the "honor" of having her in an organizational behavior class that I taught

years ago, which was a requirement for nursing majors. Along with her friend, Janice Bingham, Pat regularly disrupted this class with her stories. I must admit that I loved having Pat and Janice in this class. Janice continues to teach in our nursing program and Pat is now retired and a master storyteller –

I was able to attend David Lipscomb College, taking classes and working in a place that provided a much-needed spiritual nest for me.

I was still on the staff there when the urgent call came to assist in the beginning of a School of Nursing at Harding University in 1975. Two friends committed to come if I would. Not really eager to leave Nashville, my husband and I promised a year or two of service as if it were a Peace Corps assignment. So my two friends and I helped start the nursing program, and Guilford became the school's bus driver. That was the beginning of making a dream come true.

It was a blessing to teach at Harding with a Christian faculty and staff. The experiences students shared with us also strengthened our love for this place. Students would tell us about their interactions with teachers –

"Oh, can you believe it! My history teacher invited me to spend Thanksgiving week with his family after he found out my plans had fallen through."

"My math teacher invited me to recover in his home after breaking both of my arms. Oh, yes! The invitation included my mother so she could take care of me."

A transfer student told of trying to make an appointment at her previous school with the president with no success. "My first week here, I was invited to President Burks' home for a cookout and met him in his back yard."

Another student was excited that he got to drive the president's car home from lunch. "Oh, yes! The president took students to lunch, and he had a small morning prayer group in his office and a Wednesday night Bible study in his home!"

Some of my favorite funny memories involve chapel – stories such as dressing up Dr. Neale Pryor as a Christmas tree or positioning a teacher on a skateboard and pushing him with enough momentum to glide across the stage to knock over some bowling pins. Another funny story involved inviting the president to be in on the ransoming of a friend's favorite stuffed animal taken during Open House. Students learned that they could have fun with a little mischief.

Dr. Dee Carson was a professor of education who later accepted the responsibility as Dean of Students. She shared this memorable story with me about one of her students.

One of our students was paraplegic. I will refer to him as Aaron. Since his needs were great, I spent much time with him. I can say that memories of this young man still inspire me. He was so special! He always had a smile, always a kind word, always a "thank you" to anyone who helped him. He was smart and quick to respond. Other students couldn't wait to have lunch with him or sit beside him in chapel.

Once, because we had several students in wheelchairs, I decided to have a dinner prepared just for them in one of our special dining rooms. That night, they all came – dressed up – ready for great food on linen table cloths, along with candles and flowers. They looked so nice and I was pleased that they had come. I asked one of the young men to bless the food, and his prayer brought me to tears –"... so thankful for all the ways Harding has blessed my life."

When the prayer was over, we all put our napkins in our laps, and then no one moved. I thought something was wrong, so I asked, "Aren't you hungry tonight?" They still sat there and stared at me. Finally, Aaron grinned and said, "You know, Dr. Carson, the only reason we invited you tonight was so you could reach the salt and pepper for us. None of us can stand up!" They laughed and laughed that night, and the memory became a special bond. What a joy they brought to us all!

Board of Trustees

The truly unexpected pleasures of my time in office were the opportunities to work with individual members of the Board of Trustees. I did not know many of these individuals when I became president.

The board members in 1987 were John D. Baldwin, Pat Bell, George S. Benson, James Russell Burcham, David Paul Burton, Paul Carter, Harold Cogburn,

James H. Cone, Houston Ezell, Richard Gibson, Lewis Green, Dallas Harris, Olen Hendrix, Jim Bill McInteer, Harry Risinger, Dan Russell, Roy Sawyer and Don

Shores. It is interesting to note that after twenty-six years, only three of these individuals are on the Board today – Richard Gibson, Harry Risinger and Don Shores. All three of these men have served terms as chairman of the board.

The Board of Trustees of 2012-13 included Bruce Binkley, Bill Chism, James H. Cone Jr., Robert Diles, Harrell Freeman, Charles Ganus, Richard Gibson, Roosevelt Harris, Danny Hawk, Jim Holsombake, Gerald Morgan Jr., Lundy Neely, Roy Reaves, John Reese, Harold Redd, Harry Risinger, John Simmons, Rebecca Tubb, David Waldron, Robert Walker, Suzanne Waller, Mark Wallis and Joe Wild. In addition, Pat Bell, Bob Brackett, Russ Burcham, Mel Gardner and Don Shores were on the Senior Board.

While I had the privilege of working with all of these board members, I spent a special amount of time with the board chairs. James Cone was chair when I became president and served for ten years. I loved meeting with him at least once a month in Little Rock for lunch to talk over matters that were taking place at Harding. He was a great mentor to me and was a person of great faith who loved the mission of Harding. He and his wife, Bonnie, were ardent supporters of our work. Bro. Cone was a commercial contractor and obviously very interested in buildings. He taught me about that aspect of our work at Harding. But I must say that his primary interest was in the spiritual development of students, and that was the subject of our discussion much of the time.

Bro. Cone was succeeded by Pat Bell as chairman, and it was a joy to get to know Pat and Mary from Little Rock, Ark. Pat had been a professional accountant all of his life and served as a partner with Ernst and Young. He was highly regarded by the Board because of his skill in business, accounting and auditing. He served as chairman of the Audit Committee for a number of years. He asked good but tough questions relative to the budget and the audit. He was a blessing because of his attention to details in these important areas. While his approach was different from that of James Cone, he, like Bro. Cone, had a great love for the mission at Harding, and it was evident in everything he did. It was a blessing in my life to be able to work with this godly man.

Paul Carter from Bentonville, Ark., succeeded Pat Bell in this position and became a mentor and dear friend. He was a great encourager. It was always interesting to watch him in action in board meetings. Numerous times, people would comment about different topics and when Paul spoke on that topic, the discussion would end. Other board members had an enormous appreciation for this man. Paul was a visionary leader for the Board who helped take Harding to a new level. He and his wife, June, loved Harding dearly.

Paul was followed by Don Shores from Cave Springs, Ark. Don was on the Board the entire time I was president and was well respected by his colleagues. Don was a retired businessman who was particularly interested in the College of Bible and the spiritual values of Harding. These were uppermost in his mind as we discussed every decision. He and his wife, Lois, have been a great influence for good at Harding. He often commented that he would come to visit campus and hear the students sing, and that was his repayment for the investment he was making in the work at Harding.

Bro. Shores was followed by Harry Risinger, an executive with a business firm in Memphis. Harry was chairman and co-chairman of the Finance and Investment Committee for many years. He was knowledgeable about investments and made a great contribution to Harding with his expertise in this area. Harry was known to be the individual on the board who asked the toughest questions of the president at every board meeting. While not always fun, these questions helped advance our work in a significant way. He always

asked probing questions. Harry and his wife, Jan, also have a great love for the work at the School of Theology in Memphis.

The last board chairman I worked with was the current chairman, Dr. John

Simmons, a medical doctor who brought a different perspective of leadership to this position. Dr. Simmons was interested in making certain that every board member was heard and wanted there to be transparency in everything that was done. Because of timing, it would become Dr. Simmons' major responsibility as chairman of the Board to lead in the search for a new president. He chaired the committee and the Board as they went through this process, which eventually led to the selection of the fifth president of Harding. A passionate and emotional leader, Dr. Simmons repeatedly showed his love for Harding.

It would be difficult for me to talk about each board member, but I do want to pay tribute to Jim Bill McInteer, who served longer than any other individual. I did not know Bro. McInteer when I became president. I knew his name and his reputation, but I did not know the man, and I did not know his wife, Betty. Getting to know this couple, spend time in their home, and pray with them from time to time turned out to be one of the great serendipities of my time as president.

I learned much from Jim Bill. He served as secretary for the entire time he was on the board until his death. I will always remember the discussions that took place at the board level relative to spiritual values and the fact that, when Jim Bill would speak up on the matter at hand, it would generally end the discussion. People on the board – men and women alike – had such a respect for Jim Bill that once he stated his reasoning behind a particular point, that generally was the direction we were going to go.

I will always remember Jim Bill for his love for his wife, Betty, and the care he gave to her after she became ill with Alzheimer's disease. She came with him to board meetings, and he took care of her in such a gentle way. His comments at her funeral were simply a statement of love in the purest sense. I will always remember Jim Bill's chapel addresses as he talked about his love for Harding, his love for the church and his love for Betty.

He was also a prayer warrior as he prayed daily for specific people, including my wife, Leah, when she was dealing with cancer. Jim Bill was an encouragement to both of us in many ways.

Without doubt, Harding has been blessed with a strong and unified board, which has been a powerful influence for good as Harding has continued to advance the cause of Christian higher education. These people love Harding. I was privileged to work with this unbelievably gifted and talented group of men and women, and I will always treasure that opportunity.

What About the Future?

Harding University has been blessed because of dedicated Christian faculty members, staff members and board members throughout its ninety-year history. As all of us look back on our time at Harding, we undoubtedly have our favorites, and we probably have wondered who will take their place when they retire. I wonder who will be the next influential faculty members, who will be the next influential administrators at Harding, who will assume leadership in the future for the Board of Trustees.

I take comfort from some of the statements made by Dr. Neale Pryor in an article he wrote in the *Harding* magazine, entitled "Our Graying Faculty is Simply Passing the Torch."[3] In this article, he shared his regret that some wonderful teachers were retiring but expressed great confidence in the future of Harding because of the new people who would assume these positions. He made reference to the fact that the children of Israel probably had doubts about Joshua after Moses died. When God empowered Joshua to be the leader of His people, His first words to him were, "Moses is dead" (Joshua 1:2). Joshua would have to be his own man; he was not Moses.

We can imagine the people of Israel saying to Joshua that Moses did not do it that way. They probably asked him why he could not go into the tent of meeting and talk directly with God as Moses did. Yet, by the grace of God, Joshua led the children of Israel across the Jordan to take the land God had given them, and Israel served God faithfully as long as Joshua lived.

No, Joshua was not Moses, but he did a great work. Very likely, the next generation did not even miss Moses. Joshua was their hero. They were busy wondering who would take Joshua's place when he died.

What do you suppose the apostles thought when they saw Christ ascend from their sight, leaving them to do His work without Him? They were promised that the Holy Spirit would guide them but, in their minds, that was not the same as having the leader Himself with them. But God rose up leaders, and His work went on.

The faithfulness of the children of Israel did not depend upon Moses or Joshua. As long as they had leaders committed to God and His will, the Israelites prospered. Their success did not depend on any individual, but upon their remaining faithful to God. The same thing could be said for the early church. As long as the leaders were faithful to the word, the church grew and prospered, regardless of who the leaders were.

I believe this assessment is true for Harding. Our future does not depend upon keeping this generation of leaders but rather upon assuring that our next generation of leaders are godly, faithful members of the church who are committed to God's plan.

I am confident that we will have new faculty members, new staff members and new board members who will take Harding to an even greater level of service in the years to come.

Harding students enjoy a semester in Latin America

CHAPTER SEVEN
An International Campus

The University began its first International Campus Program in Florence, Italy, in September 1980. Since that time, six other campuses have been added, numerous special programs have been added and more than 7,000 students and faculty members have studied abroad in Harding's International Programs.

When I first was named president-elect, Dr. Don Shackelford told me he was not sure I was qualified to be president because I did not have international travel experience. He even questioned whether I had a passport. I did have a passport and was scheduled to make a trip to South Africa in the spring of 1987 to do a seminar for government officials on "The Benefits of a Capitalistic Approach to Society."

Dr. Shackelford talked me into making my first trip to Florence, so after leaving Pretoria and Johannesburg, I flew to Florence. I remember being extremely cold on the tour Terry Edwards gave me of downtown Florence. I was dressed as if it were summer. However, I was amazed at all of the sights – this was an eye-opening experience for me. I have since been privileged to make numerous trips to our HUF campus in Scandicci and have loved every minute that I was there.

The International Program model that Harding set up in the beginning still exists in essentially the same form. It is very different from the model used by most universities, where the international study office serves as a bridge between the U.S. institution and the university in another country. In 2010, eighty-five percent of all study-abroad programs followed this model. Harding has always been an exception as we have developed our own programs, sending both faculty and students abroad. Since 2010, more universities in the United States are recognizing the values of the model that Harding maintains, and the percentage of use is shifting slowly. Leading the shift are schools like Harvard and Stanford.[1]

Our model allows us to maintain the mission of Harding University. Students who choose a semester of international study benefit by extensive travel, and interactive living is just an unbelievable experience during their three months together. I believe all of our students come back with a much greater sense of self-reliance and awareness of the world because of this wonderful experience. One great benefit is that we can make connections to local churches wherever our programs exist.

PHOTO PERMISSION BY GRANT SCHOL

Harding University in Florence (HUF)

Our oldest international campus program began in Florence, Italy, at the Avanti Bible School building. After three years of successful experiences at this location, Dr. Ganus led the university to purchase a villa in Scandicci, a suburb of Florence, that we continue to use today.

Thanks to former missionaries Don Shackelford, Carl Mitchell, L.V. Pfeifer and Earl Edwards (from Freed Hardeman University), who implemented and sustained this process, HUF has a deep missional foundation.

My own family has benefited greatly from this international campus site. My oldest son, Bryan, and his wife, Laura, attended together as students before they married. My daughter-in-law, Jeanne Isom Burks, who is married to Stephen, attended several years later. Two of my granddaughters, Emily and Madison, attended HUF, so the family impact for us has been huge. Emily met her husband, Chris Meyer, at HUF as well.

The Board of Trustees granted me a sabbatical in 2002, and I made the decision to spend a month during the summer in Florence at the villa. Leah and I lived in an apartment at the base of the hill down from the villa, and I had access to an old green Panda car. I loved driving this stick shift car, although I could barely get in it. I even drove it to Venice and San Gimignano. I admit that I always had a phone close by since I did not know the language. I have been to numerous concerts in Italy, and I love the people, the food and the fellowship very much. It is easy to fall in love with the people and the hillside of Tuscany.

Robbie Shackelford serves as director of the HUF program, and he and his wife, Mona, do a great job. They have influenced students for decades in this position. I asked Robbie about some of his favorite memories of this work, and he shared these comments –

We almost always make our way to Piazzale Michelangelo (panoramic view of Florence) on our first Florence orientation to

the city walk. It is so special to see the students as we turn around a corner and see the Duomo or Piazza della Signoria for the first time. We make our way to Piazzale Michelangelo on foot or by bus. When we get there, I take time to share the site with the students, pointing out the major buildings. Usually, they all have their backs turned as I give them the information. I will never forget the time Jeff and

117

Judy Hopper first had this experience because, when they turned around after I had given the information about Florence, I saw tears streaming down their faces. They were truly thankful and moved. I often tell the students this story when we are in Manarola, one of the fishing villages of the Cinque Terre, on the Ligurian coast.

The morning after our first night there with the Hoppers and the James Walters, I decided to take a walk. This particular morning the waves were pounding the reef. Beauty! That was what my heart shouted (it often does). Walking around part of the mountain, I met Jeff, who was coming back toward me. He had been crying. He said, "Robbie, I've found it!" I asked what he had found. He said, "I found God's bass drum." He took me to a spot where the waves, crashing into a small cave, sounded just like a huge, deep-toned bass drum. As the water splashed against the back side of the cave, it sounded like a huge cymbal.

In terms of spiritual impact, Robbie shared this account –

Evernus Williams, a young man, was working with a program that allowed you to work at farms in exchange for stay in Italy. His dad called Jeff Hopper and then me, asking if there was any way Evernus could join the program for that summer. I met him at the Porciano Castle in the Casentino. Evernus wanted to meet me, and I wanted to meet him before the semester started. Evernus had had some ups and downs. He was older than the other students. He was an artist, and we enjoyed each other's company.

The last week, Evernus decided he wanted to be baptized. The group had grown to love him very much. We walked down the hill one afternoon to the "Val di Botte" Bed and Breakfast, where they had a swimming pool we could use for the baptism. Giancarlo and Helena, owners of the Bed and Breakfast, wanted to watch. It was a small, octagonal pool, and the students stood all around it. We held hands, sang and prayed together. When Evernus and I climbed into the pool, I looked at Giancarlo and Helena, and tears were streaming down their faces. That is a moment that is ingrained in my mind.

118

Students express the experience best. Kate Major Tucker made the following comments –

> *The experiences I had as a student in the HUF program in 1996 shaped a desire in me to return to do mission work in Italy. My commitment was for two years and then grew to five as I then had the opportunity to work for the HUF program. I am so thankful to God for giving me that opportunity. It was such a blessing to share the love of Christ and to see the Lord's beauty, whether in the classroom or along the trails of Cinque Terre or walking the roads the apostle Paul walked. The experience and friendships made are priceless and are treasured for a lifetime!*

Ellen Jones made the following comments concerning her experience at HUF –

> *My husband, Ben, and I had already been dating a while when we attended HUF together in the spring of 1995. It was a great experience that taught us how big God's world really is. Our time at HUF inspired us to go into the mission field and join the 1999 Avanti Italia team. Those two years had a huge impact on our lives, and we still have relationships with friends made while we were there. I'm so very thankful for Harding's international programs.*

Harding University in Greece (HUG)

The HUG campus was founded in the fall of 1994, and we rented a hotel facility just outside of Athens on a temporary basis for this program. HUG was initiated to provide a Bible-based tour for students that allowed them to go to Bible lands, meditate on their faith and increase their knowledge of the Bible. Don Shackelford and Carl Mitchell had both talked to me about the value of this program, and I had also talked on numerous occasions with Dino Roussos of Athens, Greece. I was very interested in this program because of the opportunities to travel in Bible lands. In addition to traveling all over Greece, the students are able to go to Israel – and, when possible, to Turkey, the Greek Islands and Egypt.

I love the description by Dr. Tom Howard and Dr. Shackelford in 1995 –

HUG's first class of thirty-one students participated in the program last fall. Although the program offered plenty of opportunities for fun in the sun on beautiful Greek islands, many of the students' experiences were indicative of the spiritual emphasis of the program. In fact, several students chose HUG primarily because of the opportunity to visit the Holy Lands, where they could "walk in the steps of Jesus."

Students make an eight-day trip to Israel and spend three days in Jerusalem visiting such sites as the Mount of Olives, the Garden of Gethsemane, the Kidron Valley and the West (Wailing) Wall of the Temple. A devotional on the Mount of Olives makes passages from the gospels particularly meaningful.

Students typically visit Bethlehem, Peter's house in Capernaum, the Sea of Galilee, the Jordan River, the Mount of the Beatitudes and the Dead Sea.

When possible, students take a ten-day trip to Turkey and northern Greece for a tour of the Seven Churches of Asia. While in Turkey, students visit ancient Troy and the modern Moslem city of Istanbul, where waking up to the call for morning prayers blaring from colorful minarets gave them real perspective on world religions. Paul's missionary journeys are featured in northern Greece at sites like Thessalonica, Philippi and Berea.

Students also take a four-day cruise of the major Greek islands of Santorini, Mykonos, Crete, Rhodes and Patmos.[2]

Six years after launching the HUG program, which had been quite successful, Dr. Don Shackelford was asked to research the possibility of purchasing property in Greece for a permanent year-round program. We inspected more than twenty-five properties, and I spent a month in Greece, looking at the final five or six properties and working out a deal for the purchase of the Artemis Hotel in Porto Rafti. The person who was extremely helpful in this purchase and in helping us hire the original staff was Vassilios Tsirmpas, an attorney in Greece. He continues to be a good friend and legal advisor.

I will never forget being with Dr. Shackelford and Dr. Hopper in the lawyer's office, filled with smoke, in the fall of 2000, as we finalized this purchase of property. We made the decision on faith because the documents were in Greek, and those entries are very different from those in the United States.

Mike and Beth James are the current directors of HUG. Mike said,

> I love this job because of the students who come through the portals of "The Artemis." ... I've been to Israel twelve times. I know where we are going and what the guide will say – even to anticipation of his jokes. But the visit always is fresh for me because I can see through the eyes of our students three realizations that they may never have seen before – God is real, God is alive and God is part of my life.
>
> There is no doubt in my mind that students who participate in HUG will forever read the Bible story differently because they listened to Paul's sermon to the Areopagus while in Athens, they walked where Jesus walked in Jerusalem, they reenacted David's fight

Exploring Gordon's Tomb

with Goliath in the Valley of Elah, they traversed the isle of Patmos where John received his revelation and viewed the same pyramids in Egypt that both Abraham and Moses would have seen.

Kristen Bay said of her experience in the summer of 2011,

> *The most life-changing thing about HUG was the chance to travel between Greece, Israel and Egypt and see the Bible come to life! Every time I'm in a lesson or reading the Bible, I now picture the places mentioned! It truly was an experience that has forever changed my spiritual walk. Also, spending time with and learning from people of different cultures was a blessing that helped me learn a lot about myself, loving others and understanding the world.*

Amy Crocker, at HUG in spring 2004, wrote,

> *It was my semester in Greece that began my love of living in a community and building friendships through a shared life. I bonded with a group of girls over evenings spent journaling about our trips and reading through Romans. Eventually, we began to share prayer requests and learn about each other as women. We continued to meet weekly for prayer times upon our return to campus until graduation. One of the girls in that group then moved to Africa with me. Talk about friendships changing lives!"*

Richelle Pettit, at HUG in 2012, reflected on her experiences –

> *I was blessed with the opportunity to go to HUG. While I was there, I was baptized in the Sea of Galilee by Mike James and decided to become a missionary. I gained incredible experiences that will be forever treasured in my heart, and I made friendships that will last a lifetime.*

Harding University in England (HUE)

The Harding University in England program began the same year as HUG. Harding opened the HUE program because of wonderful opportunities in business, art, music and theater for students in London and the surrounding area. We now enjoy a more than twenty-year relationship with this program and a connection with the Wembley Church of Christ, where students attend while there.

Paul and Kayla Haynie, teachers who were part of the program in the spring of 1996, wrote in the *Harding* magazine,

> *If one is to grasp a sense of time and place, to truly come to know the touch and feel of a country's history and personality, one must amble through its narrow cobbled lanes, stroll through its tree-lined park paths, pause and reflect within its gothic-spired churches and sit and dream on the banks of its quiet rivers. To have time to examine a foreign culture beneath the superficial face presented to most tourists – this is the first great pleasure Harding's semester of study in England offers those who make the journey.[3]*

Our current HUE director, Lauren Bryan Knight, writes the following about her experiences –

> *The first group was special to me in a lot of ways. Watching their eyes open to the world around them was a privilege that I can hardly articulate. While I thought through and planned elements of British culture that would impress or intrigue them, I would find myself getting caught off guard by how even the simplest things could be exciting or new. I'll never forget that, on a busy day trip to Dover and Canterbury, we made an impulsive stop along the beach. While I counted the minutes for the parking meter and calculated*

> *the distance still to travel, I tossed out a bit of conversation to a student, Brad Middleton, about how we might be able to see France.*

He replied that he was more intrigued by the water. When I asked him why, he replied that it was the first beach he had ever seen. I realized then that it's not just cathedrals and museums that students get to see for the first time – but literally, the world. We pushed back our lunch reservation and spent a perfect moment of that chilly day playing on the rocky beach and just enjoying an ordinary moment.

Harding University in Australia (HUA)

Harding's fourth international campus was started in 1996 in Brisbane, Australia. The HUA program was our first effort south of the equator and was designed to take advantage of the interest shown by Harding students in the country of Australia. Perhaps Harding students were attracted to the home of koalas and kangaroos, but I suspect the real interest simply had to do with learning more about this beautiful country. Australia offers many contrasting landscapes, from the aqua blue

oceans with brightly colored tropical fish and expansive coral reefs to the outback and the lush greenery of the tropical rain forest hidden in the continent's interior. Travel on this trip is extensive and includes stops at the Great Barrier Reef, Ayers Rock and Ooraminna Bush Camp.

I was challenged by several students on a trip to Ayers Rock to climb to the top. I did climb to the top, but I would not do it again because I am older and much wiser.

Alyne Hoover, one of the first twenty-five students to attend HUA, summarized her experience in the *Harding* magazine in spring 1997 –

124

HUA offers the opportunity to witness the country's beauty, get to know the local residents and learn about the land. Most of the Aussies we met were extremely friendly and proud of their country. Though they may complain about its problems, they would not live anywhere else on earth.

This program changes the way participants look at their entire world, from the squirrels squiring around campus to the pine trees on the interstates to their own spirituality. When reflecting on memories of crystal blue oceans, lush green forests, angry thunderheads and star-scattered nights, I know that I have witnessed God through all the natural beauties of Australia.

In recent years, Harding has incorporated an Asian component. Students visit Thailand, Vietnam, Cambodia, Singapore, South Korea, Japan and China.

Carter Wright, who attended HUA in 2010, wrote about his experience –

After studying abroad in HUA, I was able to venture outside of my comfort zone and see firsthand the beauty of vastly different cultures and the simple truth that a worldview defined by borders is becoming outdated. You cannot put a price on the realization that the world is bigger than your back yard and that it deserves exploring. Seeing the universality of our humanity in every town, country and culture is a gift I will treasure forever.

Harding University in Latin America (HULA)

HULA was added in 2002 as our fifth program. Dr. Jeff Hopper researched and selected Viña del Mar, Chile, as our program headquarters. We were looking for a program in South America, and a survey led us to select Chile as the home base. Tom Hook has been the director since the program began. He has more than twenty-five years of experience as a missionary in Chile and the region that surrounds it. The program has a good relationship with the local church in Viña del Mar.

In the *Harding* magazine in the winter of 2003, Bill Richardson was quoted as saying, "This past fall in Chile was certainly about academics, camaraderie and

opportunities for spiritual growth. It was all about combining faith, learning and living. It was indeed the very essence of Harding." [4] I could have written this sentence.

Students who attend this program stay in a beautiful apartment building, Roca Blanca, where dolphins can be seen outside the bedroom window, which overlooks the Pacific Ocean. This scene really defines dorm life for the HULA participants. Students have daily chapel, take classes and travel throughout Chile and surrounding countries.

Tom made the following comment concerning the inaugural session –

In the first HULA session in 2002, two young people from different parts of the United States met upon arrival in Chile. One was a young man from Tyler, Texas, who had already made the decision that he was going to be a missionary, determined that he would marry a local Latin American girl and spend his life somewhere in the Spanish-speaking world. The other was a young lady from Tulla-homa, Tenn., whose older brothers had already distinguished them-selves at Harding as great young Christian men and whose younger brother would follow in her footsteps and attend HULA later. As the semester progressed, it became obvious to everyone in the group that these two had formed a mutual attraction and that someone's plans were destined to change. By the time the HULA semester was completed, an obvious relationship was in full bloom, one that would eventually lead Greg McKinzie and Megan Bills to become Mr. and Mrs. Greg McKinzie.

Greg's zeal for serving in Latin America, along with Megan's desire to serve the kingdom and be Greg's partner, eventually led them to be part of the moving force behind a team of young couples who moved to Arequipa, Peru, to plant the church and to eventu-ally create and lead a thriving non-profit effort that provides many benefits to the residents of that city. Three children and almost five years later, their direct participation in that mission effort will come to a close as they prepare to return their family to the United States within the year, having already made more impact for good than many do in an entire lifetime. What a marvelous result of having a program like this in South America.

Tom's comment concerning the 2011 HULA group was also interesting to me. It was one of the smallest groups because of the economic issues in the United States –

Although there were thirteen girls, there were only five young men, and both faculty members were young women as well, leaving the director and those young men as the only male influences on the group. However, one of those young men, affectionately known as "Junior" (due to his Indiana Jones-style hat that mirrored the one worn by the director), made a great difference that semester, although he was one of only a handful of second-semester freshmen who had been part of the HULA experience. His Christian attitude made him a natural leader as would be seen later when he was elected to serve Harding as S.A. president. Will Waldron, though with somewhat limited Spanish at his command, made such an impact upon the church in Viña del Mar that his example still comes up in conversations there today.

Waldron commented on his Chile experience –

> *Harding offers an incredible array of life-changing options from which students may choose, but few of these opportunities seem to have as deep and lasting impact as the international programs. For example, if you ever get the chance (or more accurately have the patience to listen) to any students who have just returned from a study abroad, it doesn't take long to see that their trip touched them in a special way. Moreover, when two students or alumni realize they traveled on the same program, they immediately form an inexplicable bond and begin to share their stories with each other.*
>
> *While each story a student tells may be slightly different from the next student's, what lies at the heart of each story that causes them to return with such excitement in their eyes and such a desire to share the experiences? What is it that forever changes someone who has studied abroad?*
>
> *I remember the day I realized the world was much larger than I ever expected. I stood on a hill on Easter Island and looked at the island in full panorama. After taking in the view, the reality that there were no other people for 2,300 miles began to settle in my mind. Simply coming to this understanding helped me know that we live in a great world, with incredible people and places that God created, and I also knew that I wanted to better understand all of it! At some point, I think this key feeling comes to all Harding students and is one reason why these trips have such a deep impact on them.*

By the end of my three months in Chile, I became aware that what made my time abroad special was not necessarily the places I went but the people I met in those places. For one, I'd created extraordinary friendships with twenty-one others from Harding by traveling all over South America with them. Another amazing part of the international adventure is being able to reach across cultural and social barriers to form relationships with people from the countries you visit. All who participate in an international program tell stories that are full of other people, and it is these people who create the biggest difference in the lives and stories we live and tell when we come home.

Leah and I were able to visit students in 2012 and experience part of this program firsthand. We got to go white water rafting and zip lining. It was my first and last time to do this, as the water was rough and the wet suit tight. Zip lining was great for the students, though.

Harding University in Paris (HIP)

Harding began its sixth international program in 2004 in Paris, with travel all over France. This program operates every two years. Students who participate attend one of the largest congregations in France, the Paris Church of Christ. Regular fellowship meals are hosted by the congregation. Paris is a popular destination of U.S. students who study abroad. The city is full of history, wonderful architecture, music and culture. This program is particularly oriented toward students who major in French and other foreign languages.

Harding University in Zambia (HIZ)

Harding University in Zambia is a unique international program that began in 2007 after a study trip to Africa to investigate the possibility of our operating a program in a developing nation. The fall of 2007 marked the first HIZ program, and we have offered it every fall since that time. This program is integrated into a wonderful and decades-long association with the Namwianga Mission near Kalomo, Zambia. Roy Merritt, a partner in this work, is the one who formed the expression HIZ, a nice pun on the ownership of our God in this endeavor.

The HIZ program involves Harding and Zambian students in missions, church planting, cultural integration and travel experiences throughout the surrounding country. It focuses on health care, child development and interaction with young missionaries and offers a challenging academic program.

Student response to this program has been overwhelmingly positive, although the students who can attend are carefully screened and space is limited. Twenty-four students were accepted into the program for the first semester, and Janice Bingham, associate professor of nursing, has been a part of this program since its inception. Jeff Hopper, director of Harding's International Studies Program, said, "HIZ is a microcosm of all that is best about Harding." I agree with his assessment.

I love the way Brandi Clark, who was at HIZ in 2013, described the program as she recalled one special memory –

During each semester of Harding in Zambia, students travel into the bush together with Zambian evangelists. We made a week-long trek to Northeastern Zambia to experience the beauty of the country and to encourage two new churches. Near the end of the trip, we traveled a long distance north to Chambeshi. This village had been a preaching point for several months, and a Zambian evangelist and church planter, Moses Chansa, had spent several days going from house to house sharing the gospel and preparing for our arrival.

After arriving in the village, our first stop was a protocol visit to the headman and his family. He welcomed all of us and told us that he had hoped a church would come to his town. He, his wife and many children boarded the bus to go with us to an agreed-upon location where we were going to meet with those interested.

Our singing and preaching took place by the side of the road. We found a shaded grassy spot, sat in a circle and began to sing.

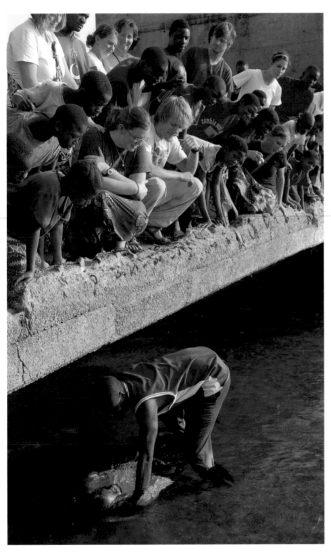

One of our students, Kayla Maynard, saved the day by helping us remember the words to a children's song in Bimba (the local language). Mothers nursed, young people and children listened, drunks heckled and Shawn Daggett preached, with Moses translating. The day was hot and dry, as Zambia was anticipating the rainy season. Shawn's text was John 7:37-38, where Jesus offered living water to Jews of His day who were waiting for rain to come. In Zambia, it had not rained for six months and thunder rumbled in the distance.

Moses offered the invitation and twelve, including the village headman, responded – some for baptism and others saying they needed to be "worshipping God." This was the beginning of the *church there. After Moses took confessions and read Scriptures that clarified what a person needed to know before being baptized, we piled into the bus and headed down to the river. The headman was the first of eight or nine to be baptized, followed by his wife, who made the decision after we got to the river.*

Villagers gathered with our group on a collapsed bridge to watch the baptisms. Hecklers sat on the far end and made jokes. A visit with the Chambeshi church, which was supposed to last just one hour, turned into four hours. When we left, we were torn and conflicted. We had a schedule to keep, but a new church had just been born. Moses assured us that he would spend the next two weeks working with these new Christians and begged us to pray that Satan not be allowed to snatch them away. The Harding students who were there that day will never forget being present for the birth of a new congregation. Theirs will forever be the memory of a self-supported preacher named Moses who traveled more than fifty miles by bicycle and devoted a month of his own time to preparing the people, teaching them and following up on their baptism. As we left Chambeshi behind and looked behind us out the back window of the old yellow school bus on which we traveled, through the rising dust we could see the joyful new Christians of that village waving goodbye to us.

Our Trip to Zambia

In November 2011, Leah and I were also able to make a trip to HIZ for the first time. We saw Victoria Falls and visited the Namwianga Mission, where it was exciting to see the work of Dr. Benson continuing to live to this day. We met with Roy Merritt and worshipped with the church in the bush on Sunday at Kasibi, where I was given the opportunity to speak. We attended the church at Johnson Hall, where I showed the video of the president of Zambia speaking at Harding when he had been there the previous year. The people had a great memory of him and loved seeing the video of Harding.

We spent time with the students in chapel as the Harding students and Zambia students sang together, led by a young man named Prince.

One of the highlights for us was the opportunity to visit Haven One, Two and Three, the homes where children are kept who are likely H.I.V. positive. While

there, we dedicated Haven Three. I got to hold a little boy named Peter, and I will always remember our visit with Peter and the other children at the Havens. Our students have been blessed by this experience.

We were also able to visit the clinic in Namwianga with Janice Bingham. I am very much impressed with her leadership in this program and the work that she is doing with health-related missions.

We were also able to go to Nairobi with Monte and Beth Cox and then travel through Kenya, including a trip to Masai Mara. Our hotel was a tent, but it was a five-star tent. The next morning we saw a lion, two cubs and many other animals, had tea on the hood of our vehicle in real china cups and then traveled to Kenya to the Siriat Bible School and Maryanne School. We visited El Doret, traveled to Nairobi and then flew back to Searcy. Our students are indeed blessed to be a part of this program.

SPECIAL PURPOSE PROGRAMS

In addition to the seven campus programs that we operate from Harding, a number of special purpose programs have been conducted, allowing students to have a global experience.

COBA/HUE

The program operated by the College of Business Administration is based in London, England. This summer-only program focuses on interaction with and visits to corporations with a significant presence in the United Kingdom.

Scotland

The Scotland program began in the summer of 2007. Dr. Mike Wood, the program's director, takes pre-student teachers to the Falkirk Schools near Stirling, Scotland, to work with Scottish teachers and become familiar with the educational system in the United Kingdom.

BAT

Bison Athletes in Training (BAT) allows student athletes to maintain a rigorous workout/training schedule while studying abroad in the summer.

Art

The Department of Art and Design has held three summer programs dedicated to art majors. Two have been based in Florence, Italy, and the other allowed the students to travel all over Europe. Stacy Schoen Gibson and Amy Cox direct the program, which provides first-hand observation of great works of art and architecture for our students.

Scholars Abroad

High school students who attended Honors Symposium in the summer following their junior year are invited by Dr. Monte Cox and Dr. Scott Adair to study abroad after their graduation the following year. This program is offered every other summer.

Personal Experiences

Dr. Don Shackelford was right. I needed more international travel experience, and I needed to have my worldview expanded. Harding University needed more international programs like HUF because of the impact these programs could have on students and faculty. I am grateful for his encouragement and that of Dr. Carl Mitchell in this pursuit.

In our travels to these international programs, I fell in love with the people in Italy, the food in Italy and the fact that they make an evening out of the late meal. I fell in love with the Holy Lands, and was able to trace Paul's footsteps in Greece – although I never got used to their eating a heavy meal at nine o'clock in the evening.

The Burks and the Mitchells enjoy an outing for dinner with Robbie and Mona Shackelford.

I fell in love with Australia, the Barrier Reef, the beauty of this country and the openness of their people.

I particularly loved our trip to Zambia, as we were able to see Namwianga and visit with the babies that were being taken care of in Havens One, Two and Three. I loved holding Peter. I loved being able to see Kenya and the animals on the safari.

I have been blessed to travel through Europe with members of our Board of Trustees as we visited the HUF program and the HUG program. I enjoyed going to our program in France and England, and I enjoyed seeing Scotland and the Swiss Alps. I have been blessed to take a trip to northern Europe and Russia and to visit with churches in all the major cities of Europe. Our trip to Chile led us to Patagonia and the lake region of Chile, along with time in Santiago and Viña del Mar. No wonder our students love these programs.

Harding is International

Because of its seven international campuses and its historic emphasis on world missions, Harding University can truly claim its place as an international university. It's difficult for some people to believe, but a student can come to Searcy, Ark., and literally see and experience the world as a result of his or her Harding experience. Add in numerous faculty members who have traveled, studied abroad or worked as missionaries, and you have all of the ingredients needed for the international education offered at Harding.

Students who take part in these experiences are changed forever. They make comments like, "Friendships made were priceless," "It taught us how big God's world really is," "I was able to walk in the footsteps of Jesus," "I know God is real and alive," "It was the most life-changing event in my life," "The Bible came to life," and "I know I have witnessed God through all the natural beauties of Australia." In Zambia, students often talk about the children at the Havens, the experience of watching churches established in the bush, and their exposure to the ministry of Janice Bingham as she helps native Africans with their health needs.

A few months ago, Dr. Mitchell shared a story with me over coffee. He said he had once showed a student through the McInteer Center, and the student made this insightful comment as she observed the world map in the rotunda – "I came to Harding and discovered the world!" That student was Karen Crabb, a sister of Dr. McLarty, Harding's fifth president.

Karen could have gone to any university, but she chose to come to Searcy to attend Harding – where she discovered the world. Her statement has crossed my lips so many times that it seems as if I actually heard her say these words myself.

The life-changing experiences of Harding's international programs help students foster close relationships with each other and reach across cultural and social barriers to form relationships with people in other countries.

CHAPTER EIGHT

American Studies Program

Introduction

The American Studies Program was initiated by President George Benson as a result of his experiences with communism and socialism while he was a missionary in China. Since its beginning, Harding has received numerous Freedom Foundation Awards for exemplary citizenship education training.

I was first exposed to the American Studies Program as a student and was impressed with the number of speakers who came to campus. I enjoyed trips to New Orleans, Chicago, Dallas and other cities as part of the program. These experiences opened my eyes to a completely new world.

I want to share some of my favorite stories involving the speakers of the American Studies Program. During my time as president, 120 speakers were invited to campus, including sixteen heads of state. I believe the Harding community and our nation benefited from the presentations made by these individuals.

The heads of state who were part of this program were presidents of the United States Gerald Ford, George H. W. Bush, Bill Clinton and George W. Bush; prime ministers of Great Britain, Margaret Thatcher and John Major; the chancellor of West Germany, Helmut Schmidt; the prime minister of Pakistan, Benazir Bhutto; the president of Poland, Lech Wałęsa; the president of the Soviet Union, Mikhail Gorbachev; the president of Zambia, Levi Patrick Mwanawasa; the prime minister of Canada, Brian Mulroney; the prime minister of Spain, José María Aznar; the president of Mexico, Vicente Fox; the prime minister of New Zealand, James Bolger; and the prime minister of Beliz, Manuel Esquivel.

Favorite American Studies Speakers

Of all the speakers to appear as part of the American Studies Program, my favorite was Lady Margaret Thatcher, who spoke at Harding April 27, 1995. She was known as the Iron Lady, and she served as the British prime minister from 1979 until 1990. Security was a major issue during her visit, as security personnel checked out our home, campus facilities and the general area before she arrived.

I had met with Mrs. Thatcher's assistant earlier, and she had told me exactly what I was to do while she was on campus. She went into great detail as to how I was to speak and what we should do during her visit. I remember her talking to me about setting up for the question-and-answer period on the Benson stage. Mrs. Thatcher was to speak for forty-five minutes and then answer questions. I was told by her assistant that I should repeat every question, even though we had microphones in the audience and everyone could hear the question. This would give Mrs. Thatcher time to compose her answer. I thought this was a bit odd since I knew she was a really bright scholar and world-renowned orator, but I did just as I was directed. After repeating the first question, I will never forget the expression of Mrs. Thatcher when she looked at me and said, "I am perfectly capable of hearing the questions they have. You have microphones in the auditorium, and there is no reason, young man, to repeat the questions for me." I knew I liked this lady, but I liked her even more after that.

Before her presentation, we had a reception for Mrs. Thatcher in our home. I was amazed at the ease with which she talked to all of the guests. At the end of the reception, our daughter-in-law, Jeanne Burks, brought in their new baby, Madison. Mrs. Thatcher held Madison for a long time and was very much at ease with her. She was down to earth and easy to visit with. The press didn't always communicate this side of her warm personality.

An article in the summer 1995 *Harding* magazine, written by Philip Tucker, summarized her presentation as she praised those who were responsible for founding our nation and drafting the Declaration of Independence. She said,

> *America is truly unique because it was founded on biblical principles. Yours is the first constitution that made it quite clear that the government was there to protect the rights of the people. No other*

nation in the world is founded on that belief. Your constitution ex-
pects each and every person to have a moral and religious approach
so that they fully fulfill the duty of citizens. That was, and remains,
the greatness of your nation.

Mrs. Thatcher also criticized some weaknesses in our country and in hers, including what she called a growing "dependency culture that doesn't want responsibility."

It's our great duty to help people get out of poverty. That we
gladly do. But we do it to give them the opportunity to become inde-
pendent themselves, for their own families – not to leave generation
after generation in dependency on the government.

A scientist herself, Mrs. Thatcher marveled at the many advances in science that have shaped this century. One, she said, is worldwide communication made possible through the Internet – but she warned that society must be careful to guard children from information on the computer network that is "appallingly pornographic and even sadistic."

Throughout the evening, Mrs. Thatcher emphasized a nation's need for personal liberty and strong rule of law. "There is no freedom without a strong rule of law," she said. "Otherwise, it is freedom for the strong to oppress the weak.

"The collapse of communism after its seventy-three-year reign," Mrs. Thatcher said, "came through the determination of countries like America and Britain, who believed it was the wrong way for people to live."

She praised her close ally, Ronald Reagan, for the decisive role he played in the breakup of communism through his Strategic Defense Initiative (S.D.I.), which she called "a piece of genius."

"Reagan's decision to go ahead with S.D.I. was the critical decision," she said. "That day when I saw Mikhail Gorbachev, he said to me, 'Will you please try to dissuade Mr. Reagan from going ahead with SDI?' I said, 'Certainly not! He's right. I'm all for it. We're going ahead with it.' Then we started on human rights and gradually we got freedom of speech and worship. Everyone should thank Gorbachev for what he has done.

"But the Russians are still Russians," she said about the country's then recent intervention in Chechnya. "We must keep a watch out – and we shall."

Mrs. Thatcher reminded the audience that she hopes the United States will always look to Britain as its foremost ally as it takes the lead as a world power in the next century. "America means a lot more to me than those countries in Europe do!"[1] she said in closing.

I was amused when a young man spoke for about five minutes during the question-and-answer session. Mrs. Thatcher's response to him was classic – she asked him if there was a question in his remarks. She made her point.

Mrs. Thatcher had not only left her mark on Searcy but once again on the world. She hit a home run in that presentation. I still have a letter from her, dated May 1, 1995, thanking Harding for the opportunity to come and speak. It is handwritten on her personal stationery and is a keepsake of mine.

I worked very hard to bring President Reagan to campus to speak in our American Studies series but was unsuccessful. I was not aware at the time that he was in the early stages of Alzheimer's, but his condition soon became public knowledge. A key player in this period in our history, Reagan would have been a great addition to our series of guest speakers.

George H. W. Bush

Harding was privileged to hear George H. W. Bush on April 24, 1997. Security was very tight since he was a former president of the United States. The Secret

Service and the state police were here for several days before he addressed the overflow crowd in the Benson Auditorium. I wondered how he would come across that evening because, for some time, he had not been portrayed well by the media regarding his ability to relate to audiences.

I really didn't need to worry, as he made an instant connection with the Harding audience. He spoke to the American Studies Board at a meeting prior to the dinner, and he was greeted and introduced by his friend, John Paul Hammerschmidt.

As he began his presentation, Mr. Bush said that retirement had been good to him – he was relaxed, he loved to travel and he loved to say whatever he wanted to say without fear of being derided by the media. He said he was a liberated free spirit – "When it comes to questions, if I like the question, fine; otherwise I won't answer it!"[2] Interestingly, he answered all of the questions that were asked that evening.

Mr. Bush was down to earth in his comments and continually poked fun at himself and his presidential term. He cautioned listeners against the danger of isolationism and urged support to strengthen ties with other nations, particularly emphasizing China. He said, "The United States/China relationship is the single most important in the world. It has more to do with peace in the next millennium than any other single relationship."

He went on to say that, with the demise of the Soviet Union leaving the role of sole super power to the United States, America must continue to lead world affairs. He told the audience, "If America does not keep its foreign policy strong and guard against isolationism, we may see a strange coalition form between the extreme right and the left."[3] It seems to me that a lot of what he said that evening has come true.

With respect to involvement in the political arena, Mr. Bush acknowledged that there was an ugly climate in Washington at the time but asked students and participants in the audience not to be turned off. He added that politics in America is a noble calling, and said, "If you good men and women at Harding decide to sit on your hands because you don't like to change, you are going to get the kind of government you deserve, which isn't a very good one."

Mr. Bush indicated that the media had charged him with being privileged and out of touch with most Americans but said his privilege came from being taught values from his parents. He said the biggest problem facing the nation is the decimation and decline of the American family.

In terms of foreign policy, Mr. Bush said,

> *I'm gratified that I had a good enough team that we were able to shape events in a way that when freedom finally prevailed in the Cold War, when the Berlin Wall fell and the Soviet Union imploded, it happened peacefully.*

What a profound statement!

He talked about the friendship he shared with Lady Margaret Thatcher and Mikhail Gorbachev. I would love to have heard more about this unlikely partnership. I am convinced that President Bush and his policies had a great deal to do with what happened as the Cold War ended.

Mr. Bush went on to say, "Character matters – and what's truly important is not the political wars you win or lose, the victories on the playing field or the marks you get. What really matters in your life are your family, your friends and your faith."

What a wonderful statement from this world leader. Mr. Bush credited faith for keeping him strong in tough situations. He mentioned that he had said many prayers the night before the Persian Gulf War began.

Mr. Bush closed by saying he hoped people would know that his administration, as well as he and Barbara, did their best to uphold the high standards that should prevail in the Oval Office. He said,

> *What I really hope history will show is that Barbara and I conducted ourselves with honor in the White House and upheld the integrity of the office. Let history decide whether I was a good president or a bad president, but I was a better president because I had faith in the Almighty.*

Mikhail Gorbachev

Mikhail Gorbachev was president of the Soviet Union from 1985 until 1991. He came to the Harding campus to speak Oct. 15, 1998. He was the most unlikely American Studies speaker to be a part of our program. I would not have dreamed of inviting him to this program while I was a faculty member prior to the fall of the wall in Berlin in 1989.

In 1987, Reagan stood at the Brandenburg Gate, looking over the Berlin Wall and made the oft-repeated statement,

> *General Secretary Gorbachev, if you seek peace, if you seek prosperity for the Soviet Union and Eastern Europe, if you seek liberalization, come here to this gate. Mr. Gorbachev, open this gate! Mr. Gorbachev, tear down this wall!*[4]

On Nov. 9, 1989, the borders in Germany were opened and Germans, both Eastern and Western, swarmed the old symbol of division and repression with hammers and chisels, and the wall came down.

Perhaps with this background of events taking place in earlier years, you can understand why this presentation was so important and seemed so unlikely to me. Again, security was very tight for this presentation. Mr. Gorbachev stayed in the Harding Heritage Inn while here, and this suite has since been referred to by his name.

We had a large reception for Mr. Gorbachev at our home, with the food set up in the back yard. It was the biggest reception I remember having during my presidency for any guest. I will never forget Mr. Gorbachev asking me, after all the people had gone through the line, where he could find a drink. Not realizing immediately what he was asking, I responded that the drinks were in the back yard and that there were several choices for him. The drinks we were providing were not quite what he expected. He was surprised, but I noticed he had an alternative source in his coat pocket.

Before his presentation, we were privileged to hear from a combined chorus, and he was very moved by the singing that evening. His comments were interpreted simultaneously, so we had the volume turned low for him as he spoke in Russian and turned up for the interpreter. It worked pretty well.

In Mr. Gorbachev's opening remarks, he said,

I like Americans because they feel that they are free citizens. They don't have to pretend – freedom is in their blood. This is something I have always been aiming for in Russia. It is difficult after centuries of slavery and then almost 100 years of the communist regime, which suppressed the human spirit just like the system of slavery suppressed human initiative.

Mr. Gorbachev talked about his dream of changing the Russian system so that democracy could be established, along with free speech, elections, free press, free

opinion and freedom of religion. He talked about establishing the freedom to leave and return to the country and promoting a step-by-step transition to a market economy.[5]

He said he knew Americans better at the time of his presentation than before, and that the farther you go from Washington D.C. and New York, the more you like America. The crisis of the old system in Russia is what made perestroika necessary, he said, explaining that perestroika meant "changes in the domestic life of our country, which destroyed the totalitarian regime."

In my mind, it was important to look at the messages that were brought to the Harding audience by Margaret Thatcher, George H. W. Bush and Mikhail Gorbachev as a package because all were heavily involved in the peaceful resolution of the Cold War. What a blessing to have the opportunity to hear these key world leaders on the Harding stage.

I vividly remember a trip we took to Germany in June 1990, six months after the fall of the Berlin Wall, along with board chairman James Cone and his wife, Bonnie. While in Berlin, we were able to work with A.B.C. to film an American

Studies video at the site of the Berlin Wall and Berinauser Square. This was the highlight of the trip for me. You could see the wall with its death strip in between and guard towers close together. The wall was painted white on the inside so the Russians could easily see any movement between the walls. The wall was 104 miles long and well lit. Wire fences were included at some points on the inside, and land mines were on the east side of the fence. We picked up pieces of the wall to bring back as souvenirs. Tom and Lou Ann Sterner were our hosts while we were there, and they were very gracious to us.

Barbara Bush

Harding hosted Barbara Bush, former First Lady, as our speaker on April 11, 2002. Mrs. Bush was a wonderful communicator, and the audience instantly loved her. The visit was accompanied by the usual amount of Secret Service, security and a lot of excitement. It was obvious to all that Mrs. Bush was a strong lady and a very important part of the Bush legacy. She shared her opinions about family and life in the White House and talked openly about the importance of character and faith.

George W. Bush

A third member of the Bush family, George W. Bush visited Harding April 22, 2010, after serving as the 43rd president of the United States. This was his second time to speak at Harding – he had spoken in the Heritage Auditorium when he was in Searcy campaigning for the election of his dad. Mr. Bush talked openly about the challenges he faced as president. He was optimistic throughout the evening. It was easy to see the resemblance between George W. and his father. At the conclusion of his question-and-answer period, the

combined chorus sang "The Lord Bless You and Keep You," which was very touching to him and the entire audience.

A portrait of the three Bush personalities who visited the Harding campus was painted by art professor, Beverly Austin, and presented to Mrs. Bush. The painting was later sent back on loan from the Bush Library so that it might be displayed on the Harding campus. It hung in my office until I retired in 2013.

Condoleezza Rice

Harding was honored to have Dr. Condoleezza Rice speak March 19, 2012. Dr. Rice formerly served as Secretary of State and advisor to President George W. Bush. I was most impressed with her background and success. It is interesting to read her book and learn about her background and the opportunities provided by her determined parents.[6] Dr. Rice spent much of her presentation talking about growing up in Birmingham, Ala., in a divided and segregated society, and going to college and eventually becoming the Secretary of State. I loved that she was a dedicated pianist who apparently planned for a long time to make that her career. She decided later

that she loved international relations, and that became her area of specialty.

Her presentation, "Looking Back and Moving Forward to a Stronger America," was one of the best I have heard at Harding. The question-and-answer was world class in every sense of the word, as she is so knowledgeable.

Benazir Bhutto

Benazir Bhutto spoke Sept. 26, 1991. It was my joy to serve as host to the former prime minister of Pakistan. She loved southern accents, she loved people and she connected with people easily. Because of her royal position, we were told not to touch her hand and given other instructions on proper procedure for her visit. It turns out that she was one of the easiest individuals to like and be around that I have known.

One of the first things she wanted to do when she arrived on campus was to have her hair done. At the last minute, we got her an appointment at Mr. Mac's, her hair was styled and she paid $25. She noted that she had gone to the beauty parlor the day before in New York City and it cost $125.

Leah and I enjoyed hosting her for a reception in our home, and she presented Leah with some beautiful pillowcases that we still cherish. What a gracious lady.

Unfortunately, when Mrs. Bhutto was killed as part of the unrest in Pakistan, it felt as though we had lost part of our family, as we had drawn close to her as a result of her visit on our campus.

Malcolm Forbes Jr.

Malcolm Forbes Jr. was president, C.E.O. and editor in chief of Forbes Magazine. He spoke Nov. 8, 1994, and again in 2008. He flew in on his private jet, "Capitalist Tool." I loved visiting with him and enjoyed the time that he spent with the American Studies Institute Board.

We were in the middle of a national election, and he was very knowledgeable of the election and its pending results. In fact, he spoke on election day and before the polls closed, he predicted the outcome by percentages of all the races across the nation. He was right on target.

Dan Quayle

Former Vice President Dan Quayle was our speaker April 14, 1994. He is one of the top ten speakers to be a part of the American Studies program. I was impressed with him personally, with the content of his presentation and with the positive response from the large audience.

Mr. Quayle addressed a number of topics, and his comments of some twenty years ago still ring true. With respect to family values, he said,

> *We're essentially talking about a breakdown in civilization,*
> *where we have dysfunctional families with no one assuming respon-*
> *sibility. We see crime, violence and drug addiction, and we ask,*
> *"Why?" You can trace it time and time again right back to the family.*

On the matter of education, he said, "Our education system today, unfortunately, is a monopolistic system that breeds mediocrity. Excellence is not rewarded or recognized." To encourage a high-quality system, Quayle expressed support of a plan allowing parents to choose their children's public schools.

With respect to health care, Quayle disagreed with the focus of the current health care reform debate, believing that the crisis lies in the health insurance

148

industry. He suggested regulatory laws that would require insurance companies to accept and manage risk. He indicated that this could be done without a grandiose health care plan that cannot be made to work. He said we already have the best quality of health care anywhere in the world, and he did not want to change that. He guaranteed that, if the government was running things, we would not have the security of timely access to health care. He asked, "When has the government done anything less expensively or simply?"

With respect to foreign affairs, he said he was in favor of a strong policy.

> *The stronger America is, the better it is for the American people. We can recover from mistakes in health care or in tax and education policy, but if we make serious misjudgments in foreign policy, sometimes it takes a generation or more for a nation to recover.*

He concluded by saying, "Even though we have won the Cold War, the world is still a very dangerous place. If we're not willing to support our military operations and we become weak, then we'll become irrelevant."[7]

Dr. James Dobson

Dr. James Dobson and his wife, Shirley, came during Harding's 75th anniversary celebration on April 22, 1999. Dr. Dobson was widely known as an author and founder of Focus on the Family, headquartered in Colorado Springs, Colo. He has written numerous books and is considered one of the foremost experts on the subject of family. Dobson's presentation addressed faith – not just family – because he was so impressed with Harding's commitment to faith development.

General Colin Powell

Gen. Colin Powell spoke Oct. 24, 2000. A retired general and retired chairman of the U.S. Joint Chiefs of Staff, he was being considered as a candidate for president of the United States at the time. He talked forcibly about foreign policy and national security.

Ben Stein

Ben Stein spoke at Harding Feb. 10, 2009. A columnist, author and actor, he surely is one of the most unusual individuals to speak as part of the American Studies program. He stands alone as the speaker who wore tennis shoes. His Arkansas ties to in-laws in Eden Isle and his reference to Sonic as his favorite restaurant in this area made him a hit with students.

Dick Cheney

Former Vice President Dick Cheney spoke at Harding Nov. 4, 1993. He spoke about national security and urged people to get involved in political life. It is strange what you remember from some speakers. I remember his saying that he had thousands working under him when he was Secretary of Defense, and as vice president, he did not have a single person working under him. He was a down-to-earth person who served as vice president from 2001-2009. Later, we were privileged to have his wife,

Lynn Cheney, speak at a graduation exercise, and she was outstanding as well.

Other Favorite Speakers

Other favorite speakers who visited Harding include former Secretary of Education William Bennett, who spoke on three different occasions. I remember numerous discussions with him at receptions and in a car with him as he talked about national policies. His book, *The Book of Virtues*, is quite excellent.

I loved having Robert Bork here in 1989. He was a Supreme Court nominee. I found his book, *Marching Toward Gomorrah*, to be outstanding. I have quoted from it in many presentations since he was on our campus. Admiral William Crowley, former chairman of the Joint Chiefs of Staff, spoke in 1990. Robert Novak and Bob Beckel were here for a debate on American issues in October 1992. They broadcast their program from the Harding campus.

Cal Thomas was one of the more interesting speakers who came in 1993. He was a syndicated newspaper columnist. One of his books, *The Things That Matter Most*, is one that I have thoroughly enjoyed reading. Michael Medved, film critic and author, talked about Hollywood's glamorization of violence, promiscuity, profanity and anti-social behavior of every kind as being tantamount to cultural pollution.

151

One of my favorite speakers to be on the Harding campus was Coach Bobby Bowden from Florida State University. I admire him greatly for the work he did, not only as an excellent football coach but as a man of great character.

A very emotional presentation was given by Deena Burnett, widow of Tom Burnett, who was a passenger on Flight 93 on 9/11. She spoke in February 2004. Gen. Tommy Franks was a popular speaker in April 2004. The U.S. general who led the attack on the Taliban in Afghanistan, he was considered a soldiers' general.

We were privileged to have Don Soderquist, an executive officer with Walmart, in November 2006. I loved listening to him talk about the Walmart culture and his work with Sam Walton. I also enjoyed hearing Karl Rove talk about political analysis Oct. 16, 2012. He was a senior advisor to President George W. Bush.

The American Studies Institute Advisory Board

In 1987, we created an American Studies Advisory Board to help provide wisdom and guidance for the ongoing operation of the program.

I will never forget flying to Bentonville, Ark, to meet with Paul Carter, Sam Walton and Jack Stephens. We met in Mr. Walton's small office, and there was barely room for the four of us. The result of that meeting was the creation of the advisory board with Mr. Stephens and Mr. Walton agreeing to serve as co-chairs.

The original board included influential national leaders – Paul Carter, president of Walmart Realty; James Cone, president of James Cone, Inc., and a member of the Harding Board of Trustees; Dr. Bill Cox, former A.S.I. director; Jack McNutt, former president of Murphy Oil Corporation; John Steuri, retired chairman and C.E.O. of Remington Products, Inc.; Barger Tyygart,

president and C.E.O. of J.C. Penney; Donald W. (Buddy) Wray, president of Tyson Foods, Inc.; and Dr. Stanley Marshall, former president of Florida State University. Dr. Carr, Dr. Bob Reely and Dr. Ganus served in an ex-officio capacity.

Jim Carr and I share an interesting memory from a visit we made to see Victor Kiam in New York City, a member of our A.S.I. board. He was the owner of the New England Patriots and while there, we were his guests at a game. After the

game, we met a number of the players in the locker room as we visited with Mr. Kiam. We happened to witness a discussion between a woman reporter and Mr. Kiam related to the place of women in a locker room setting. Mr. Kiam was quoted incorrectly in the paper, based on what we heard, and he was very upset over the incident. He took out a full-page ad in the Boston Globe, denying the statement, and used Jim Carr and me as witnesses to validate his statement.

The Sino-American Studies Institute

In 2002, the Sino-American Studies Institute was formed at Harding to bring Chinese students to Harding for the first time. This was a major development for Harding, given that for many years, students from China were not allowed to do their higher education in the United States.

In 2003, Harding received the first group of sixteen students, who pursued a master of science in education degree.

In the spring of 2013, we had 147 students from China. From inception, we have received 424 students from China, and 277 of

these students have graduated. A number of these students have been baptized into Christ as a result of their study here.

It has been amazing to see this development on the Harding campus. The involvement of Harding faculty and staff and members of the community has been remarkable.

The Walton Scholarship Program

The Walton Scholarship Program began at Harding in the fall of 1985. It was started by Sam and Helen Walton, who wanted to make a difference in Central America. Sam and Helen were friends with Gabriel Galindo, a wealthy Panamanian diplomat and businessman who helped negotiate the Panama Canal Treaty. He and Sam loved to fish together in Panama.

On one of their fishing trips, Galindo persuaded the Waltons to fund a scholarship program to counter the influence of communist governments who were edu-

cating the brightest students in Central America. Upon returning from one of these fishing trips in the summer of 1984, Mr. Walton said, "I feel that it is very important to do all we can to help the countries of Central and South America to develop their economies and improve their standard of living."[8] The result of that resolve on his and Helen's part was the inauguration of the Walton Scholarship Program.

I remember talking with Mr. Walton about this program in the summer of 1984. I was meeting with him to present a proposal for them to endow our American Studies Program. I was excited about this proposal but, as I talked with him about it, I learned about his great interest in a program for students in Central America. He asked if we would like to be a part of that program with the University of the Ozarks and John Brown University. We were happy to be included in this new experiment in international education.

As of 2013, more than 1,300 Walton students have studied at Harding, and 392 have graduated from this program. Almost all of these students have returned to their home countries and are making a tremendous impact on the economy. This was Mr. Walton's dream. The program requires that graduates return to their home country for a minimum of five years. This is one of the most successful programs of its type in any university in the nation.

The students who attend Harding – or one of the other universities as part of this program – are selected on a competitive basis from a large group of candidates. The following students attended Harding as Walton Scholars.

Carolina Cardona, who graduated in 2010, said,

> *Attending Harding University and being a Walton scholar changed my life. I was scared because it was going to be a big change in my life. I was leaving my small town in Guatemala, a place where the living conditions were quite different. We only had running water for two hours a day; we didn't have any restaurants; washing machines were considered a luxury, and bicycles were our main form of transportation. All of a sudden, I found myself in Arkansas, enrolled at Harding University and taking classes in a foreign language that I barely understood. I was immersed in a different culture and living in a dorm filled with things that overwhelmed me.*

Slowly, the obstacles began to fade, and all of my fears disappeared. At Harding, I found people, who, with a smile, were willing to help me with all of these challenges. I found people who loved God and demonstrated the fruit of the Spirit. I remember the first day in chapel when Dr. Burks asked the students how to spell "camaraderie." At that time, I had no idea what he was talking about. However, at the end of my four years at Harding, I not only knew how to spell this word, but I had learned the true meaning of the word. Camaraderie was present everywhere on the campus, and it helped me to claim Harding as my second home.

After my graduation, I returned to my beautiful country. There was no question what my mission was to be. I had to serve the poor in my country, and God opened the doors for me to work for a non-profit organization where I am currently working with missionaries who come to serve the poor people who depend on the Guatemala City garbage dump for their survival.

Carlos Velasco, from El Savador, graduated in 1999. He provided the leadership to begin the JESUS Project, which has been so successful that it now includes three colleges. Current students and alumni still go there during the summer to assist with this program. The following quotation was sent to Dr. Nicky Boyd in March 2014 concerning this part of Carlos' experience at Harding –

An important principle of Sam Walton was that Walton scholars would return to their countries after graduation to create a positive impact on their local communities. This concept was of significant motivation and made me think that, as Waltons, we could start creating this positive impact even before graduation. This principle, along with the high-quality Christian education received at Harding, helped me create the JESUS Project in 1997 while still a sophomore. At that time, the JESUS Project was mainly a once-a-year mission trip by Harding students to El Icacal community in the country of El Salvador. Now, the JESUS Project is a legally established non-profit organization that supports about 300 students in rural communities.

American Studies

I don't know how you can measure the impact of the American Studies Program for Harding University, its students and faculty, our community, our nation and the world. Citizenship education has always been an important part of our mission at Harding University. Dr. Benson and Dr. Ganus set the standards very high.

We were blessed to hear from sixteen heads of state during my time as president. I especially treasure memories of hosting Margaret Thatcher on our campus. I loved hearing Condoleezza Rice's personal story about growing up in a racially divided Birmingham, Ala.

Harding is also stronger because of our Walton Scholars Program, which brings students here from Central America and Mexico, and our Sino-American Studies Institute, which brings students to Harding from China.

Pharmacy students don their white coats for their final year

CHAPTER NINE

New Academic Programs

While Harding continues to emphasize liberal arts education, which I believe in strongly, we have seen a dramatic increase in the professional and graduate areas of instruction. Business and education comprise a major portion of the undergraduate student body, and engineering has been added in recent years. At the graduate level, numerous professional and graduate programs have been added to meet the needs of students, including new programs in the Allied Health area, with the creation of the Center for Health Sciences.

Degrees Conferred

	1987		2013	
Undergraduate	517	86%	784	65%
Graduate	86	14%	409	34%
Totals	603		1,193	

Many of the degrees conferred in 2013 were to students with a major that had been added during this twenty-six-year period. At the undergraduate level, 257 degrees out of 784, or thirty-three percent, were new majors. At the graduate level, 352 degrees out of 409 total degrees conferred were new, which represents eighty-six percent of the total. Overall, 609 of 1,193 degrees awarded were new, which represents fifty-one percent of the total.

According to a report issued by the Provost, twenty-nine new undergraduate majors were added during this twenty-six-year period, and eighteen new graduate majors were offered.[1]

New Undergraduate Programs

The College of Arts and Humanities added majors in interior design, general studies, criminal justice, interactive media, electronic media production and Web design. This represents ninety-five new degrees (fifty percent) out of 187 degrees earned in 2012-13.

In the College of Allied Health, Communication Sciences and Disorders offered a non-clinical route for their degree. In Bible and Ministry, a new preaching major began being offered in 2011.

In the Paul R. Carter College of Business Administration, new programs included professional sales, international business, health care management, finance and global economic development. In 2012-13, forty-six of the 151 degrees conferred were from these new majors, representing thirty percent of the total.

In the College of Sciences, new programs included athletic training, exercise science, child life development, computer engineering, electrical and mechanical engineering, interior merchandising and software development. In addition, biochemistry and molecular biology, molecular and cellular biology and recreation management were added. Forty of the degrees conferred in 2012-13 were from these new programs.

A new Degree Completion Program was added in 2005 to make it possible for adults who had dropped out of college to complete their degree at Harding, with its Christian emphasis, by doing work both online and in residence. A total of 113 individuals have graduated since 2007.

One of our employees, Kevin Davis, completed his undergraduate degree in leadership and management through this degree completion program. He later earned his Juris Doctorate from the U.A.L.R. William H. Bowen School of Law.

A major feasibility study was conducted during the 1991-92 year concerning the possibility of establishing a branch campus in Florida. A board committee helped with the study and the location chosen as a possible site was a small community between Mt. Dora and Eustis. While there was a lot of enthusiasm for this venture, the final decision was not to proceed, primarily because of funding. We felt we could operate a two-year program economically, but the four-year program desired by people in Florida would be difficult to finance and operate efficiently.

Honors Symposium

In addition to the new undergraduate degrees, an Honors Symposium was started in the summer of 1993. This program targeted college-bound potential honor students to introduce them to Harding and university life. Invitees were select students who had finished their junior year in high school.

The Honors Symposium is a life-changing journey for the students who attend, as they are able to witness in a few days what Harding University is all about. They are engaged with wonderful professors and mentored by student counselors. They attend stimulating academic classes and participate in fun activities designed to develop group bonding and sharing.

A key element of the symposium is the tabernacle experience led by Dr. Monte Cox.

Interestingly, the goal for Honors Symposium attendance that first year was twenty-five students, and forty-two attended. In the summer of 2012, 200 students attended. More than ninety percent of the symposium attendees have gone on to enroll at Harding.

Honors College

While not a new major for a degree, Harding established an Honors College in 1989 under the direction of Dr. Larry Long. It was felt that Harding's most talented and scholarly students would benefit from a special program that would allow them to approach their studies in an advanced, interactive way. This program began with nineteen students who have since gone on to become lawyers, doctors, business leaders and college professors. By 1998, this program had expanded to more than 500 students and was transformed into

its own college at Harding. The Honors College now has more than 1,000 members, with about 150 who are part of the upper tier Honors scholars group.

New Graduate Programs

Much of Harding's growth in the last ten years has centered on the development of new graduate and adult professional programs, which is consistent with trends in higher education in America. Eighteen new graduate programs were added during the last twenty-six years, and in the 2013 year, 409 students graduated with a master's or professional degree.[2]

College of Bible and Ministry

The master's degree in marriage and family therapy began in 1994. Dr. Carl Mitchell was the champion for this program, as he had a keen interest in providing this service, particularly for the church constituency. Designed as a Christian-based M.F.T. program specifically to help people who work with church members in Christian counseling, the facilities for this program

were provided in the new McInteer Center. The degree involves an intensive two-year, full-time program.

In 2005, a master of ministry degree was begun online on the Searcy campus in the College of Bible and Ministry. Dr. Bill Richardson now directs this program, and fifteen degrees were awarded in this area in 2012-13. Thirty-eight students were enrolled in the graduate program in Bible on the Searcy campus in 2013.[3]

Paul R. Carter College of Business Administration

Harding began a master's degree in business administration in 2001. While many of our students choose to go to a different university for a graduate degree, others want to stay here to finish their degree requirements. This program graduates about ninety students each year, and since inception, 888 master's degrees have been conferred. The emphasis of the degree program is Christian ethics, and it is offered both online and face to face.[4] The M.B.A. was the first Harding program to be approved by the Higher Learning Commission to be fully online.

School of Theology

Our oldest program in graduate studies is offered by our School of Theology in Memphis, Tenn. This program began in 1958, and the M.Div. degree is the major degree offered at this location. Two other degrees have been added – the M.A. in counseling in 1996 and the M.A. in Christian ministry in 2003. A significant development for the School of Theology was the offering of many of their courses in an online format or in intensive one-week seminars. The School of Theology has 1,625 graduates and 4,379 alumni serving churches all over the world.[5]

Cannon-Clary College of Education

One of our largest programs in graduate studies is the College of Education. A number of new degrees have been offered, including the M.A in Teaching and the M.S. in Professional Counseling: Clinical and School, in 2002. A specialist degree in educational leadership was started in 2005, and a second specialist degree was offered in counseling in 2007. Harding's first ever academic doctorate, the Ed.D. degree, began being offered in 2007.

The process of developing Harding's first academic doctoral program began in 2005. After two years of extensive research by Dr. Tony Finley, dean of the Cannon-Clary College of Education, Harding approved the establishment of a Doctor of Education degree in educational leadership. In January 2008, eight candidates made up the first cohort under the initial courses required for the doctoral degree.

The first graduate of this program was a former Harding student, Bruce Bryant. When Harding announced in 2007 that we would offer this doctoral degree, this unique degree was of great interest to him, and he believed that God was truly directing his steps as he returned to Harding to complete the degree. Dr. Bruce Bryant was the first person to defend his dissertation and receive the Ed.D. degree from Harding. He is now a member of the Harding University Cannon-Clary College of Education faculty.

Master's programs are offered in Searcy and in professional center locations in North Little Rock, Ark; Northwest Arkansas in Rogers; and the School of Theology in Memphis. Courses are also offered at other locations in the state, including Clarksville, Pine Bluff and Paragould. Currently, the Cannon-Clary College of Education offers two education specialists degrees and thirteen master's degrees in various areas. In addition, the Master of Science in Education offers twelve areas of study and the Master of Secondary Education offers nine areas of study.

One hundred twenty-one degrees were awarded at the graduate level in the College of Education in the 2013 academic year. The largest program was the

Harding in Rogers, Ark.

164

Master of Arts in Teaching, with sixty-seven degrees conferred. Harding's graduate program in education is one of the largest in the state of Arkansas.[6]

Health Sciences

Harding's Strategic Plan in the new millennium called for adding a number of programs in the Health Sciences – Physician Assistant Studies, Communication Sciences and Disorders, Pharmacy and Physical Therapy. Additional degrees have been approved in Occupational Therapy and Nursing, which have not yet been implemented. Other programs have been evaluated, including a College of Osteopathic Medicine, which may be considered in the future.

Physician Assistant Program

The first new degree in Health Sciences to be added was the Master of Science in physician assistant studies in 2006. Thirty-five students received their degrees in 2012-13, and 200 students have received degrees since its inception. This is the first program to offer degrees for physician assistants in Arkansas.

I enjoy reflecting on the initiation of this program and how it came together. Unknown to me, Dr. Dean Priest, who was academic dean at the time, was conducting a study regarding the possibility of this program being added to the Harding curriculum. He talked to a number of people and made a visit to a college campus to discuss their program in Tennessee.

At the same time, I was in Arlington, Texas, with my wife, Leah, who was ill with cancer, and she was meeting with her primary doctor, Dr. Blumenschein, and an additional professional. My wife loved both of these individuals and assumed that the second person was a doctor as well. It turns out that she was a P.A. and a wonderful provider for my wife. It was then that I learned about the extensive manner in which P.A.'s serve the medical profession. I came back to campus and talked to Dr. Priest to see if he would be willing to pursue the possibility of this program for us at Harding.

I learned that Dr. Priest was already pursuing this option. We proceeded to conduct a feasibility study and visited several campuses to learn more about the

program. We recommended it to our Board of Trustees, and it was approved in 2004.

A key to our beginning this program was finding a director, and we were fortunate to find Dr. Mike Murphy, along with his wife, Marci, who were able to come lead this program. Dr. Murphy is a medical doctor with background in teaching and the perfect person to come and plan the program. We leased space off campus to house the program for the first several years until it moved into facilities in the new

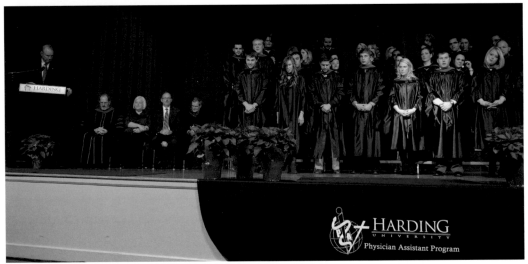

Farrar Health Sciences Building. This competitive program receives about 600 applications for thirty-six new positions each fall.

Perhaps the best way to illustrate the impact of the Physician Assistant program is to share a story about one of the students in the program, Lauren Bump, who was scheduled to graduate in 2014 but was tragically murdered in her hometown of San Antonio, Texas, during the Christmas holidays of 2013. Part of her story is described by Caitlin Anderson, also a student in the Harding University P.A. program.[7]

Caitlin recalled getting a phone call on New Year's Day, learning of Lauren's murder and wondering if this could be real. Her classmate had been murdered while running one day. Caitlin described Lauren as a shining example of hope –

Lauren's story is one worth telling. Beyond her flawless grace and appearance, she carried a mission in her heart. Her blonde hair and blue eyes paled in comparison to the beautiful ways she interacted with the world around her. Lauren's mission was simple. She pursued people with the love embedded in her from her God.

Meeting Lauren Bump changed lives. Her presence invoked an emotional response from people – a response of hope because of her careful attention and her gentle confidence.

In clinical rotations, Lauren treated more than 1,000 patients. Her compelling characteristic as a student was her devoted curiosity for each individual's deepest needs. She endured through didactic and clinical work as a student devoted to never failing her patients.

Regardless of personal struggles, Lauren kept her faith in her work, a characteristic precious in today's health care field. Patients and physicians observed in Lauren a model of fierce patient advocacy as she embraced the potential influence she could have on others.

Caitlin concluded her comments with her own statement,

The defining moment in my P.A. education was the moment of realization that health care is more than a career. It's motivated by more than friends, family or patients. It's about choosing to celebrate life, especially in the memory of a stolen sister. We persevere in this exercise of endurance, grace and compassion by being joyful in Lauren's legacy. Losing our P.A. classmate comes as a shock and a blow to our hearts.

I agree with Caitlin's assessment that "Lauren's story is one worth telling." What a sad and tragic story. In one sense, it is also a story of great hope and faith. It

167

is what our Physician Assistant program is all about. It's what health care education at Harding is about.

I learned from discussions with Dr. Bill White, one of Lauren's professors, that after his wife, Neva, died last year, Lauren and a group of other students, came to visit with him in his home each week to encourage him. They offered to bring a meal. It is my understanding that they just came to clean the house and learn more from Dr. White about his memories of his wife. They were simply ministering to one of their professors in a simple, yet profound way. I think this example speaks to the heart of the program and to the heart of Lauren Bump, who wanted to serve others. I am glad that Dr. McLarty, Dr. Murphy and others were able to go to San Antonio to participate in her memorial service. I didn't know Lauren, but I have heard a great deal about her life since her death and feel that her legacy will live on as an example of what our Physician Assistant program at Harding means.

Communications Sciences and Disorders Master's Program

A new graduate program in speech-language pathology was approved in 2006 and the Department of Communication Sciences and Disorders was expanded with Dr. Beckie Weaver as chair of that program. The first cohort of fourteen students entered in the fall of 2008, graduating in the spring 2010.

In 2010, the College of Allied Health was established with Dr. Beckie Weaver as dean and Dr. Dan Tullos as chair of the department. Full accreditation was granted to the program in 2013 when the sixth cohort of fourteen students entered.

Because of the increased demand for facilities to serve undergraduate and graduate programs, the department moved into new space provided by the addition of the Swaid Swaid Health Sciences Building in the fall of 2013. These facilities include a fully equipped speech clinic, along with offices for faculty and classrooms.

As the new program began, discussion centered on ways to make the program distinctive from other programs operating in the state and region. Emphasis was given to adding an international dimension in connection with Harding's program in Zambia, which was in the development stage. Since the national language of Zambia is English, there would be no language barrier.

In October 2007, the late president of Zambia, Levy Patrick Mwanawasa, visited the Harding University campus, accompanied by many of his government's ministers – Honorable Professor Geoffrey Lungwangwa, Minister of Education and the Honorable Dr. Brian Chituwo, Minister of Health. Professor Lungwangwa and Dr. Chituwo discussed with Dr. Weaver the serious need of speech therapy services for the citizens of Zambia. A proposal was made by Dr. Weaver to allow American faculty and student clinicians to come into Zambia to train the Zambian teachers and students in communication disorders.

In the summer of 2008, Dr. Weaver, Dr. Tullos and Sara Shock traveled to

Zambia to determine if this program would be advantageous to the speech-language pathology graduate students and George Benson Christian College, a Zambian institution that trains native teachers and students. George Phiri, Namwianga Mission superintendent, and Fist Chona, director of the college, approved our suggested training program. The training program began in May 2009 with an introductory course offered to students at George Benson Christian College. HIZ-Path graduate students also began offering speech therapy services to the citizens of Zambia at that time.

The story of the HIZ-Path program has been shared at national and international professional speech-language and hearing meetings and conventions. With the assistance of Dr. Hopper, a video of the workings of the program was premiered at the 2011 American Speech-Language-Hearing Association annual convention. In the audience that day was an undergraduate student from Bakersfield, Calif. The mission of this program and the opportunity to share his faith while honing his clinical skills was appealing to him.

At the conclusion of the session, Jake Severson approached Sara Shock and said, "Where is Harding and how can I be a part of this graduate program – because

I have to go to Africa with you?" She gave him information and the Web address. Four months later, we received an application for graduate school from Jake, who was highly qualified and readily accepted into the program.

On the first day of graduate orientation, Jake asked when he could sign up to go to HIZ-Path. He was the first to submit all of his paperwork, and he eagerly prepared for the trip. The trip became a family affair when his mother's sixth grade class decided to make the Haven their class project for the academic year.

College of Pharmacy

Our most ambitious new program in the health sciences was the establishment of the doctoral program in pharmacy in 2009. This four-year program enrolls sixty students in each class, and fifty-four degrees were conferred in 2013. Fifty-five students had been awarded degrees in 2012, which was the first year of graduates in this program.

I am very much encouraged with the mission of this Christian-based pharmacy program at Harding. It is only the second Pharm.D. program in the state of Arkansas, with the other being at the University of Arkansas for Medical Sciences.

While the program began in 2008, we actually began work toward this program in 2005-06. The first objective was to recruit a dean, and we were fortunate to find Dr. Julie Hixson-Wallace to lead this program. She was instrumental in finding the faculty for us to inaugurate the program.

This was the most difficult new program for Harding to establish. We faced a number of obstacles in this new professional program, even a change in our charter. Accreditation challenges were significant, and we had to arrange all of the clinical rotations that were needed in the program. Assembling the faculty was and continues to be a challenge, but the long-term benefits of the graduates of the College of Pharmacy will be a blessing to Harding and our nation as these graduates practice their professions all over the country and the world.

The mission of the College of Pharmacy is holistic in nature, which makes the program special. The mission makes the program appealing to a number of students who want this kind of pharmacy education experience. One student – Brian Grace – an Arkansas resident, could have chosen to attend a state-funded college of pharmacy, but he was looking for a school where he could develop his skills as a pharmacist while pursuing his passion for medical missions. As a part of his pharmacy education, he participated in medical missions to Guatemala, Honduras and Zambia.

Brian went on medical mission trips out of a deep desire to make a difference in the lives of patients in these medically underserved areas, but he received a great deal in return. The medical mission trips enhanced his communication skills, empathy and cultural and spiritual awareness. He saw firsthand the dramatic difference medications like antibiotics and vitamins can make in a patient population with underserved health needs.

His education at Harding, which allowed him to pursue his passion for medical missions, was helpful to him when applying for and securing a highly coveted residency position. His education at Harding provided him with the knowledge to become a pharmacist, as was reflected in his NAPLEX scores as he ranked in the top four percent in the nation.[8]

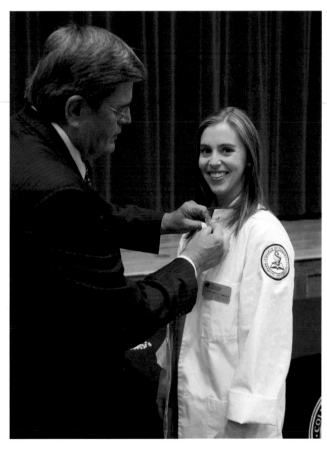

Harding students have the opportunity to learn more than just medical techniques and pharmacology. They learn how to make a difference in the physical and spiritual wellness of their patients.

Even though this program at Harding is very young, I am encouraged by the accomplishments of our graduates. Another Arkansas resident, Celia Proctor selected Harding because she wanted opportunities to develop in teaching and scholarship. A natural leader, she was instrumental in developing our student research program and presented a poster about this research at the national A.A.C.P. conference. During the course of her pharmacy education she helped create a product – a new topical anti-infective wound treatment. This product currently has a patent pending, with the potential to lead to multiple products. What an achievement from a student this early in the history of our pharmacy program.

After graduation, Celia completed two years in residency at Johns Hopkins University, where she also earned an M.B.A. in Hospital Management.[9]

Physical Therapy

Harding began a doctoral program in Physical Therapy in 2011-12 after a four-year preparatory study. We were able to hire Dr. Mike McGalliard as director of this program, and he has assembled an excellent faculty. I am excited about the Christian nature of this program – that it is designed from the ground up as a Christian, professional doctoral program in physical therapy.

Dr. McGalliard said of his decision to come to Searcy to direct the program –
When the opportunity to come to Harding initially came, I was
not looking to make a move. I was happy in the job I was in. We
were well established in a community where we had been living for

*the better part of sixteen years. At the time, my wife certainly did
not want to make a move. God had different plans, however. I had
always been looking for a way to combine my profession – physical
therapy – and ministry in a meaningful way. Although this is possible to some extent anywhere, many road blocks to this existed at the
state institution where I was teaching.*

*When my wife and I came to visit Harding in the spring of 2010,
we immediately saw that this is what God had been preparing us for.
Harding is a place that encouraged and expected ministry from its
faculty. This was and is the perfect place to make a lasting impact
for Christ on the lives of physical therapy students in a manner that
is not possible anywhere else. We made the move in the summer of
2010 and have never regretted it. It is a place that the worldview of
students can be shaped so that they view physical therapy as their
way to serve both God and man. The physical therapy program at
Harding exists to prepare students to be the hands and feet of Jesus
Christ in the health care system in this country and around the
world. Harding truly is a great place to be.*

Leah Avery shared this story about her experience in our new Physical Therapy program. She came to Harding without a relationship with Christ –

*My experience in the Harding University Physical Therapy
program is not one of only academic and professional growth; it
is a journey that began with a skeptical outlook and ended with a
true and deep relationship with Christ. I was raised by the standard
mantra, "Always be a good person and say your prayers." Although
my life was surrounded by some of the kindest, most warm-hearted
and loving people, church was rarely attended and prayers were
sparsely said.*

*I attended a large, public state university for my undergraduate
career. During my first four years, not a single church service was
attended, and prayers were only said on the infrequent occasion
when I felt the need. Things began to change when I met my boy-
friend – now husband. During the last two months of my undergrad-*

uate career, he ever so kindly asked me to attend church with him nearly every Sunday. To be quite honest, I attended each service without any intention of rejoicing in the Lord or listening to the word of God.

When the time came that I was accepted at Harding, I was thankful to be a part of a P.T. program. I was skeptical, however, to be in a curriculum that claimed to be Christ-centered. At the start of the program, I was uncomfortable when prayers were said and Bible verses were read. As the stress of a doctoral program began to set in, I started to struggle. I found myself looking to my fiancé at the time for comfort. He gradually taught me about the goodness, grace and peace the Lord could provide me. When he spoke of these things, for the first time I was not afraid or uncomfortable. I found myself wanting to attend church on Sundays and actively listening to the word of the Lord. I slowly began to pray with my professors at the start

of every class and exam. The Bible I have was given to me as a gift from my mother-in-law for completing my first semester of physical therapy school. It was the first Bible I had ever owned.

Before I could grasp the depth of the journey I was on, I found myself praying for salvation on a Sunday service after a long and stressful week of exams. On April 14, 2012, I was baptized. From that point on, my outlook was changed. I knew I was no longer in control; God was in control. Through Christ, my spirits were lifted.

On my clinical rotations, I found myself wanting to care for patients in the way Christ would. I wanted to treat them in the godly way my professors spoke of on a daily basis. I was praying for my patients even months after I had treated them. As a graduate of Harding University, the love of Christ has been instilled in me and my service to Him will continue to flourish.[10]

Physical therapy students, like those in pharmacy and communication sciences and disorders, also have elected to spend a rotation in Zambia, which gives them

a great experience in cultural missions. The first class graduated in 2014. The program is housed in a remodeled facility on Main Street next to the White County Medical Center south campus. Classrooms, office space and room for a gross anatomy lab are provided for this program and a closely related master's program in occupational therapy.

New Programs

Academic programs change rapidly. Half of the degrees awarded by Harding in 2013 were new to Harding during the last twenty-six years. At the graduate level, eighty-six percent of the degrees awarded were new because so many new graduate programs were developed.

I am amazed with the stability of the academic leadership team and faculty during this period. In terms of leadership to expand its offerings, Harding has had only five chief academic officers since its inception in 1924.

Our mix of programs at both the undergraduate and graduate level is diverse, and I think it meets the needs of a much larger number of students today. Harding continues to focus on the core residential, undergraduate liberal arts program while also addressing the growth of programs for students who desire graduate and professional programs.

Computers affect every discipline in the academic world

CHAPTER TEN
Internet Changes Everything

<u>Harding's Earliest Information Technology</u>

Today's college campus scene is one of computers on every desk and practically every device known to man at your fingertips. Some of my golfing friends can even look at their watch and tell how far it is to the green. But if you go back to 1975, you would find us with no cell phones, no cable television, no telephones in dorm rooms and the only calculators available could barely add, subtract, multiply and divide. I can even remember using a slide rule, which I loved.

In 1975, the I.B.M. equipment housed in the basement of the Administration Building and an AT&T telephone system housed in the Heritage Center with 273 extensions made up most of the technology on the Harding campus. The accounting office and the cashier's office used accounting machines that would total columns on large ledger sheets.

Computers became commercially available in the mid-50s, but it was only with mass production in the 60s that schools and businesses could consider owning a computer. Harding set out to purchase its first computer in the mid-70s. Dr. Billy Ray Cox, then vice president of Harding, chaired the committee, and I was privileged to serve on this committee.

I remember receiving bids from I.B.M., DATA General and Digital Equipment Corporation (D.E.C.). D.E.C. was a leading candidate because of its use on college campuses, and it was a time-share with multiple systems. We purchased a D.E.C. PDP11/45 computer, had our own computer room with a raised floor and were proud to have our first computer.

Technology in 1987

By the time I became president, technology had already exploded on the Harding campus. It continued to grow in unprecedented ways for the next twenty-six years. During this first year, a decision was made to combine the academic and administrative computer operations into one organization. We had been operating with separate computing operations for the academic system and our administrative offices.

Also, an Apple Macintosh Computer Laboratory was established in the Ganus Building, consisting of twenty computers, four dot matrix printers and a laser printer networked together in a local area. Macintosh computers were also added in the English Department for the writing lab.

The Internet Arrives

Perhaps the announcement of the funding of ARKNET Network Consortium by National Science Foundation was the most exciting event to take place in the early 90s. Through this grant, nineteen colleges in Arkansas were interconnected with a computer network called ARKNET. The ARKNET in turn was part of an international network. Via this network, Harding faculty and students were able to access a wide variety of resources that were available only at much larger urban universities. It was the beginning of an entirely new day at Harding University.

Harding's academic VAX was first connected to this worldwide network on January 29, 1992. The President's Report in 1992 stated,

Electronic mail has now been sent and received from individuals from most of the fifty states, as well as from several countries, including Italy, France and Russia. Access to libraries all over the world is also being utilized. Some people subscribe to electronic discussion groups on various topics. In the few short months that the Internet has been available, it has become an essential resource for many students and faculty here at Harding. With the anticipated installation of the campus-wide network, the Internet resource should be available to every person on campus. [1]

It is hard to believe this all began in 1992.

In 1993, the VAX 3600, which served the new academic computer lab, was installed during the summer, and it effectively doubled the VAX capacity for academic computing needs. A major project for the Department of Information Services at this point was the installation of a fiber-optic network that allowed us to connect the academic and administrative computer center and the library by fiber-optic cable. Later, this would be expanded to every building on campus.

In 1998, a new D.E.C. VAX 3600 was purchased and dedicated to academic computing. It provided a five-fold increase in computing capability. About 200 personal computers were installed in various places on campus, including forty Apple IIs, thirty Apple Macintoshes, forty D.E.C. Rainbows and nearly 100 I.B.M. PC's or compatibles.

The advent of the network increased academic interest on campus in a significant way, and the Department of Computer Science was created. Faculty access to the Internet and administrative support data caused a thirty percent increase in the number of faculty computer customers. Majors in information systems and computing engineering were also added.

Harding's first presence on the World Wide Web occurred in 1996. The public relations office was responsible for the content, and the administrative computer center furnished the hardware, maintenance and support to serve it on the Internet community so that it could be seen throughout the world. It is hard to imagine operating without this kind of Web access today.

Mike Chalenburg, Harding's vice president for computer services, said,
Students now have access to information and capabilities that

were inconceivable twenty years ago. The available technology has opened the door to tremendous learning opportunities. No longer are teachers and librarians the keepers of knowledge nor are employees involved in every aspect of a student's business with the school. Now, so much knowledge and tools are readily available that they have become guides to finding knowledge and teachers of how to understand and evaluate information for validity and relevance. The kind of education that Harding could only offer in Searcy, Ark., has become possible throughout the world. It will be fascinating to see how Harding will grow in this new world in which we find ourselves.[2]

Reorganization of Department

The Strategic Plan for the five-year period beginning in 1999 called for a reorganization of the Information Systems and Technology area, with a chief information officer to manage the program. Keith Cronk was selected as C.I.O. and vice president, and the department was organized into the functional areas of Management Information Systems, Academic Information Systems, Desktop Computing and Network Operations. Funding was also improved to implement a modern library access system, and a completely revamped Harding Web site was implemented in 2000. When students arrived on campus in the fall of 2000, they were greeted by a remodeled student center that included a cyber café.

Technology Fee

Perhaps the most far-reaching decision was the approval of the Technology Academic Enrichment Fee. In the year 2000, more than $1 million was collected for technology purposes. A large part of this fee was allocated to specific departments to be used for technology and academic enrichment. The remaining thirty percent was distributed via a competitive bidding process. The technology fee has proven to be a dependable source for the advancement of technology across the University, both academically and administratively.

Resource Planning System

A major development in 2001 was the purchase of the S.C.T. Banner Enterprise Planning System. This came after a long-term study to determine the best vendor to provide a corporate information system built on a modern database management system that would be our Web interface. This new system was made possible because of the money available through the technology fee. Banner runs on top of the Oracle database management system.

I remember the final decision to approve the purchase of the Banner system, a major expenditure for Harding. To secure maximum discounts, the contract had to be signed quickly after the decision was finalized, so Keith Cronk brought the contract to me for signing on the thirteenth tee box at the Course at River Oaks. We did receive the discounts.

Banner

Banner has been the launch pad of much innovation and change at Harding. It led to the development of our own portal that has proven to be more resilient and reliable than any other commercial product we tried. The portal is known as Pipeline. Students are able to register for classes, select chapel seats, allocate meal plans, obtain parking permits, pay accounts, check grades, order transcripts, develop study programs, apply for financial aid, track intramural games and scores, and even buy and sell things. A wealth of information and processes are also available to faculty in Pipeline.

This system also led to more accurate and trustworthy data for decision making. One of the first instances of this is what became known as "the clicker," which provided real time, up-to-date enrollment data, especially during the crucial early days of the fall semester. Initially, there was some suspicion about these numbers, as they did not seem to compare properly with previous years' reporting methods. Over time, the numbers proved to be accurate and with some refining, aligned with the official IPEDs reporting numbers. The first two years they were produced, they were scrutinized regularly at joint meetings that took on the name of the old "smoky room" meetings in which important decisions were hammered out.

E-Learning and Classroom Technology

The most visible change in our classrooms is the standard technology equipment. At the end of the 1990s, only two classrooms on campus had digital projectors. Now, every classroom is equipped with a computer, audio system, digital projector, Internet connection and document camera as standard equipment. This includes the classrooms in Searcy, North Little Rock, Rogers and Memphis. The Foreign Language and Interior Design departments are effectively using flipped classrooms to further enhance their learning. The introduction of health science disciplines led to the equipping of highly specialized labs and classrooms. The Patient Skills Facility in the Farrar Building is a state-of-the-art model for teaching in pharmacy and the physician assistant programs. IS&T provides specialized help in establishing the "wet lab" for the physical therapy program, which uses specific digital cameras that record work on cadavers.[3]

Harding began using a learning management system (L.M.S.) in the early 2000s. Initially the L.M.S. was introduced to facilitate online learning. Over time, it has been included in most classes, including on-ground classes. Harding has used a number of L.M.S. products with the current one being Canvas. L.M.S. has changed classes and learning in many ways, but one of the most significant has been the testing lab, which allows faculty to set up tests and students to schedule a test in a secure and monitored testing lab. This has returned many class hours to the classroom, replacing hours previously used to conduct testing.

In 2011, the Center for Learning with Technology was formed to meet the growing demands for instructional design of courses that are offered as online or blended courses. The Center provides one-on-one instructional design consultation with faculty, offers professional development programs to keep faculty informed and competent with educational technology, and conducts a colloquium program for faculty to share their scholarship as it relates to learning with technology. A highlight of the year for the Center is the Technology Showcase, where faculty share what they are doing with technology in their classes.

<u>Brackett Library</u>

In an innovative realignment, Harding moved the library under the umbrella of IS&T. With the rapid march toward online digital holdings and other technology connections in modern libraries, this proved a successful move.

For a time in the late 1990s and early 2000s, students were not using the library as the academic hub of the university. Plans were put in place to turn this around. The books underwent heavy weeding to remove holdings that were not used or could now be accessed online. Bookshelves were removed to make more space for student seating. The decor was upgraded and modular furniture installed so students could use computers at the tables and rearrange them to suit different study group sizes. This was in recognition that faculty are giving more group work assignments and that students are more engaged in social learning than in the past.

To help create a modern learning environment, a coffee shop was built inside the library. Students returned to using the library so much that there is now a need for more space for both group/social study areas and quiet study areas.

Network Connections

There is no denying the impact that the Internet is having on teaching, learning and dorm life. Harding installed a robust network around the campus and has been improving its connection to the Internet regularly. There have been some rough spots in this process, mainly with our Internet service provider, but Harding is now in the position of having the bandwidth needed to conduct our business and academic activities, even as they have demanded more and more bandwidth for accessing media-rich learning mate-

rials. The bandwidth also supports dorm life, and students use the Internet to watch television and movies.

From 2007 on, the demand for wireless network connections has skyrocketed. This has been driven by the mobile technology that has become available. All the dorms on campus have high speed wireless connections through a network of 837 wireless access points. The campus is now bathed in a high capacity wireless network, providing secure access for students, faculty and staff, as well as access for visitors to campus. Access of visitors peaks during events like Lectureship, Homecoming and Spring Sing.

Equipment Refresh Cycles

Harding officials early recognized the cost of technology equipment obsolescence. Along with the introduction of the tech fee, a cycle of equipment maintenance was instigated so that faculty and staff could work with reliable, up-to-date equipment. It meant our servers, storage equipment and network equipment remained reliable and efficiently maintained.

Harding is the Internet

Technology has exploded on the Harding campus. The Internet arrived in 1992, and nothing has been the same since. Students now have access to information and capabilities that were unknown twenty years ago. A great benefit to Harding is the opportunity to offer educational experiences for students throughout the world.

We now have a technology fee to support these investments. Terms like Banner, E-learning and Pipeline are commonplace. We have "smart classrooms" and wireless Internet. What an amazing development. Technology is vastly improving our access to information.

Special events add to the excitement of life at Harding

PART FOUR

Living

Harding students assist victims of Hurricane Katrina

CHAPTER ELEVEN

Students Who Serve

Introduction

I have always loved working with Harding students. That was the best part of my job when I taught and served as dean in the College of Business, and I wondered what would happen when I became president. While it was very different because I did not have students on a regular basis in class, I found that working with students was still an extremely enjoyable part of my work. I love the energy, enthusiasm and passion for life that students bring to the table. It is hard to describe, but when they are gone during breaks and summer, the campus seems dead. We could not possibly experience camaraderie without our incredible students.

Working with Student Leaders

Having served as S.A. president during my senior year in 1964-65, I knew something of the value of the Student Association to Harding. I had watched the S.A. very carefully during the intervening years and knew the positive contribution they made to the atmosphere at Harding. Having also spent time at Florida State University when there was tremendous unrest across the nation among the students, faculty and administration, I was aware that life would be very different at Harding if we did not continue to build positive relationships among the student body, the faculty and the administration. I have always marveled at the partnership that exists between students and faculty at Harding.

When new leaders were elected by their peers to serve as president of the student body, they invariably came to visit me, and I talked to them about the partnership relationship between the Student Association and the administration. I was privileged to work with some of the most wonderful people in the world. Many became dear friends.

I asked a few of those who served as S.A. president to relate their experiences to me. Jimmy Huff served as president during the 2004-05 year, and he became a dear friend. Today, he is a member of the Harding faculty –

I was elected with the platform of "building bridges," a call for each student to intentionally pursue the unity of Christ with those who were different.

This campaign platform became something profound and personal to me after my initial meeting with Dr. Burks. Before this meeting, I had rarely spoken with Dr. Burks. I had a pit in the bottom of my stomach as I walked into his office for this meeting.

I knew that, as a student body president, part of my job would be to meet with him regularly on behalf of student concerns, but in my anxiety, I could not really think of any meaningful words to say to him. Fortunately, my nervousness was assuaged as Dr. Burks spoke with me as a fellow leader rather than a wide-eyed student. In that moment, an esoteric university president became a fellow human and brother in Christ. He continued a reflexive dialogue with me about his own journey in leadership, remarking about how a fellow board member had given him the advice to "lead in a way that you can sleep at night."

190

On one occasion, I discovered that bridges could be built when I least expected them to be. I found myself delivering cookies to freshman students as a way of welcoming them to campus. I knocked on the door and a student, whom I refer to as Ali, answered. In the course of some brief conversation, I learned that Ali had come to Harding from several states away and had mostly spent time in his dorm room since arrival. Ali grew up in a family that was Muslim, and he had felt warm toward Harding but also a bit isolated from the campus. He had decided to come here after a cursory examination of promotional materials that he had come across, and he was a bit surprised to learn that this was a Christian university. I was touched by his story and sensed that Ali needed, more than cookies, the consistent presence of a friend. In that busy year, I could hardly guarantee a steady presence, but perhaps through the prompting of the Spirit, I suggested that we meet weekly. This weekly get-together morphed into a Bible study. We read the gospel of John, and a regular group of four freshman guys started to attend. In these Bible studies, a friendship that was forged by compulsion became something that was genuine. I became refreshed with this text in reading it through Ali's eyes. He spoke with considerable excitement about how we came to understand Jesus by understanding stories of his life... The biblical text came alive to him – and to me – as we encountered these stories of God manifested in the form of Jesus Christ.[1]

Michael Campbell was president during the 2003-04 year. One of the things I remember most about Michael's year was the Texas vs. the World competition, which became a huge success as one of many service projects conducted by the Student Association over the years. He said,

Since that February was our big push for the year, we kind of coasted to the end when Sam Shewmaker came to me with a need from Africa. There was a village in Kenya that needed a water well and a hospital in Sudan that needed a bunch of medical supplies. The good news was 1) the water was already in the ground *in Kenya; we just needed $8,000 to dig a well and get it out, and 2) the medical supplies were already donated; we just needed $17,000 to pay to have them shipped in a huge container across the ocean and trucked into the barren interior of the African continent! Well, from that one conversation, we birthed the Umoja project. Former S.A. president Nathan Mellor had offhandedly mentioned the idea of*

doing a "Texas vs. the World" competition, so we ran with it. We challenged all of the obnoxious, prideful Texas students, about 500 out of 4,000, led by me – a proud Arkansan. We sold about 1,000 T-shirts, got ticket receipts from a movie, took donations, had a "Battle of the Bands," ran a 5K and did several other small things – all in the course of a few weeks. We had a LOT of help. One student, a native Texas football player, called some big wigs from the Lone Star State and told them that someone had the audacity to challenge TEXAS to a competition – we got several $500 checks just because of that young man. In the end, God showed me how all my planning and preparation during the month of prayer didn't matter near as much as His power at work through the students and loved ones of Harding. We reached our $25,000 goal almost perfectly (Texas lost by $1,000!), and I give all the credit to Him. It all happened far too well for my own efforts.[2]

Steve Cloer served as S.A. president in 2000-01. I remember Steve working hard to begin the "Bisons for Christ" effort as a service project for Searcy and White County. An entire day was devoted in the spring for the faculty and student body to do service projects all over our community. It was a great success, and this project continues today. Steve has been preaching at Southside Church of Christ in Fort Worth, Texas, since August 2006 –

> *I was privileged to be able to serve as Student Association president my senior year. Dr. Burks graciously worked closely with me*

*and allowed me freedom to lead as I felt God calling. Being pres-
ident provided a chance to sharpen my ministry skills. The chance
to think through vision, delegation, mobilizing students for ministry,
assessing spiritual needs, learning to bring groups together, and
balancing other responsibilities with leadership was a challenging
task. Yet, as a preacher, I find that I am dealing with the same challenges on a regular basis.*

*I believe Harding helped shape my faith during the four years
I was there. The farther I get away from that time, the more I am
thankful for the mentors, friends and opportunities that I had that
helped me shape, develop and act out my faith in Christ. God used
this as great preparation for ministry in His kingdom!*[3]

Going to an earlier point in history, I remember Nathan Mellor's year very
well. Nathan and I got to be friends, and he later worked in my office for a number

of years before leaving to take a preaching
position. Nathan was one of the strongest
leaders I have ever known. He was mature
beyond his years from the first day I met
him. I remember working with him closely
on the dedication of the McInteer Center,
as he spoke on behalf of the student body.
I also remember Nathan leading a group of
students on a service project in Alabama,
and at the end of one of the days of service,
everyone jumped in a pond of water that
was filled with mud. I was there that day for the service project, but you would not
have found me in the pool of mud. Nathan was later instrumental in the research
and development of the Institute for Church and Family.

Susan Vaughn served as S.A. president in 1989, and I remember Susan making a recommendation to the administration on behalf of the student body to change
our shorts rule. Up until that time, we did not allow shorts to be worn by men or
women on campus at any time. As many will remember, it can be very hot during
the summer in Searcy, Ark. The recommendation from Susan was that we allow

Bermuda shorts to be worn for recreational purposes after 4:00 in the afternoon. She personally guaranteed to me, on behalf of the S.A., that students would wear Bermuda shorts that came about to the knee, which was the style at that time. I remember making the change with the approval of all parties involved, and then reading in an editorial in the *Democrat Gazette*,

> *The calendar says 1990, the mercury is rising above the 90-degree mark and Harding University in Searcy has finally noticed both. Last Monday, the school – renowned for its strict, traditionalist standards in adherence to its Church of Christ affiliation – unbuttoned its stiff collar and relaxed the campus dress code a tad, announcing that students may henceforth wear shorts without risking reprimand. There's a catch, of course – not just any shorts will do; they must be of the "walking" variety, which, according to the code writers, restricts the hemline to two inches above the knee. OK, maybe three. Plus (and this is a major plus), the shorts will be allowed only at club meetings and similar extracurricular activities, during physical education classes, when going to and from P.E. class or when going to and from campus (When Harding says "walking,'"it means walking). Oh, and shorts are O.K. on weekday evenings after 6.*
>
> *Since the school rarely bends any of its rules, we have to cheer reason and progress wherever we can find it. Congratulations to Harding University for proving that old dogs can learn new tricks, even if they're only simple tricks.*[4]

Would you believe that that turned out to change through the years? To be certain, I thought they made a great deal more out of this than they should have, but as long as Harding maintains a distinctive code of conduct that is different from the culture, we will be subject to comments like this from outsiders.

Charlie Walker served as S.A. president in 2006-07 and will always be remembered for his leadership in persuading the faculty to approve two extra holidays – the Martin Luther King holiday in January and a one-day fall break. Student leadership ideas make a difference at Harding –

> After much discussion, Dr. Burks allowed the S.A. to present their proposal to his cabinet. The S.A. officers formulated a proposal that would dismiss classes for Labor Day or a fall holiday and M.L.K. Day in the spring. S.A. officers ran the figures for the number of school days Harding has and the holidays we recognized as compared to other Church of Christ schools in Arkansas and those within the top tier according to U.S. News and World Report. Dr. Burks' cabinet met to discuss our proposal and determined that it could only fully endorse recognizing M.L.K. Day, not a fall holiday. Dr. Burks, however, wanted the faculty to support the cabinet's decision. He allowed the S.A. officers to submit our proposal to the entire faculty. If the faculty supported both holidays, he would acquiesce. But he warned us to only expect M.L.K. Day at best, and that would only happen if the faculty supported it.
>
> The S.A. officers presented our proposal with our research to the faculty during a spring faculty meeting. We were asked to leave and allow the faculty to discuss the proposal and vote on it. The S.A. waited anxiously in the S.A. office to hear word from the S.A. sponsors. The proposal passed! We were thrilled and Dr. Burks reported the change in Harding's policy for the 2008-09 school year.[5]

This is a great example of the value of the S.A. and the partnership that can exist among students, faculty and administration, even when the parties do not all agree.

On a much lighter note, Charlie also recounted his love story –

> Erin, my girlfriend, was on to my original proposal idea – a

quiet picnic at Marlsgate Plantation in Scott, Ark., (where she had always wanted to get married and where Dr. Burks officiated our wedding ceremony a year after my graduation proposal). She had seen the notes I had written in code on a "to do" list on my desk in

the S.A. office. Thus, I needed a back-up plan that was sure to surprise her!

I nervously scheduled a meeting with Dr. Burks' secretary. When the time came for the meeting, I told Dr. Burks I needed "one more favor, and I promise you won't have to deal with me again." I came into the meeting fully expecting him to say, "Absolutely not." I told him my idea and that I didn't want to detract from the ceremony or anyone's graduation experience, but I really needed to surprise Erin. To my surprise, Dr. Burks loved the idea! He then chided me for not proposing sooner. I think his exact words were, "It's about time you decided to propose!"

At graduation, the only people aware of my plan were the jeweler, Dr. Burks, my parents and Erin's parents. The plan was executed perfectly! Dr. Burks played it off great and, most importantly, she said "YES!" To say the least, it would have been a disaster if she had said "No." But like any good lawyer, I have learned not to ask questions unless I already know the answer.[6]

One of the student leaders I worked with a lot during the early days of my presidency was Terry Davis. Terry continues to be a good friend who works in Atlanta, Ga., with a non-profit organization. Terry served as the S.A. committee

chairman and with the Student Association for several years. I enjoyed his organizing cookouts at our house, but my wife learned quickly that she needed to talk with Terry as often as possible if she was to know how many people were coming over for dinner.

Terry also helped select students who attended a focus group with me to see how things were going at Harding. He would just stand at the entrance of the cafeteria and choose a random group of students. I continued this practice throughout my term as president.

Terry organized concerts for students and shared the following regarding his favorite concert moment –

> *Having Bill Cosby perform two shows in the Benson Auditorium was the highlight of my time as S.A.C. chairman. Dr. Burks said he had tried to get Bill Cosby to come as an A.S.I. speaker but had never been successful. Let the records show that I was able to get him, and we did not lose money from having him on the campus, even after paying his fee. Dr. Burks later expressed to me that he thought we would clearly lose money. The show was great, and I am glad he was here.[7]*

Bryan Clifton served as S.A. president in 2009-10 –

> *During times of hardship, it is the connections I formed at and through Harding that have helped me push forward. Knowing that others surrounded me when I needed them most is more comforting than words can describe. These moments specifically are the times when I knew friendships were based on much more than position or title. They are rooted in*

197

a deep-felt respect and mutual admiration for each other. This is
not a normal college experience, because Harding is not a typical
university. It is a place where personal transformation and life-long
connections are formed.[8]

I am glad Bryan felt the connection at Harding and that he benefited from the Harding experience, but I would suggest that those of us who have the opportunity to work with student leaders are the ones who really benefit. It really is a two-way street, but I have benefited greatly from working with these leaders and many others who are not mentioned here. My life has been positively influenced because of the opportunity to know these students.

Student Organizations/Social Clubs

Students can elect to be involved in many organizations and activities as a member of the Harding community. Through these experiences, students draw close to each other as they learn about teamwork, traditions, loyalty and acceptance. Students often develop a servant lifestyle as a result of these experiences.

One of the important activities for students at Harding comes through the social club system, which has been an important part of the Harding scene since our beginning. We have thirty social clubs, which involve more than 2,000 students every year. Participation in clubs is very strong, and these club members do a lot of activities together, including devotionals, athletic events and service projects. For many students, camaraderie would be defined by the club they were in. But the beauty of the Harding community lies in the greater sense of fellowship found in being part of a community that honors God above all else.

Spring Sing

I really can't imagine Harding University without Spring Sing. I always look forward to the presentations, and I was delighted that more than 1,000 students were participating in this activity each year. I loved the fact that social clubs can come together in a meaningful way in stiff competition. I loved the way the community was involved with the charities who benefited from gifts presented to them.

I loved the Spring Sing hosts and hostesses – their professionalism and ability to perform in front of large audiences. I loved the fact that members of the community could come and enjoy the program. I loved that guests, parents and friends from all around the area could enjoy the talents displayed by our students.

The Saturday night performance was always very special to me. I had the privilege of assisting with handing out the awards each year, and the stage was just electric with excitement as a result of all the hard work that had been put into the performances. This is one of those times when camaraderie actually can be spelled out, it is in the air, people see it and the fellowship is just magnificent. I am grateful to Dr. Jack Ryan, who began this program in 1974; Steve and Dottie Frye, who have directed it for the past 20 years; and a host of other people who assist. I am particularly grateful for all of the student leaders who have been in charge of the club productions. What a cool experience.

Homecoming

In the fall, I look forward to the presentation by our students of the Homecoming musical. I love Homecoming and the fact that it brings so many alumni together on campus, but I must admit that I most look forward

199

every year to the musical production. Our drama department produces a professional performance every year. I have seen the interaction between the actors and actresses on stage, the orchestra and the behind-the-stage crew who do the lighting and props.

My favorite musical, "Joseph and the Amazing Technicolor Dreamcoat," was performed twice while I was president. I was honored to have a small role in each one, where I made a brief appearance. My thanks to Robin Miller and all the people who work with him in making this musical such a marvelous occasion for all of us.

Intramurals

Our Intramural Sports Program involves about sixty-five percent of the student body each year. We have wonderful facilities and offer all kinds of opportunities for students to participate in a variety of sports. Club competition is also a part of the intra

mural program, but students do not have to be a member of a social club to participate in the intramural program. The level of competition for the A and B games and many of the intramural sports is really intense. An intramural athlete of the year is awarded every year. Jim Gowen has directed the men's program for eighteen years.

At one swim meet, one of the clubs wanted one of their members who was a paraplegic to swim in a relay. I asked them if he could swim and if they would stay with him until he finished the lap. They assured me that they would, so I put his club's relay team in an outside lane, and we started the relay. He was going to swim the last lap. As the other clubs were finishing the race well ahead of him, I was recording the time for the other clubs when I became aware

of a rising level of cheering in the room. As I turned around, I saw
everyone in the building standing, applauding and cheering him on
to complete the relay.[9]

After almost every game or match, teams or individuals who
had competed fiercely to win, circled up, put their arms around each
other and prayed together.

Wonderful relationships are built through this strong program.

Other Activities

Other activities that involve our students include band, chorus, professional clubs related to one's major, debate, business intercollegiate competition, student publications, and political and civic organizations.

Many relationships are also formed as a result of residence hall living experiences. Harding is a traditional residential campus, with more than 3,150 students living on campus, plus at least 250 others in campus apartments. Late-night discussions, devotionals and activities in the residence halls are important components of student life at Harding.

Wanise Lemmons, a residence life coordinator for Armstrong Hall, shared this story about one of her R.A.'s –

I always had about ten Walton scholars in my dorm. Their room
assignments would be spread out so they would have a chance to
make friends with Americans. One year in the spring, I had a Walton
scholar turn in an application to be an R.A. In the application, he
said that the reason he wanted to be an R.A. was because his R.A.
was so helpful to him as a freshman coming from another country,
and he wanted to help others in the same way.[10]

Service Projects

Service projects were common responses by Harding students when they became aware of a disaster or personal problem. While their efforts were supported and encouraged by Harding administrators and faculty, they were generally student-led. These projects represented Harding students' commitment to serve others.

One of the most memorable service projects occurred early in my time as president during the 1993-94 year. The theme for that year was taken from He-

brews 10:24, "Let us consider one another in order to stir up love and good works." In the student body that year was Rich Little from Capella Queensland, Australia. After a terrible flood near St. Louis, Rich contacted the Arnold, Mo., Church of Christ. Grady Miller, minister of the congregation, immediately went to work organizing an operation from his end, lining up specific work sites for the students and planning meals and sleeping arrangements. He told Rich that the congregation could manage up to 120 students.

The S.A. made a chapel announcement asking for volunteers to go to Missouri for a weekend to shovel mud and load sandbags into trucks, hoping that at least 120 would come to the organizational meeting. They were overwhelmed when more than 600 students showed up. When the Searcy group arrived at the Arnold church on Friday, Sept. 10, all arrangements had been made for the volunteers who made the journey.

The students who took part in this experience were changed by what they saw. They found fields of mud, personal belongings scattered around neighborhoods, basements filled with water, thousands of sandbags and people who had lost nearly everything they owned. A beautiful article, "The Flood of Help," written by Phillip Tucker and Allen White, appeared in the winter 1994 *Harding* magazine. Rich commented on this effort –

> *There are many, many great memories that stick in my mind during my student years at Harding, but none represent the heart and mission of Harding more than this memory, for it epitomizes what Christian community is intended to look like. It demonstrates*

how servants of Christ, irrespective of age, race, national origin, major or gifts, can work together to serve a broken and hurting world to show the love of Jesus. And it is a reminder that God has ordained Harding to excel at the creation of Christian community where people can really find their identity in Christ as they serve alongside others for the cause of Christ.[11]

I could hardly believe the response of the Harding student body. This turned out to be the first of many large-scale efforts to do service work for people in need. I was amazed at the response of our students to this effort. I still have a "sandbag plaque" given to Harding after this disaster.

Another major disaster in 2009, Hurricane Katrina, prompted an unbelievable response from the Harding student body. As Hurricane Katrina evacuees returned to New Orleans to salvage what they could from water-damaged homes, dozens of University students spent their weekends joining in relief efforts. More than 100 students, staff and faculty drove into a deserted suburb of New Orleans to clear out debris and offer support to victims of the storm. In addition to the weekend trips, one group spent the week of Thanksgiving break working in the area.

Students worked primarily in conjunction with the Tammany Oaks Church of Christ, which headquartered relief efforts in their building in Mandeville, La. I will always be grateful for the leadership of Andrew Baker and others who organized this relief effort on behalf of Harding students. I was able to go and be a part of it for two days and was simply amazed at the amount of damage you could see in this place. An article in the *Harding* magazine, written by Jennifer Lashley in the fall of 2009, outlined the Harding response.

Other relief projects included tornado relief in 1999, led by Brian Bush; an ice storm relief effort in Northwest Arkansas in 2009, led by Bryan Clifton; and a tents and tarps effort for Haiti in 2010. As recently as 2014, Tyler Gentry led a relief project for tornado relief in Vilonia and Mayflower, Ark.

Prayer Groups

Perhaps the best way to illustrate my involvement with the students and the fact that they influenced me in a positive way would be to share a story with you concerning prayer groups with students over the years. I tried to select six or eight students each year to be part of a prayer group. We would meet in my office, typically early in the morning, and we would pray for forty-five minutes or so before chapel would begin at nine o'clock. This gave me an insight into what was on the students' hearts. I learned more about what they wanted to do in life by listening to these men pray than any other single activity I have ever been a part of. It bothers me that some people put students down today. If they knew our students, they would be optimistic about the future. They would be encouraged about what they will be able to accomplish. They would realize that these students are the leaders of the Lord's church for the future, and they would be encouraged as they listened to these men pray.

Harding is Students

Students are the reason for our existence, and we are blessed with wonderful, caring, serving individuals who have chosen Harding for their university family. I love working with them as they bring so much energy and passion for life with them when they enroll.

Working with the elected S.A. presidents was a wonderful experience for me. Watching students participate in so many activities that comprise their Harding experience was exciting.

Most of all, Harding students love to serve others, whether they are in Searcy or other countries. I have watched students in mass go to Missouri to help with flood relief, to New Orleans to help with the damage from Hurricane Katrina and to Clinton, Ark., for tornado relief work. Our students simply have a heart for service to others.

Intercollegiate athletics arouse school spirit and camaraderie

CHAPTER TWELVE
Student Athletes

Intercollegiate sports are important to the life of students at Harding. I can best illustrate this by sharing some information about the 2014 conference tournament for men's basketball in Bartlesville, Okla.

It was an awesome tournament for the Harding men's basketball team. The team, consisting of only eight men, entered the tournament with a 13-14 record, having lost their last five games in a row but only by a total of thirteen points. With only eight players, they weren't expected to win the tournament, but outsiders were not aware of the heart, the courage and the determination of this very special group of men and their coaches.

In the first game against East Central, senior Hayden Johnson scored twenty-four points and senior Weston Jameson had seventeen points to lead the Bisons to a 77-65 victory in the quarter finals of the tournament. In the semi-final game, Harding played Arkansas Tech and connected on thirteen of twenty-five attempted three-pointers, defeating the number one seed, 83-64. They had lost both games with Arkansas Tech during the regular season by one point.

This victory set up Harding to play Henderson State in the championship. The game was tied at 74 at the end of regulation and at 81 at the end of the first overtime. Blake McNair, who scored a career high twenty-five points, opened the second overtime with his sixth three-pointer of the game. Weston Jameson, the G.A.C. tournament M.V.P. followed that with another three-pointer. In this double overtime, fifty-minute game, Harding had all five starters play forty-two minutes or more. Harding won the game and the championship 93-86. Coach Jeff Morgan said, "Today was all about going on guts and adrenaline. What a great college basketball game!"

I was privileged to watch this amazing feat by these eight special players – Antoine Burrell, Will Francis, Jacob Gibson, John Hudson, Weston Jameson, Hayden Johnson, Blake McNair and Tarrale Watson. I loved watching their courage, unity, ability and determination. I was so proud of our players and our coaches. This is high-spirited fellowship at Harding, and this is camaraderie at its best. But the real story is not that these men won the tournament – the real story is who they are and what they stand for. These men love God and represented Harding in a wonderful way.

Intercollegiate Athletics

As I assumed my new position as president, I was aware that Harding had a good intercollegiate program in athletics, and I was keenly aware of the role played by Dr. Ganus in promoting Bison sports. I also knew I was not an athlete and I knew very little about athletic administration – so I had a lot to learn. Some people even suggested that Bison athletics would suffer under my direction. But I loved watching Harding sports, hardly ever missed home games and was determined to see these programs flourish. I knew I could count on Dr. Ganus' support, and I knew he would always know how many people were on each team, how much each player weighed and how fast they could run. I made no attempt to compete with Dr. Ganus in this regard.

In 1987-88, Dr. Harry Olree was athletic director, and I had enormous respect for him and his leadership ability. We competed in the N.A.I.A. and were members of the Arkansas Intercollegiate Conference (A.I.C.), which was one of the best small conferences in the nation. About 200 students participated in athletics and 106 were on athletic scholarships. All of this would change rather dramatically in just a few years.

The once strong Arkansas Intercollegiate Conference was dissolved in 1994, just seven years after I became president. We were having serious discussions in the conference about changing from N.A.I.A. to N.C.A.A. affiliation, but we presidents were not pursuing a different conference. We were surprised when Henderson moved to the Gulf South Conference, which led to the demise of our A.I.C. conference. Some of the remaining colleges later joined the Gulf South Conference, while Harding and Ouachita joined the Lone Star Conference in 1997 after being rejected by the Gulf South Conference. Harding also became a member of N.C.A.A. Division II in 1997.

Because of travel considerations, Harding later joined with former A.I.C. colleges in the Gulf South Conference, which played in two divisions. This change reduced travel for athletes. Harding remained with the Gulf South Conference until the fall of 2011, when we became a founding member of the newly established Great American Conference. We joined former Arkansas and Oklahoma colleges

in the new conference with the intent of having divisional play with less travel for athletes.

Athletic Director Greg Harnden played a key role in the formation of this new conference. He has been a joy to work with, and all of our coaches have worked hard to develop our athletic program at Harding.

In 2012-13, more than 400 students participated in intercollegiate athletics at Harding. These athletes are a very important part of the Harding fabric, and intercollegiate athletics has added a great deal to life at Harding.

We are blessed with coaches who understand and love the mission of Harding and who have been here for a long time, with great success working with student athletes.

Football

I love to watch football at First Security Stadium because I love the sense of brotherhood that has been developed by Coach Ronnie Huckeba and the more than 130 players on this team. Coach Huckeba and his assistants have done a marvelous job in building a sense of family as they embraced the mission of Harding in the football program.

One of my favorite football memories was a game with rival University of Central Arkansas in 1989. The Bisons defeated U.C.A. 16-11 in Conway in the last game of the regular season to tie for the conference championship. It was our first win over the University of Central Arkansas since 1976. Coach Huckeba recounted this game as one of the important games in his memory –

We needed to win this game to tie U.C.A. for the championship and advance to the national playoffs. That night, U.C.A. dominated the game statistically, but we played great defense in the red zone and forced eight turnovers. We won the game 16-11 and claimed the conference championship.

Our defensive ends, Matt and Kenwick Thompson, were exceptional that night. Lee White, Tommy Shoemaker, Lance Rodgers and Pete Phillis all had great individual efforts. One of our leaders, John Spann, was injured early in the game and left a tremendous void at

the linebacker position. That void was filled in an unbelievable way by our remaining starter at linebacker, a young sophomore named Pat Gill. Pat had thirty-one tackles that night, one of the most amazing performances I have witnessed as a player or a coach.[1]

Coach Huckeba also recounted the 2010 season when Harding ended the year with exciting wins at Delta State and the University of North Alabama at home. Both of those teams were in the N.C.A.A. playoffs, and Delta State eventually played for the national championship. Coach Huckeba also recalled the seasons of 2012 and 2013, finishing both years with identical 9-2 records and a trip to the national playoffs in 2012 and an exciting bowl victory in 2013. To say the least, these were exciting seasons for Harding football, and I was very proud of our team.

It is particularly interesting to me that Coach Huckeba said his most memorable season as head coach was 2011, a year when we did not have a great deal of success on the field. The year began with a bang as we defeated S.A.U. on the road, scoring sixty points with more than 600 yards in total offense. The season ended with a disappointing 4-7 record, largely due to the fact that we had the dubious honor of leading Division II in turnovers.

At the end of the season, Coach Huckeba shared with the team that he had fully expected them to be in the N.C.A.A. playoffs that year for the first time and that the poor results on the field had shaken him. He told them that, as Christian men, they had to accept the responsibility for their choices and persist. He closed by saying,

> Ask me in twenty years how these young men on our team are doing because that is a true reflection of the kind of year that we have experienced. If they are still persisting in the right things – following Christ and leading their families, then we have had a great year.[2]

What a great attitude. That is exactly what Harding athletics must be!

Men's Basketball

Jess Bucy and Nicky Boyd coached our men's basketball team from 1987 to 1993. Coach Jeff Morgan became the head coach in 1993. Under his leadership, Harding University has the highest winning percentage of any four-year college in the state of Arkansas – and I believe the best student body support in the state of Arkansas.

In terms of special memories, Coach Morgan shared the following –

> As far as game memories, the one that stands out is the 2008 Christian Brothers game when it came down to the last possession in overtime. We were down by one and Matt Hall got a great shot from the top of the key for the win. He missed, but Jesse Bynum got the rebound and made the shot at the buzzer for a 64-63 O.T. win! The crowd stormed the court, and that game helped us win the G.S.C. West Division Championship!
> One of the best things about that game was that Jesse's mom made

the trip from Austin, Texas. She had been battling cancer and had a free weekend, so she told her family, "I'm feeling pretty good this week; let's go to the game!"[3]

Coach Morgan noted the Henderson State series of games that began in 2003 when the last game of the year was for the G.S.C. West championship. Henderson beat us by three, but the gymnasium was full and the atmosphere was incredible. This carried over for several years, and we had to start ticketing the Henderson State game. The series culminated in 2008 with a nationally televised game on C.B.S. Sports.

Remembering a particular game, Morgan noted the 2007 G.S.C. Tournament game against Valdosta State,

We were down to Valdosta by fifteen with ten minutes to go. Down three with six seconds to go, Reggie Bibb missed two free throws but got his own rebound on the second miss and was fouled with four seconds to go. He made the first free throw, missed the second free throw on purpose and the rebound went out of bounds off of a Valdosta State player. We were still down two now with two seconds to go and taking the ball out under our basket. Reggie Bibb banked in a three as the buzzer went off for the win!

In terms of exceptional players, Coach Morgan said,

It is difficult to single anybody out, but it would have to start with Matt Hall. Being a three-time player of the year in the G.S.C. and representing Harding the way he did was awesome. That was evident from the first week he was on campus from a special conversation in the library at study hall with Jay Brogdon when Jay was considering being baptized! Matt was instrumental in Jay making that decision!

Aaron Farley's free throw streak was a lot of fun and brought great attention to our program. He made eighty-eight free throws

in a row before missing, coming up ten short of the record for most consecutive free throws made in games. He missed while shooting a technical free throw. I remember the collective gasp from the crowd and being asked after the game, "Why did you put him at the line for technical free throws with no one on the line?" Only thing I could think of was that coaches always put their best free throw shooter at the line for technical free throws.

Stephen Blake will be one that many people forget because he was so quiet and unassuming. What a great player and even better young man! He had an incredible senior season, which all came together in the 2011 G.S.C. tournament. One of his best individual performances was when we were at University of North Alabama that year. We were down nine with three seconds to go, and Stephen made a three and the very next possession made a three and got fouled for a four-point play. He scored seven points in a matter of about ten seconds, and Sam Brown ended up making a three to send the game into O.T. and – we won in O.T! Stephen is such a great representative of Harding!

Weston Jameson also has been a big part of our program for five years. He has been a great ambassador for Harding and our program. I believe if we looked in

WE WON!

"BEST ROAD TRIP DESTINATION IN COLLEGE BASKETBALL"

the dictionary for what a student-athlete at Harding is all about, his picture would be there! I have often referred to him as a Peyton Manning on the court! He makes all the right calls for us offensively and defensively.[4]

Coach Morgan summarized his feelings about intercollegiate basketball –

I believe our program is important to Harding because it has the potential to reach across the entire campus and involve the student body and faculty! It really does encompass "high-spirited fellowship'"and is something that brings us all together. It gives us the opportunity as a campus and program to honor Christ with the talent he has given us and to show athletics in a different light to our culture.[5]

In 2013, Harding won the G.A.C. regular season championship with guys such as Bradley Spencer, Matt Walters and Zach Roddenberry, earning our fourth trip to the N.C.A.A. tournament and being voted "Best Road Trip Destination in College Basketball!" All of that came to fruition with the last home game of the year when they were filming the special for C.B.S., it was Senior Night and the G.A.C. championship was on the line! We played great, and it ended up being one of those games we will remember for a long time! Another great memory game was beating Central Missouri State in the N.C.A.A. tournament to reach the regional semi-finals for the first time.

A sports writer for the *Log Cabin Democrat* in Conway, Ark., wrote, "Rhodes Field House is the most exciting, most dynamic and most thrilling experience for the college basketball fan in the state. There is currently no second-place candidate in the ball park, including the University of Arkansas."[6]

Lady Bison Basketball

Our women's basketball team was coached by Greg Harnden from 1989 to 1997. They competed in the N.A.I.A. National Tournament in 1997 and 1999, with outstanding players like Angie Dugger and Bridget Benson.

Coach Brad Francis became head coach in 1997, and Coach Tim Kirby assumed these responsibilities in 2005. Under his leadership, the team had a marvelous year in 2013-14, winning the first conference championship in the history of women's basketball. They were ranked in the top ten nationally in the final *U.S.A. Today* coaches poll, ranked number two in the final regular season *U.S.A. Today* coaches poll and won the most games in the history of the women's basketball program with a record of 29-3. What a great year for this team of talented students!

In the Great American Conference tournament, the Lady Bisons won their first game against Ouachita Baptist 60-57, which brought their record to 28-1 on the season. During the semi-final game, Harding beat Arkansas Tech 81-48 to improve the record to 29-1. The Lady Bisons held Tech to only seventeen points in the first half.

While the Lady Bisons fell to Southwestern Oklahoma in the final game, 78-74, it was only their second loss of the season, and they still hosted the Regional N.C.A.A. Division II Tournament at Harding.

I had an opportunity to get to know some of these Lady Bisons as they represented Harding over a number of years. Kristen Celsor was a leader on the team and excelled in every aspect of the game. It is a blessing to have student athletes like Kristen represent us at Harding. In her blog at the end of the season, she made the following statement –

> *I owe a lot to my time as a Lady Bison. I am so thankful for the friendships I have developed along the way and the teammates that I know will be lifelong friends. That's the awesome thing about Lady Bison basketball… you aren't just teammates… you are sisters. I love every one of my teammates, past and present, and would do anything for them. I know without a doubt that they would all do the same for me. I had two of the most amazing coaches out there.*

217

*As a Lady Bison, it was my job to represent Christ in my actions
and in the way I played. It is about more than just winning or losing
a basketball game. It's about remembering who you are and Whose
you are as you are playing. When we step on the court, we have the
opportunity to shine our light for all of those little kids who support
us wholeheartedly season after season. We have the privilege of
showing respect and class to our opponents in frustrating moments,
imitating God in our actions. At the end of the day, no matter the
score, I would consider it a loss if I failed to show Christ throughout
my actions in the game.*[7]

<u>Volleyball</u>

The women's volleyball program is a strong program at Harding. If you look
in the trophy case in the Rhodes Field House, you will find it jam packed with
awards dating back to when Harding was a member of the A.I.C. and the N.A.I.A.
We had multiple N.C.A.A. Division II National Tournament appearances and consistent and repetitive conference championships, including five A.I.C. titles, seven
Gulf South Conference titles and two Great American Conference titles. During the
2013 season, the Lady Bison volleyball team had the longest conference winning
streak in school history.

Dr. Karyl Bailey was head coach for our volleyball team from 1989 to 1994.
The team enjoyed championship seasons in 1989, 1990, 1991, 1993 and 1994. Out-
standing players during this time included Amy Devel, Regina Huddleston and Lori
Hendricks.

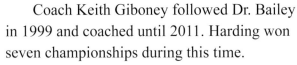

Coach Keith Giboney followed Dr. Bailey
in 1999 and coached until 2011. Harding won
seven championships during this time.

Meredith Fear was a member of the Harding volleyball team who returned to Harding as
head coach in 2012. She mentioned three individuals that received All-America recognition
– Veronica Piech, Manuela Nesheva and Mollie

Arnold. Each of these All-American athletes wrote about special moments during their careers as Lady Bison players –

Veronica Piech said,

> I am so grateful for my four years of college and volleyball at Harding. Looking back, it shaped me more than I realized. From the moment I walked onto campus, Coach Giboney made me feel a part of the volleyball team, and more importantly, part of his family. We were close as a team both on and off the court, and that started with Coach Giboney's leadership. The relationships formed from that team continue to this day. In fact, four of us who were seniors in 2003 get together every year for a Girls' Weekend. The friendships I made while at HU are priceless![8]

Manuela Nesheva said,

> I grew up in Bulgaria, so coming to Harding was a little intimidating because I had never been in the States before. I was blessed to have my coaches, the people from church, friends and my teammates help me adjust to the new culture and lifestyle. Being at Harding was a great experience for me overall. I received a great education, got to play the sport I love, met some wonderful people, and most importantly I accepted Christ as my personal Savior.[9]

Mollie Arnold also shared her feelings –

> The best memories I have were my junior and senior years as we set the conference winning streak record by going undefeated in conference for two straight seasons! Over my four years as a Hard-

ing volleyball player, I made memories that I will cherish for a lifetime, and I will always be a faithful fan and supporter.

As you can tell from these statements, Harding volleyball is about much more than winning. Coach Fear remembers watching Manuela's baptism and being overjoyed as her teammate. She also recalled two of the players in 2012-13 deciding to be baptized and asking her and her husband, Robert, to do the honors. She said, "This is what Harding volleyball is all about!"[11]

Cross Country/Track

Harding has a rich history in competition in men's and women's cross country and track and field. Coach Ted Lloyd was a legendary coach when I first became president and had unbelievable results from his student athletes. Coach Bryan Phillips worked with the team from 1991 to 2002 in addition to his academic responsibilities. Coach Steve Guymon became head coach in 2002. I have been privileged to attend several national meets with our students and Coach Guymon.

Reflecting on twelve years at Harding, Coach Guymon said that one of the biggest highlights for him came in the fall of 2003 when they were at the N.C.A.A. Cross Country Championships in North Carolina. The Women's team that year came in second at the conference meet and finished fourth in the N.C.A.A. Region meet, earning the last spot for the National meet by just four points. The men's team had won the conference in the regional championship. It was a bright, sunny day and the women ran their race first. Janet Kogo ran an outstanding race, finishing as runner-up (highest finish of any Harding University athlete in history). The other six ladies, made up of two juniors and four freshmen, had solid races.

Coach Guymon was in the woods, yelling at the guys as their race was about to begin, when the announcer read off the women's team scores. He recalled, "I heard some young ladies screaming and running toward me – as they leapt into my arms, they said we are fifth! This is the highest N.C.A.A. finish of any female team in Harding history." He continued, "The men continued to race well and ended

third in the country, with Jacob Rotich earning the runner-up spot and five men named to the All America team, along with Janet Kogo for the women." As a side note, Janet Kogo went on to win three individual titles in track that year and, as Janet Kogo Bawcom, represented the United States in the Olympic Games in 2012. She ran in the 10,000 meters and came in twelfth. Coach Guymon recognized her as the best runner he had ever coached.

Coach Guymon also has great memories of track and field. Hosting a meet on our home track in 2013, Guymon said Tiffany Chambers sailed over 12"6" in the pole vault, and a minute later, he heard the crowd roar as Kristen Celsor cleared

5'8" to set a Harding University high jump record. The best part was that her dad, Steve Celsor, was present, and he still holds Harding's men's high jump record.

In terms of highlights, Coach Guymon shared the story of one of his students from Poland that he had the honor of baptizing. He said she was a sophomore and on one Saturday evening, she called him and asked if he would be willing to baptize her on Sunday night. That night, in the Harding swimming pool, the track team came to see Kalina give her heart to God. What a great memory to have of one's experience as a cross country coach.[12]

Men's and Women's Soccer

Harding added women's soccer as an intercollegiate sport in 1998 and men's soccer in 2000. The teams enjoy their own field as a result of generous gifts from supporters of the program, including Mark Stevens, after whom the field and the teams' field house is named.

The highlight of the women's soccer program came in 2004, when Harding tied for the Gulf South Conference regular season championship, going 15-4-1 overall and 6-1-1 in conference play. The Lady Bisons earned the program's first N.C.A.A. Tournament trip and played in the regional tournament in Miami Shores, Fla. The top player on that team was Kendyl Washburn, a freshman who scored thirteen goals that season and earned mention in *Sports Illustrated's* "Faces in the Crowd." Washburn, a native of Midland, Texas, holds Harding's record with forty-eight career goals.

Until 2001, Dr. Greg Harris coached both the men's and women's teams. Coach Harris was an outstanding soccer player who did his graduate work in marriage and family therapy from 1994-1996 and came back to coach at Harding in 2001. He said,

> *There is no doubt that the Almighty has shaped me in my journey while working at Harding. I arrived with the mindset to change the soccer program into one that could compete with anyone on a national level. Although the soccer program has been blessed by His hand and has changed during these years, the greatest transformation has been within me. These students have challenged me*

*with their faith and selfless acts and taught me to grow and blend
my faith and athletics; and the journey has been remarkable. When
I am discouraged or am presented with an opportunity to leave
Harding, without fail, an angel from our Father in the form of a
student shines through and gives a smile and an unexpected, "Love
you, Coach!," and then I wipe my eyes and settle back into my chair.
That is Harding!*[13]

In 2011, Harding hired Jeremy Bishop to coach the men's program, and in
2012, former Bison player Odie Guzman became the head coach. Ben Faris, who
played from 2002-05, is Harding's career goals leader, with forty-one in his career,
twenty more goals than any other player.

Men's and Women's Tennis

During all of my time as president, Harding's tennis team was coached by the
legendary David Elliott. He started working with our tennis program in the early
70s and has watched it grow from a non-scholarship, walk-on program to one that
is highly competitive in Division II of the N.C.A.A. and against many Division I
programs.

In the early 80s, Coach Elliott evaluated what was taking place around the country and decided he needed to add some international players. Most of the win-

ning programs were almost 100 percent made up of international athletes. Coach Elliott decided to seek some international students, and in the late 80s and early 90s, had a number of players from Mexico who were very successful.

He particularly mentioned Leoncio Dominquez coming to Harding for tennis. Leoncio became a Christian while here and was able to convert his family as well. He also mentioned Carolina Banuelos. He stated that she was able to convert her father before he died a few years ago.

Coach Elliott recruited a number of students from Brazil, including Catherine Carui, a transfer from Arkansas State University, and Karina Gomes Swindle. Karina introduced Coach Elliott to Marco Ruiz, an outstanding student player, who is now the tennis coach. Marco came to Harding, became a Christian and has made a marvelous contribution to Harding.

Coach Elliott talked about a lot of conference championships but said, "Nothing measures up to the influence our teams at Harding have had on the lives of other people."[14]

The tennis teams and individual players have had great success on and off the court, and I respect Coach Elliott for his leadership in Harding's tennis program.

Women's Softball

A decision was made in 2011 to add women's softball to the array of programs offered at Harding University. Phil Berry was selected as the inaugural head coach to prepare for the first season of competition in 2013-14. A lot of work was put

into this program effort, including the building of a beautiful new stadium, which holds 314 people. Complete with batting cages, it is one of the finest facilities in our conference. Construction began on this field in April 2013 and was completed in time for the first practice in September 2013. The first official game in the program's history was Feb. 8, 2014, against Northeastern Oklahoma State University, and Harding won the game 6-4. The first home game and our first Great American Conference series took place in February against Southern Nazarene. Harding won the series 3-1.

Harding started its first year on a high note, even though they were picked to finish last in the preseason G.A.C. poll. The Lady Bisons qualified for the conference tournament as the #4 seed. What a great beginning for this program.

Baseball

The most exciting baseball games I remember happened in Millington, Tenn., in 2002. This was the Gulf South Conference tournament, and in that game, freshman Justin Cone hit three homeruns and drove in eight runs as Harding picked up a win. Cone also picked up a win as pitcher for the most outstanding player honor in the 2002 Gulf South Conference tournament. It was an exciting game. Coach Pat McGaha provides leadership for our baseball program. He shared this story –

The first memory may not seem like a highlight because it was a horrific situation, the scariest of my coaching career, but it turned out to be such a blessing for our team. During my first season at Harding, we played Crichton College in 2006. We won the first game by a score of 10-2 and played very well. In the second game,

225

*we gave up five runs in the second inning and trailed by one run
when we got into trouble in the fifth inning, so I brought Jordan
Blake to the mound in relief of our starting pitcher. Jordan forced
the hitter into a grounder for the second out of the inning, but the*

*next batter he faced hit
a line drive that struck
Jordan just above his left
temple. I knew it was a
bad situation immediate-
ly! When Doc Lambeth
and I got to Jordan in
front of the mound, he
was attempting to stand
but we kept him down.
Jordan was rushed to the
hospital. When the ball
struck Jordan, it created*
*a spider web of small fractures in his skull right at the speech center
of his brain. Jordan spent the better part of a month in I.C.U. unable
to speak. Obviously, this was a very trying time for Jordan, his family, our players and coaches. However, the Lord's presence during
this time was so obvious and the faith of our players and all the
Harding students who were concerned was so uplifting. Our team
came together as a family through this tragedy, realizing just how
fragile life is and how powerful the Lord is. So many life lessons and
faith discussions occurred during the time that Jordan was recover-
ing in the hospital, and I was reminded just how special a community of faith Harding University really is.*[15]

In terms of memorable wins, Coach McGaha referenced the 2011 season.

*It proved to be the best in history as Harding set a school record
with forty-two victories, the first forty-win season in program history; won the Gulf South Conference West Division regular season
championship, our first baseball championship since 1984;*

An Open Letter to Coach McGaha

Coach McGaha,

Well, the numbers on the scoreboard weren't what I would have liked yesterday for the Bisons. I'm sure they were not what you or your team liked either.

However, a very important aspect of the game for me was not on the scoreboard. It was listening to two men behind me who were talking about their baseball experiences. The father of a Bison player was saying that he would not trade his son's experience at Harding for anything.

"Oh, they've fallen on some hard times lately," he said, "but the relational experiences my son as had here at Harding – with the team and the coach – have been the best! I wouldn't have had him anywhere else. Coach is just an extraordinary man."

As I walked across the parking lot after the game, a woman whose son has been at Harding for three years raved about the coach and the Harding experience. "He has had such a great experience that now his two younger sisters both want to follow him at Harding," she said. She shared a story about attending one of his games his freshman year at Abilene. "I almost cried when we went into church that Sunday morning," she said. "There was the whole baseball team sitting in front of us."

On a scale of 1 to 10, it seemed our Bison baseball coach scored a 10. It wasn't posted on the official scoreboard, but it seems that it was recorded in the hearts of the players and their parents. To me, that was the most impressive stat from the game yesterday.

Thanks for being a first-class coach at Harding. Go, Bisons!

Pat Rice

advanced to the championship game of the G.S.C. Tournament for the first time; and received our first ever South Regional Tournament bid, earning the #3 seed. At the South Regional Tournament, we won our first game against the University of Tampa, which marked the first time a Harding University men's athletic team had won an N.C.A.A. post-season tournament game in any sport. Additionally, we were ranked as high as #16 in the Collegiate Baseball News Poll.[16]

Prior to Coach McGaha, Harding's baseball team was coached by Dick Johnson, Steve Smith, Jess Bucy and Shane Fullerton.

Golf

Harding's men's golf program will celebrate its 50th anniversary season in 2014-15. Under the direction of Coach Dustin Howell, who was hired in 2008-09, the men's team won the G.A.C. Championship in 2012-2013. The Lady Bisons program began in the 2005-06 season, and the team became successful quickly. They also won the Great American Conference championship in 2012 and 2013.

Harding is Athletics

Some of the most exciting times for the Harding family center around inter-collegiate athletic competitions as we watch students we know and love compete with others. While all of us love winning, we know the real story has to do with the lives of the students competing. As we see these athletes reach their potential in competition of any type, we cheer them on and recognize their achievements.

Our men's and women's basketball teams in 2013 are great examples of Harding athletics. Knowing the athletes is really what matters. Knowing they love Christ and have a servant heart is what matters. The fact that they won a lot of games is just icing on the cake. I am so proud of our student athletes in all sports.

I'm also proud of our coaches. These men and women have a truly unique opportunity to transform the lives of young men and women. However, I am biased, but I believe Harding has the best team of Christian coaches to be found at any university in our nation. They have a heart for serving others and sharing Christ with the student athletes.

Students come to Harding and discover the world

PART FIVE

University Growth

Casual visits contribute to Harding's family environment

CHAPTER THIRTEEN
Enrollment is Life

Introduction

In recent years, I have used the phrase, "Enrollment is life" to talk about my belief in the importance of enrollment for a private university. This phrase came from a book by Dr. Stephen Trachtenberg, who has been president of three private colleges.[1] It really sums up my thought process on enrollment from my early days as president. I have always wanted Harding to have an impact on as many students as possible with the gospel message. I was also aware that, as a private university, we are very much tuition-driven, with a large percentage of our total revenues coming from student tuition and other fees.

When I was interviewed by a committee of the Board of Trustees in 1986, one of the major points I shared with them was my commitment to intentional and gradual enrollment growth. I had studied enrollment management at Florida State University, and I knew the importance of enrollment to the success of higher education. I subscribed to the view that colleges are either going forward or they are going backward because it is nearly impossible to stand still. My experience is that colleges that try to remain constant end up being elitist and expensive; therefore, many students who could benefit from that college experience are excluded in the process. I was strictly in favor of a growth strategy.

After an involved strategic planning process, the committee concluded – in a report dated March 29, 1986 – that enrollment growth should be our priority for the next five years. Noted in this report as a result of a major effort to identify strengths, weaknesses, threats and opportunities was the fact that Harding had experienced a declining enrollment for the previous five years. Enrollment was listed as the number one weakness for the University. Consequently, as I talked to the Board Search Committee and later to the faculty through the strategic planning process, I emphasized the need for a proactive approach to be taken relative to student recruitment.

Proactive Approach

In keeping with my statement to the Board, I asked Dr. Jim Carr, who was working at that time with the American College Testing Program in Florida, to join

my team at Harding as Vice President for Educational Services and to lead an aggressive approach to recruit more students to the Harding campus. Dr. Carr, along with Jim White, Mike Williams and Glenn Dillard, provided the key executive leadership for this effort over the entire twenty-six-year period. I believe they developed one of the finest student recruitment programs to be found anywhere in America.

We have been blessed with professional staff in admissions who have represented Harding well. Morris Seawel is a good example of an individual who has been the face of Harding for a large number of students coming from the Southeast. I am especially grateful to all of our admissions representatives for a job well done.

In 1987, Harding's enrollment was 2,997, with 2,709 undergraduate students and 288 graduate students. Students were enrolled from forty-eight states and twenty-five countries. We had some concern about enrollment because it had peaked at 3,260 in 1980 and then decreased slightly in each of the following six years. We wanted to reverse this downward trend.

Our proactive strategy continued to emphasize the recruitment of students from churches of Christ. A nationwide recruitment effort was assigned to work with churches and Christian academies to attract students. We knew we needed to identify these students and aggressively persuade them to choose Harding for their higher education option.

The top priority in following this proactive approach to student recruitment was the recruitment of Christian students who would fit in with the mission of Harding. I wanted to be certain that we continued to recruit students who would benefit from the Harding experience and who would make us a better institution.

I traveled all over the United States for Harding receptions and talked with students about opportunities at Harding. We were blessed with wonderful alumni volunteers who hosted these receptions. Because more than two-thirds of our students come from states other than Arkansas, a nationwide strategy was critical for our success. Harding was blessed to have alumni in all fifty states.

I loved sharing the Harding story of camaraderie with prospective students and alumni at these receptions. We often took current students with us to share their experiences at Harding. I always wanted the students to share their experiences first because their message was so real and from the heart.

I was able to get to know a lot of students as a result of these trips. I remember meeting Ryan Rummage as he traveled with us to Nashville, Tenn., for a reception. We later became friends, and he worked in my office during his senior year, helping with Spring Break Missions.

I always talked about both the spiritual and academic nature of Harding, the true integration of faith and learning. I think it is easy to follow the lead of higher education in general and talk only about academic excellence. While Harding offers wonderful academic programs, I always wanted prospective students and parents to understand Harding's commitment to spiritual values as we defined our mission.

One of the challenges we have always faced has to do with Church of Christ membership and the fact that it has been static and/or declining over this period of time. It is hard to know how many Church of Christ college-bound students choose to attend one of our Christian colleges. For years based on anecdotal data, most of the Christian college presidents assumed that about twenty percent of these students enrolled in one of our colleges. In 2007, Dr. Flavil Yeakley was commissioned by the presidents to conduct a comprehensive study to more accurately assess the number of college-bound Church of Christ students going to one of our Christian colleges or universities. He found that the percentage was actually thirty-seven percent, not the twenty percent we had assumed.[2] While encouraged, I believed we still had a wonderful opportunity to increase the number of Church of Christ members attending Harding or other Christian colleges by simply doing a better job of communicating with our fellowship the quality and benefits offered by Christian higher education. Recent meetings of our Christian college presidents have included this important discussion.

We also need to realize that the chief competition for Harding and other Christian colleges is not with each other but rather with other institutions of higher education, particularly public institutions. Generally, the cost to attend is lower for public universities, perceived academic quality is good, universities are bigger and these universities are seen as prestigious in the eyes of peers. I am always amazed at the number of conversations that suggest that the primary competition for students is among Christian colleges. While this has occurred and while students often send applications and test scores to several of our colleges, I believe our strongest competition is with public universities in all fifty states.

In recent years, this challenge of recruiting students from churches of Christ has been heightened because of the polarization and internal conflict among autonomous congregations of churches of Christ. The challenge for our Christian higher education institutions will be to effectively communicate to these individuals that we are still committed to maintaining the mission and that Christian higher education is worth the investment on behalf of the students and parents involved.

International Students

Harding is blessed with students coming from fifty nations to be a part of the Harding family. This has been a long tradition at Harding. Some come from Central America and Mexico because of our Walton Program. In an effort to make an impact in China, Harding was privileged to enroll about 175 students from there in 2012-2013. We have always enjoyed having students from the continent of Africa.

Costs to Attend Harding

Harding has always tried to keep the price as low as possible so that more students who have limited financial resources can attend. For example, for the 2012-13 academic year, the cost to attend Harding, including tuition, tech fees, room and board, was $22,534 at the undergraduate level. At present, the average cost to attend a Christian college associated with churches of Christ is $29,927. Of the Christian senior colleges, Harding is the second lowest in terms of total cost to attend. The average for all Arkansas private colleges in 2012-13 was $31,934. This cost comparison would be similar for the entire twenty-six years, with Harding being at the low end of the spectrum. Graduate tuition rates are higher and vary based on the program involved.

Net Cost to Attend

The cost to attend Harding involves a great deal more than just looking at the total gross tuition, room, board and fees. Many students receive financial aid, which lowers the cost of attendance in a significant way. I always talked to parents in terms of looking at the net cost of attendance, i.e., total cost less scholarships and other forms of assistance available to students. An increasing amount of scholarship assistance is provided by Harding and its donors.

Financial Aid				
	1987-88	#Students	2012-13	#Students
Federal Pell Grants	$1.2 M		$4.7 M	
Total Scholarships	$2.2 M	1,876	$21.9 M	3,600
Loans	$5.5 M	1,640	$26.3 M	2,480
Federal Work Study	$408,000	650	$337,000	421
HU Work Study	$447,000	817	$2.2 M	1,330

Harding students receive Federal Pell Grants based on need. As can be seen in the chart above, these grants have increased in dollar amounts, but the percentage of students receiving the grant over these twenty-six years has remained constant at twenty-nine percent.

The biggest increase in financial aid was for scholarships given to students primarily because of academic ability. These scholarships, provided by Harding, amounted to $21.9 million in 2012-13, benefiting 3,600 students. Loans also increased substantially, with fifty-nine percent of the student body taking out loans in 2012-13. Federal work study funding decreased, while Harding-funded student work scholarships increased to $2.2 million by 2012-13.

Altogether, $9.9 million in financial aid was awarded during the 1986-87 year as compared to $61.2 million awarded during the 2011-12 school year. Included in these awards are athletic, departmental, trustee and other special or program-related scholarships.

Importance of Retention

Near the top of the list of importance relative to an aggressive approach to recruitment is an effort to retain students once they arrive on campus. This involves the entire faculty, student services and really the entire Harding community. Our retention rate for the 2013 year was eighty-four percent, in contrast to a retention rate of seventy-one percent in 1986-87. Retention is an extremely important part of the recruitment process and represents a lot of effort on the part of the entire Harding community to make this positive number possible.

Many factors have an impact on retention, including satisfaction with instruction, residence hall life, involvement in student activities, code of conduct and even food in the cafeteria. The appearance of the campus makes a difference as well.

<u>Special Efforts</u>

I have always been impressed with the creativity of our admissions team in coming up with different ways to help get the Harding message out to a wider audience. One that I remember with fondness involved sending a personalized Christmas video to each prospective student. These videos depicted scenes from the Harding campus and each video was personalized with a message from the admissions advisor who worked with that potential student. Letters have often been sent directly from alumni to students, and I appreciate the work on behalf of many people who made this initiative possible. Student leaders on campus have been utilized effectively in calling prospective students and, in general, a proactive effort has been made to reach students who have expressed an interest in Harding.

Sometimes a staff person makes a special effort. The following letter is from the father of a student who was about to graduate –

In two weeks, my first child will graduate from Harding! Like her dad, she squeezed four years into five! She has had a wonderful experience, hates to leave but did find a fiancé. Nursing has been a challenge for her, but she has demonstrated her determination. Our son will graduate the following year, so we will certainly get a raise!

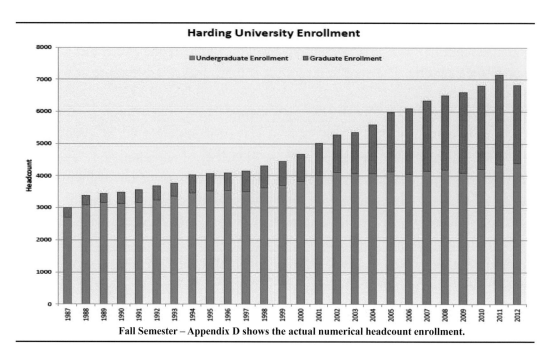

Harding University Enrollment

■ Undergraduate Enrollment   ■ Graduate Enrollment

Headcount

Fall Semester – Appendix D shows the actual numerical headcount enrollment.

I simply could not let her graduate without saying a special word about a special person who has made the lives of parents so much better while their children are at Harding. I am talking about Ann Guffey in Financial Aid. I can't say enough good about this dear, sweet lady. She understands when parents are frustrated with a confusing process, returns calls, explains things in English and represents Harding extremely well.

Just couldn't let my daughter graduate without telling you this. You know you have some exceptional people at Harding. Ann is certainly one of them!

Enrollment Results

The results of this aggressive recruitment strategy are reflected in the chart above, which shows an increase in undergraduate enrollment from 2,709 in the fall of 1987 to 4,390 for the fall of 2012. As you can see, this growth was gradual over the twenty-six years of my presidency. Graduate enrollment increased dramatically from 288 to 2,425 because of the additional programs offered. Total headcount enrollment increased from 2,997 in 1987 to 6,815 in the fall of 2012.

The record high enrollment of 7,155 was reached in the fall of 2011, but dropped in 2012 and 2013 because of a decrease in summer graduate education programs funded or promoted by the State Department of Education.

It should be noted that the average A.C.T. score for the incoming student also increased during this period of time from 19.9 in 1987 to 25.1 in 2012. Further, the number of National Merit Finalists enrolled at Harding from 1987 to 2002 was impressive as it grew from six in 1988 to a high of twenty in 1998.

Many people in the Harding family referred to rankings by *U.S. News & World Report* as evidence of Harding's success, not only in admissions, but in our entire program. We have been consistently ranked in the top twenty universities in the South in this publication. We have also had a high ranking for years in *Peterson's Competitive Colleges* guide.

My response has always been guarded with respect to these reports. While I am grateful that Harding is recognized, I do not believe these reports measure what Harding is about. We are primarily a private Christian university, and our goals are not measured by any standard in these publications. Harding's success in its mission cannot be measured by just looking at our retention rate, class size, student/faculty ratio, average ACT scores or alumni giving rate. We are all about intangible factors that lead to heaven itself. It's impossible to measure these intangible but critical components of a Harding education.

Another result of the growth in enrollment, especially regarding on-campus residential components, was the need for expanded student housing. One of the truly significant investment decisions by our board was a major decision to build or renovate existing housing for students. We now have more than 3,400 students living on campus.

It should also be noted that this growth periodically resulted in calls from some people to cap our enrollment. This topic was discussed every time a new strategic plan was proposed, and the decision was always to pursue intentional growth to provide the Harding experience to more students. However, we did limit enrollment in some years because of space limitations.

Of course, the number of students enrolled does not even begin to tell the story of the importance of the Admissions program. We are about working with young people as they come to the campus, and our prayer is that they will have a wonderful experience as a student at Harding as they learn more about opportunities to serve in the Lord's kingdom. Let me share just a few stories about students who have made the decision to attend Harding.

Glenn Dillard, our assistant vice president for enrollment management, told me about Eric Kee, a Native American, who grew up on an Indian reservation in Arizona. A year or two after Eric's high school graduation, a current Harding student was serving as a missionary on the reservation where Eric and his family lived. At the end of the summer, the young woman needed a ride back to Searcy and asked if Eric could drive her.

On the drive back, the girl talked to Eric about Harding and encouraged him to visit with someone in the Admissions Office. She brought him in to visit with Glenn, who showed him the campus and discussed financial aid availability. Eric was convinced that he wanted to be here but didn't think it was possible since he had no clothes or any other belongings in Searcy. After talking with his parents, people in the Admissions Office took Eric to buy basic items at Walmart, and Eric stayed to attend Harding. He later graduated from Harding and served as a missionary in Italy. He met and married his wife, another Harding University graduate, and they are both serving Native Americans in Arizona.[4]

Another story was shared with me about Dr. Melanie Lowry, who is a faculty member in our Communication Sciences and Disorders Program. Melanie came to Harding from Temple, Texas, having been named a National Merit Finalist in high school. While many of her friends were heading to state universities, she made the decision to come to Harding because, as she said, "I wanted to go someplace where it was cool to be good." We are delighted that she came to Harding and that she is now on our faculty.

Kellum Tate from Kimberly, Ala., came to Harding as a freshman in the fall of 2008. She had attended our Honors Symposium the previous summer, and she related her experience, which solidified her decision to enroll at Harding,

Honors Symposium was absolutely fantastic! To be completely honest, I think that's the most fun I've had in my entire life. I feel like I know my friends from the symposium better than I do the people I've spent my entire high school career with. The people there were absolutely amazing, the teachers' classes were challenging and the activities were so much fun... I had a blast! I really can't imagine someone NOT having a good time. I'm already seriously considering signing up for HUF in summer 2009 just because of how much fun I had at symposium.[5]

Morris Seawel worked with Kellum, and she was able to attend Harding on a Trustee scholarship. She had a wonderful Harding experience and is now a nurse at St. Vincent's Hospital in Little Rock.

Morris shared this story about Phillip Mion from Miami, Fla. Phillip came to Harding as a freshman in the fall of 2009. He was a 5'7" football player who graduated from Killian High School. He has been a campus leader at Harding and a member of the football team. He didn't know much about Harding until they came to visit and fell in love with Harding. Coach Paul Simmons says that Phillip was a game changer on several occasions during the 2012-13 school year. [6]

 Scott Hannigan tells about Emily Cook's decision to attend Harding in 2009. As she was completing her application, her dad, who was the pulpit minister at the West End Church of Christ in Knoxville, Tenn., was diagnosed with a brain tumor. Emily was able to enroll in the fall of 2010.[8] Her dad passed away May 21, 2012, at the age of 58.

Another student came to Harding on an athletic scholarship. Bruce McMullen came from Cape Town, South Africa, to play golf for Harding. While he was here, he was converted and baptized on a snowy day in the fountain in front of the Benson. He later became president of the Student Association and graduated in May of 2013.[7]

Many other students have benefited from being enrolled at Harding. Many have gone on to be school teachers, missionaries and professionals in numerous areas. I wish all of you could hear the speeches given by seniors in chapel as part of the Senior Week program every year. I am amazed at what these students have accomplished and will continue to accomplish in the Lord's kingdom.

Harding is Growth

I would like as many students as possible to experience Harding. I have always been in favor of intentional growth for our student body. We are offering a Christ-based experience that can change the world for good.

We have been blessed with growth at the undergraduate and graduate levels. A proactive strategy has been in place to attract undergraduate students. We have attempted to keep tuition as low as possible to allow as many students as possible to attend. Scholarships have been increased dramatically to help students attend. New programs have been offered at the graduate and professional levels to attract these students and better prepare them for their professions.

CHAPTER FOURTEEN

Investing in Harding

Harding University has been blessed since its inception by people who believe in its mission. These individuals have made sacrificial gifts to the University, especially during hard times, which have allowed Harding to survive and even prosper. They have given liberally from the heart so that more and more students could experience Christian education at Harding. They have invested their time and money into students who are the future leaders of the church and the nation.

I often have spoken to students and donors about the joy of giving. The message in the gospels includes a stern warning, coupled with a marvelous promise. In Matthew 6:19,[1] we are warned about storing up for ourselves treasures on earth where thieves break in and steal. The message of verse 20 is to store up treasures in heaven, for where our treasure is – that's where our heart is. In verse 33, God extends a promise to us when he says, "But seek first His kingdom and His righteousness, and all these things will be given to you as well."[2]

A similar warning and contrasting promise is recorded in Mark 10:23.[3] Jesus uses the illustration that it is difficult for the rich to enter into the kingdom of God. In fact, he says is it would be easier for a camel to go through the eye of a needle than for a rich man to enter the kingdom of God. Then comes the promise in verses 29 and 30 –

No one who has left home or brothers or sisters or mother or father or children or fields for me and the gospel will fail to receive a hundred times as much in this present age: homes, brothers, sisters, mothers, children and fields – along with persecutions – and in the age to come, eternal life. But many who are first will be last and the last first.[4]

A similar message is recorded by Paul in 2 Corinthians 9:6. But one of the most famous passages dealing with wealth is in Matthew 19:16-27, where we are taught about the rich young ruler who would not give up his wealth.

It would be a huge mistake to read into these passages a health-and-wealth gospel, as so many people have done, but it would also be an injustice to suggest that giving is unimportant. I am convinced that we cannot outgive God, and it is an important requirement for Christians to give generously and eagerly. I love the statement by William Arthur Ward in the book, *Give to Live*, which says,

> Each of us will one day be judged by our standard of life – not by our standard of living; by our measure of giving – not by our measure of wealth; by our simple goodness – not by our seeming greatness.[5]

In the same book, Henry Ward Beecher wrote, "There never was a person who did anything worth doing who did not receive more than he gave."[6]

I really believe the key to understanding the Bible message on giving is found in looking at the heart. If we are giving for the wrong reason, the result of the giving will still bless the receiver but may not bless the giver. If the giving is done with a pure heart for the right reason, I believe God will bless the individual who makes the gift. Certainly, Harding has been blessed by gifts from generous individuals since our inception in 1924.

Total Gifts

From 1987-88 through 2012-13, gifts totaled $288 million, an average of $11 million annually. This included $60.4 million in annual fund giving, $74 million in capital fund gifts, $95 million in endowment gifts, and $59 million in restricted gifts. Harding's endowment, including all funds, was $18.7 million on June 30, 1987, and grew to $105.2 million by June 30, 2013, as donors invested in the future of our work. In addition, numerous individuals have put Harding in their wills, which will result in future gifts for the University.

Many people at Harding have been a part of the process of talking with people about making a gift to support the work at Harding, but I am particularly indebted to the work of Floyd Daniel, who has served as a major gift officer in an exemplary way. During the time that I was president-elect, I talked with Floyd about this re-sponsibility and indicated to him that I had very little experience in fundraising. He assured me that he would do his part and, true to his word, he was a major factor in our effort to secure gifts for a rapidly growing program. He was all about fundrais-ing. What a blessing Floyd has been to Harding University as he has built relation-ships with individuals and asked them to invest in our mission. I am also indebted to Dr. Clifton L. Ganus, Dr. Jim Carr and Dr. Mike Williams, who played a key role in many of the gifts received.

Annual Fund Giving

Annual Fund gifts bolster student scholarships, help us balance our operating budget and keep tuition at a lower level.

An important part of the Annual Fund drive has been contributions/gifts made

by current faculty and staff members or retired faculty. We have always con-ducted a campaign by first asking our own people to help. Of course, these people are already helping in a very sig-nificant way by their full-time service as faculty or staff members. Nonethe-less, we always ask them to be on the front line in giving for any new campaign effort. Many of these individuals have given sacrificially every year.

We also made it a practice to go to the residents of the city of Searcy, and Lott Tucker directed this effort for many years. In fact, Lott directed four of the five-year campaigns. He was well known in the community, and he organized efforts to contact business leaders in Searcy. Community leaders were also helpful in meeting the campaign objectives. The Searcy Campaign generally led to $2 million in gifts for each five-year campaign. Reynie Rutledge, president of First Security Bank, was the campaign chairman for the last two campaigns, and we are indebted to him for his leadership. The community of Searcy has been very helpful to us in raising needed funds.

The President's Council, which began in 1965 under Dr. Ganus' leadership, continues to be an invaluable group of men and women who help Harding achieve its mission. The 1,200-plus family members of this volunteer council assist us with the recruitment of students, fundraising and public relations. We always count on these members as a core support group for the annual fund, particularly in regard to student scholarships.

Harding is also a member of Arkansas Independent Colleges and Universities, which supports private and independent education in Arkansas. Funds raised by this organization come to Harding to support our annual fund. This group also assists with legislative efforts in Arkansas, with the intent of getting private colleges included with public universities for student scholarship funds.

The Associated Women for Harding make a strong effort every year to raise money for scholarships for students. They raised $1.6 million over the twenty-six years of my administration, including gifts and merchandise sales. This money goes entirely to A.W.H. scholars. Liz Howell is the liaison person with A.W.H. and volunteers who work diligently on behalf of Harding students to raise money for these scholarships.

A significant part of the annual fund effort has been conducted by the Harding School of Theology to raise money in the Memphis area and from alumni of their program. In recent years, they have raised in excess of $450,000 annually.

In 2011, a special event called "Say Thanks Day" was developed by our Advancement office to communicate to our students the importance of giving to the University. Clearly one third of the cost to attend Harding is made up of donations or gifts to help us keep tuition as low as possible. Students were asked to "say thanks" to our donors by writing notes to them or by making calls of appreciation.

Capital Fund Giving

A long-standing policy of our Board has been to use donated funds for any building to be constructed at Harding, excluding residence halls, where we use debt repaid by designated student revenue sources. We have been blessed to have generous people invest in these projects so that we could have the facilities needed for our students.

Visitors to campus can take a tour and read the plaques in the halls of almost every building, placed there to recognize people who were instrumental in making the project a reality. You will be encouraged as you reflect on the gifts that are representative of the many gifts that have been made to assist us with our mission.

A visit to Keller Hall, a residence hall for 200 men, will inform you of the generosity of Mrs. May Keller. I only met her twice, as she lived a quiet and fru-gal life. She was seldom on campus, but Floyd Daniel visited with her on a regular basis. At a glance, you would have no idea that she might make a sizable gift to Harding in her lifetime, but I don't know if you could ever find anyone who was more genuine in her faith and more committed to helping others – Harding in particular – than she was. Keller Hall is named in her honor, but this hardly begins to tell the story of her life, which Floyd could relate for hours on end. Mrs. Keller is representative of many people who invested in Harding students because of her commitment to God.

A visit to our Brackett Library will remind you of a wonderful example of love for the university by the Brackett family. I remember the announcement as though it were yesterday, when on the first day of class in the spring of 1990, a gift was presented by the Bracketts to build a new library. In addition to the gift for the building, the Bracketts – on faith – pledged an additional $10 million to endow the library. This was the largest gift in the history of Harding to that point. It represented a significant endorsement of the mission of Harding University.

This gift came during my first five-year campaign, an exciting time for the entire university. Floyd Daniel said,

During my first visit with the Bracketts in February 1988, I recognized that Bob and Sandy were people with great faith and love for God and a strong interest in young people. This is reflected in their work with the local congregation. I found them to be quiet but very generous and effective workers for the Lord. They also had a great belief in the benefits of a Christian education at Harding. Working with them is a joy.[7]

The most significant part of this gift was that they made so much of the endowment gift on faith, realizing that they would need blessings from God to be in a position to give the amount of money they had pledged. With complete trust in God, they made and gave the money that is now part of our permanent endowment for the library. What a blessing this has been and will continue to be.

The plaque displayed in the Student Center recognizes two earlier supporters of Harding – James T. and Oral Cone. Their love of young people and Harding College has been expressed in many ways. Before his death in 1968, Jim Cone served as the vice chairman of Harding's Board of Trustees. Oral Cone served faithfully on the President's Development Council. It was her generous gift that challenged Harding's alumni and made possible the construction of the Student Center.

When we added on to the student center in 1992, we were privileged to name it after Charles Kenneth and Marie Schell Hammon, in honor of their commitment to Harding and its students. Both Charles and Marie had a deep love for and trust in young people, and they believed that much great and lasting good could be done through encouraging students to live at their highest levels and realize their full potential. Mrs. Hammon provided the initial funds and momentum to make this addition possible.

As the addition was being made to the Student Center, a special request came from students to have a small chapel in the building. Members of the Shores family generously supported this venture and allowed us to name the chapel in honor of their parents, Carl E. and Mary C. Shores, both of whom were active in support of Harding. Bro. Shores was an active businessman, song leader and member of the President's Council. He and his wife were killed in an automobile accident on Sept. 18, 1971.

A plaque at the entrance to the president's office in the Heritage Building is very special to me. It recognizes the generosity of Don and Lois Shores in helping us make the American Heritage Building addition possible. What a blessing they have been to us in our work at Harding. Bro. Shores serves on our Board and was chairman for four years.

A visit to the east side of campus will bring you to the J.E. and L.E. Mabee Business building, which was enlarged in 2012, and the School of Business was

named in honor of Paul R. Carter. Paul was the perfect example of a successful Christian businessman, and his ideals represent what the College of Business attempts to teach. As you view the building lobby, note the plaque honoring some of the people who helped make this project possible, including Rodney and Suzanne Waller, David and Donnie House, Mark and Angela Stevens and Bob and Sandy Brackett.

One of Paul and June's greatest desires was to create an endowment fund for scholarships to be given to students majoring in Bible. They had a great love for the Lord's church and wanted young people who wanted to go into ministry to receive scholarship help. Numerous students have been assisted from this fund. Paul and June have been great believers in the mission of Harding, supporting it in every way imaginable.

Cone Chapel is my favorite room on campus. Numerous weddings and receptions are held each year in this chapel, which overlooks the front quadrangle of the campus. It is named in honor of James and Bonnie Cone, who loved Harding and were active in supporting Harding in many ways. James was chairman of the Board when I began and a great mentor to me. Cone Chapel was dedicated to the late James H. Cone Sr. and Bonnie Cone Hooper in appreciation of their leadership and support of Harding University and their special support to the addition of the American Heritage Center. Prior to his death in 2001, James Cone served for almost three decades as a member of the Board of Trustees, including ten years as chairman. Bonnie has had a significant leadership role in the Associated Women for Harding, especially with the Little Rock chapter. Together, the couple provided leadership during a dynamic period of growth for Harding.

Our Health Science Building, which houses our Physician Assistant and Pharmacy programs, is named after Dr. Henry and Grace Farrar. Dr. Farrar graduated from Harding in 1948 and earned a medical degree from the University of Tennessee, after which he practiced medicine for fifty-six years. In 1964, he and Grace moved to Nigeria, West Africa, to begin the Nigerian Christian Hospital and outpatient clinic in a response to an outcry from missionaries in the area to help the country's many suffering people. This work continues today, and the 110-bed facility serves 30,000 patients each year.

In addition to their work in Nigeria, the Farrars helped start the Christian Mobile Clinic in Cameroon, South Africa, and worked at the Chamala Mission Hospital in Tanzania, East Africa. In 1982, they served in China, where Henry was a visiting professor of surgery at China Medical University. Grace was a nurse who served with Henry in a beautiful fashion.

As I talked with Dr. Farrar on many occasions, he would inevitably hold out his surgeon's hand, which was steady as a rock. He and Grace made a wonderful team who truly represented the nature of Christian servants. We were blessed to know them.

The Farrars were a wonderful example of a giving spirit for Harding University. As patriarchs of medical missions, Dr. Farrar and Grace spent much of their time in Africa helping needy people. They were genuine, generous Christian people – the kind of examples that make our work possible at Harding. I was pleased that our Board of Trustees wanted to honor Dr. and Mrs. Farrar by naming the new Health Sciences Building after them.

Next to the Farrar Center is the new Swaid and Christy Swaid Center for Health Sciences, which houses our Nursing and Communication Sciences and Disorders program. We are grateful to Dr. and Mrs. Swaid for their commitment to Harding and to health sciences. A well-known Christian neurosurgeon, Dr. Swaid practices in Birmingham, Ala. As you tour this beautiful new facility, you see plaques honoring oth-

ers – Ashley and Eleanor Thomas, Rodney and Suzanne Waller, Mark and Roxie Crews, Lois Howe, Harrell and Carlton Freeman, Bonnie Cone Hooper, Don and Lois Shores and many others – who made the building possible. Because of generous people, our students are blessed with this modern, well-equipped building.

A visit to the west side of campus will bring you to the Thornton Center for Education. Because of our relationship with Jack Stephens, we were privileged to name this new center in honor of his sister, Wilma Stephens Thornton.

A special memory of mine happened at the groundbreaking ceremony. Mrs. Thornton, members of the Stephens family, faculty for this building and a host of friends were present as I jested – I thought gently – to Mrs. Thornton that I could help her with the shovel to break the dirt for this ceremony. She quickly reminded me, in front of the entire audience, that she was highly capable of digging up the dirt on her own and that I should stay put. She had the last word.

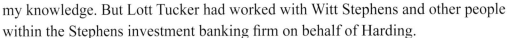

Our relationship with Jack Stephens had begun when Dr. Benson was president. An admirer of Dr. Benson, Jack had never worked directly with him to my knowledge. But Lott Tucker had worked with Witt Stephens and other people within the Stephens investment banking firm on behalf of Harding.

I remember meeting with Jack on many occasions to talk about our mission at Harding, and he was always interested in the efforts we were making in citizenship education and conservative government. I loved to have lunch with him at his office because he always served the best cornbread to be found anywhere in this region of the world. Dr. Carr and Lott Tucker were often with me and could confirm my assessment of the cornbread.

Mr. Stephens was helpful to Harding in a number of ways. He helped arrange visits by Vice President Dan Quayle and Admiral William Crowell, he provided transportation for Margaret Thatcher when she visited the campus, and he arranged transportation for a number of others who spoke as part of the American Studies Program.

I remember visiting with him in detail about his Cities and Schools Program. A man by the name of Karl Hochradel worked with him and later worked on the Searcy campus to develop a Stephens Scholars Program for students from the Delta region to attend Harding. The program was funded by Mr. Stephens, and we continue to use this endowment fund for scholarships today.

I have wonderful memories of visiting with Mr. Stephens on a regular basis. I remember feeding quail in his back yard, going to the Augusta tournament when he was chairman, and having a part with him in the dedication of the Cathedral School in Little Rock, one of his major interests. Mr. Stephens was a good friend of Harding.

Importance of Charitable Foundations

We are indebted to a number of foundations who have provided gifts for our building programs. Many of these gifts have come as "challenge" gifts, requiring that Harding raise a matching amount of money from other donors if we were to receive the foundation gift. These gifts have often sparked the success of the total campaign.

The J.E. and L.E. Mabee Foundation generously gave to Harding during my time as president, and their gifts were always a matching challenge.

I remember the very first gift made from the foundation after I became president. It was to help with the  C.L. Kay Plaza in front of the McInteer Center and Student Center. C.L. Kay, a good friend of mine and a friend of Joe Mabee, assisted with this gift. Gifts were later made for the J.E. and L.E. Mabee Business Building, the American Heritage

Center, the Thornton Education Center and the Swaid N. Swaid Health Sciences Center. We are indebted to this foundation for their significant help over a long period of time.

Harding's association with the Kendall Foundation began with Dr. Benson and continued with the assistance of Dr. Ganus. The Kendall Trust was established in the early 50s and was eventually dissolved and the money given to Harding. The $11 million given to Harding when the trust dissolved is part

of our permanent endowment. In addition, the Kendalls have been generous in contributing to the annual fund. Dr. Ganus continues to work with George Kendall, and we are grateful to the Kendall family for their confidence in Harding and its work.

The Walton Scholarship Program for students from Central America began in 1985 and continues as a strong program today. We are grateful to the Walton Family Foundation, established by Sam and Helen Walton and members of their family, for generous gifts that fund this program. Their gifts support sixty students each year with full tuition, fees, room and board, as well as travel funds to come to Searcy. What a blessing this program has been to Harding and to the countries of Central America and Mexico.

The 1996 school year began on a high note with the announcement that Harding was receiving a $5.9 million gift from the Donald W. Reynolds Foundation to build a new music and communication center on campus. It was long hoped that we might be able to construct a building for this purpose, but we were not certain how to raise the money for it. Jack Stephens was helpful to us as we made connections with Fred Smith of the Reynolds Foundation, and they were generous in giving us

this grant, contingent upon our raising money for endowment so that we could maintain the building in first-class shape. We did raise $1.2 million for the endowment.

The Donald W. Reynolds Foundation provided the support for the Reynolds Center for Music and Communication. Donald W. Reynolds, a businessman who believed in high ideals, built his success around free enterprise and a strong work ethic.

Harvey and Bernice Jones were pioneers in the trucking industry, and they built the Jones Trucking Lines into one of the most successful companies in the nation. The Joneses had a love for America and particularly for the state of Arkansas. They were a caring couple whose philosophy of life was, "Do to others as you would have them do to you." This couple was instrumental in helping Harding build our Marriage and Family Therapy Center, which is located in the McInteer Center.

Designated Giving

Harding has been blessed by the generosity of parents, alumni and other donors who have seen specific needs and been willing to fund them. Of particular note are our athletic facilities and the Jim Citty Football and Athletic Training Complex, led by football players and their parents, with others joining in – and we have a marvelous football facility. The same could be said for the Soccer Complex, led by Mark Stevens, and

the baseball facility for which parents took the lead in making possible the improvement to the stands, the field and the indoor practice facility.

Endowment Giving

One of the important parts of any giving program is permanent endowment to provide funds to ensure the long-term liability of the University. Many of these gifts come in the form of estate gifts or annuities.

The Endowment Fund was $18.7 million in June 1987 and $105.2 million in June 2013. Donations received are invested under the oversight of the Finance and Investment Committee of the Board of Trustees, and five percent of the dollars in the fund are used for operating purposes each year. Although the fund took a hit during the 2009 recession, it has since recovered.

This fund reminded me again of people like Dr. Henry Farrar and his wife, Grace, who on a regular basis, gave annuities to the University which, at their death, went to endowment for the specific purpose they had designated. Their generosity will benefit students continuously for as long as Harding exists.

A significant endowment fund was established in 1998 in honor of Dr. Kenneth Davis and his wife, Betty. Created by friends of this wonderful couple, this fund was designated to ensure the quality of the Donald W. Reynolds Center for Music and Communication. Dr. Davis directed Harding's a cappella chorus for thirty-five years. Former members of the a cappella chorus donated to this fund.

We are grateful to Ashley and Eleanor Thomas for their commitment to Harding and their belief in helping us with our endowment. This couple, who always loved children and young people, were never blessed with children of their own. They have been both parents and mentors to scores of young people throughout their lives. In recognition of the importance of education, they were led to help many young people – some of whom they never met – obtain college degrees. As they learned more about Harding and its mission, they funded various projects and scholarships for Harding students. The Thomases consistently looked beyond their own needs to those of others, serving as an example of generosity and enthusiasm in giving of themselves as well as their financial resources. Ashley expressed it best when he said, "We have been blessed in so many ways. We feel a responsibility to give back to help others."

This fund reminds me of people like Dr. Joan Coleman, now gone on to her reward, who left much of her estate to Harding. Many other individuals have also left Harding in their wills and/or made designated gifts for endowment.

I am also grateful for the Dr. Clifton L. and Louise Ganus Endowed Scholarship Fund, which provides significant scholarships for students to attend Harding. This fund was made possible by generous people in honor of Dr. and Mrs. Ganus. It is representative of many individual endowment funds that help students attend Harding.

Every Gift Matters

I often read the list of donors to Harding that is published in the *Harding* magazine each year. I appreciate every single donor. It's easy to read the top categories and think in terms of major gifts received, but I think it's important to recognize every gift, even the smallest gift made.

Dr. Mike Williams loves to share the following story, which I love as well –

> *Lillian Darr was a woman who believed in Christian education. Her first gift to Harding was given when she was ninety-three years old. Her final gift was received a few months before her 106th birthday. The final gift came with a personal note, which said I am enclosing a check for $10 – that is all that I can give… I wish it was more." The gift reminded me of the passage in Mark 12 where Jesus has robust praise for the widow who gave all that she had. Harding is a school built on the sacrifices of people like Lillian Darr.*[8]

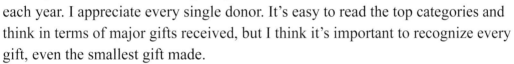

ASSET GROWTH		
	1987	2013
Total Assets	$90.5 million	$352.6 million
Buildings	$45.5 million	$202.2 million
Endowment	$18.7 million	$105.2 million

The Jennings Osborne family from Little Rock, Ark., donated their time and barbeque dinner to students and faculty for many tailgate parties in recent years. Dr. Ganus joined them in serving.

Harding is Blessed

Gifts represent about one-third of the total budget needed for Harding's annual operation, and we have been blessed with generous donors who make our work possible. Donors include faculty and staff members, parents, friends, alumni, foundations and corporations.

Gifts for the Harding Fund support scholarships for students, making it possible for them to attend a private university. Gifts for buildings have allowed Harding to develop a functional and attractive campus to accommodate varied program offerings. Gifts for permanent endowment help us provide stability for the University.

A walk through our campus reveals the names of some people who have been recognized with respect to various building or endowment projects. We are grateful and blessed by each donor. One of the great blessings of my life has been the opportunity to get to know people who have a heart for God's work.

The tower at Legacy Park reflects the classical design of that campus addition

CHAPTER FIFTEEN

A Beautiful Campus

Building a beautiful campus requires the efforts of the entire Harding family. Dreams have to be put on paper, architectural plans must be drawn, funds must be raised from donors and buildings can then be constructed to meet the needs of a growing campus. Maintenance of the existing campus, remodeling or renovation of existing buildings and landscaping are major parts of the challenge to have a truly beautiful and effective university campus.

When I became president, I had little idea as to how much of my time would be spent building and expanding the campus. I knew I would need to spend significant time in fundraising and other activities, but I underestimated the amount of effort that would go into the building program. I must admit that this was an experience I enjoyed very much as I worked with various architects, faculty, staff and students. I enjoyed the strategic planning, and I enjoyed the fundraising that made these buildings possible.

In fact, I had dreamed of being an architect, but I passed on that dream early in life when Harding did not offer this major. It is probably a good thing because I doubt that I could have made a living as an architect. As it turns out, I was able to be part of the design of the Harding campus over a twenty-six-year period, and I loved working with the team of people on building projects. I especially enjoyed working with Mike Steelman, the principal architect for these projects.

One of my resolutions as I began my presidency was to do everything possible to preserve the heritage of Harding and the look of Harding. We continued to use the red brick that had been used to build the Harding campus and tried to preserve as many of the existing buildings as possible. We only deviated from red brick at Legacy Park because we desired to develop a unique village.

Much of the planning was devoted to the concept of a small community. We used a map of the campus and drew ten-minute circles around the center of the campus so we would always know the walking distance from one building to another. We wanted the campus to continue to be a residential community where people could easily walk from one point to another.

The cost of construction projects for new facilities and renovations during my twenty-six years was $250 million, not including land purchases or regular maintenance work on the campus. I estimate that we spent an average of $12 million annually on building additions or renovations.

Pattie Cobb Hall

The first project I was involved in as president was the remodeling of Pattie Cobb Hall, which had served as both a residence hall and one of two cafeterias

for many years. The building had a distinctive architecture that we wanted to preserve as we redesigned it into suites for girls. The decision was made to close the cafeteria and use only the dining hall in the American Heritage building.

The challenge for this project was maintaining the historic nature of the building as one of the oldest buildings on campus and still providing for the needs of students. Almost everything had to be done by special order because nothing was the same size. Further, the building had a major problem with water leakage in the basement.

Brackett Library

The building of the Brackett Library was quite a challenge. I had always felt that the library was the heart of the campus and a very important tool for learning. How then do you move 300,000 volumes to another location for a full year while you construct a new library in exactly the same location? After much consideration, we decided to move all of the books in the library to the Administration auditorium so

265

students could still have access to them during the construction process. A temporary floor was put in the auditorium and shelving was added. Students had to check books out through the librarian because they could not get through this area to do it on their own. I was simply amazed at the ability of our library staff to make this change work, but we had few problems with it. Winnie Bell and Suzanne Spurrier were wonderful in helping us facilitate this process.

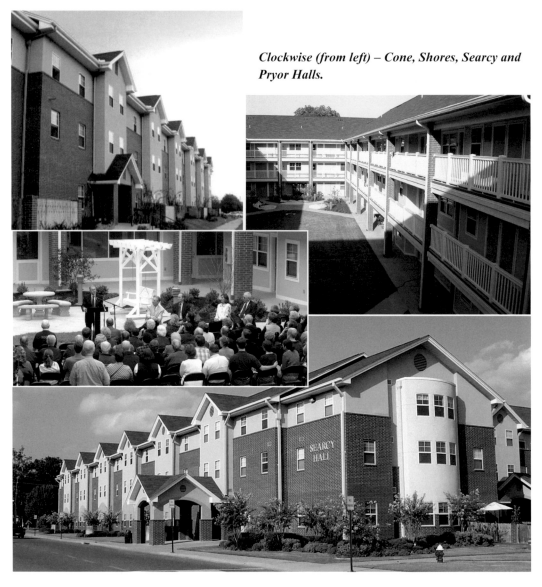

Clockwise (from left) – Cone, Shores, Searcy and Pryor Halls.

New Residence Halls

One of the great tasks during this early period of growth was building additional residence halls to accommodate increasing enrollment. After visiting with students, faculty and staff, decisions were made to build different styles of residence halls to try to better meet the needs of students. Built in 1996, Searcy Hall was an effort to provide housing for female students in a suite arrangement with a partial kitchen and living room. Cone Hall was built for men, using a similar concept. Shores Hall was built in 2001 and Pryor Hall in 2003, both with full-sized kitchens so that students were not required to eat any meals in the cafeteria. Shores and Pryor used a similar floor plan, opening to a common atrium in the middle.

It became necessary to provide additional married student apartments, so in 1996 and again in 2000, apartments were built at the new Harding Village on the east side of campus. Most of these were two-bedroom apartments, but a few were one- and three-bedroom apartments.

Relocation of Physical Resources

With our growth, the south side of the campus was changing dramatically. The old boiler room and swimming pool were ultimately removed, and Park Avenue

was changed to go around Shores and Pryor Halls so that students would not have to cross a busy street. All of this necessitated that the Physical Resources buildings be moved. A new facility was designed on the renamed Jimmy Carr Drive, expanding campus facilities further south. The new

facility houses Harding Press and Physical Resources. The facility was dedicated in honor of Lott R. Tucker, who had managed facilities for many years.

At the same time all of this work was being done, a major effort was undertaken to relocate all the utility lines underground. Once all the buildings were finally connected with underground cables, we were able to remove all of the telephone poles and wires from above ground, which made a dramatic impact on the appearance of the campus.

The primary factor in relocating the utility poles was to provide a safer environment for uninterrupted power. We had had a problem for some time with squirrels being fried on top of a utility pole, causing the connection to be lost. I am grateful for the squirrels that made it necessary for us to remove the telephone poles so that we might have more dependable power and a far more beautiful campus. Squirrels are still plentiful on our campus.

Removal of Railroad

One of the biggest challenges I faced was the removal of the railroad that ran

down Park Avenue from Benton Street on the east side of campus, through campus and down Pleasure Street to the main part of town. A line also went south from Park Avenue across Beebe Capps to the old industrial park in Searcy.

This is one of the largest projects I worked on because it took years to work through the details with varied businesses –

Union Pacific Railroad, the city of Searcy and individual property owners – to get permission to remove the tracks. In 1999, we were finally able to remove the tracks and replace them with a sidewalk that runs from east to west along Park Avenue. We had a ceremony, entitled "The Tracks Came Up," on May 14, 1999, as we celebrated the removal of the DK&S tracks from the middle of the campus. I still have a plaque in my office that reminds me of that significant day.

Remodeling of Alumni Field

Alumni Field received a major facelift in 1990. We built a new stadium on the home side, new seats on the visitors' side and a press box. We also remodeled the concession stand and restrooms. The greatest visual impact resulted from putting brick on the back of the visitors' bleachers and constructing a wrought iron fence around the stadium. Artificial turf was added, giving Harding a field for year-round use. Our soccer teams used the field before we were able to provide them their own facility. The Harding Academy Wildcats use the field for their home games. A generous gift from Reynie Rutledge, president of First Security Bank, prompted us to change the name to First Security Stadium.

The Plaza and McInteer Center

The most significant construction project during my early time as president was the construction of the McInteer Center and plaza. One of my early goals was the construction of an academic facility for the College of Bible and Religion that was second to none. The Bible department had been housed in the Ezell Building for many years and had outgrown its capacity with our increasing enrollment.

Dr. Carl Mitchell, dean of the College of Bible and Religion, worked closely with me and his faculty on this project. We decided to build the facility directly across from the Benson auditorium, with the plaza between them. This required closing part of Center Street and the relocation or razing of three houses on the north side of that street.

The design for this building included a circular entryway that is three stories high. It was designed so that the Great Commission could be shown in letters

around a map of the world in the center of the room. Flags representing all of the countries our students come from were hung from the high ceiling. We wanted every student at Harding to understand that evangelism is at the heart of Harding's identity and mission.

As the project neared completion, I was concerned that we did not have any kind of fountain or structure planned for the middle of the plaza. We did not have the money to put in the fountain because the building project was costing more than anticipated. Leah and I happened to be in Branson before the project was completed and saw a number of fountains at the Grand Village. I came back to Searcy, determined to find a way to build a fountain for the plaza. I met with Mike Steelman and asked him to design a fountain similar to one I had seen in Ephesus, with the exact dimensions of a baptistery, with steps going up and back out on one side of the fountain so that it could be used as a baptistery as well as a focal point for the plaza. We were able to find some additional funding to build the fountain, and one

of the joys of my life has been to watch scores of people baptized in this fountain since 1994.

I will never forget the day of the dedication of the McInteer Center. The decision had been made to name the building in honor of long-time board member Jim Bill McInteer. He chose the scripture that is engraved on the front of the building, "But thanks be to God, who gives us the victory through our Lord Jesus Christ" (I Cor. 15:57). On that day of dedication, we had a combined chorus singing, with some of the chorus members on the balcony, and the plaza full of guests. Bro. McInteer spoke to the group, a memory that is etched in my mind forever.

The Fire at Memphis

Fires are just horrible, but this one at the Harding mansion in Memphis turned out to be a blessing. The old mansion was the centerpiece of the Harding Graduate

School of Religion. It was the old King mansion, which included a chapel, faculty offices, admissions, financial aid offices and dean's office. It was a beautiful old structure, but it was in need of significant work that would be quite expensive.

Early in the morning on July 29, 1993, I got a call that the mansion was on fire, a crisis for the graduate school. Dr. Jack Lewis had his entire library at that location, and many of his books were severely damaged by water as the firemen worked to extinguish the fire. Books were freeze-dried, and a lot of effort went into preserving as many books and other materials as possible, but the mansion itself was unusable after the fire.

In the true spirit of Harding, the faculty and students worked together to make adjustments so that the mansion could be rebuilt. We had good insurance on the mansion and were able to restore the historic building.

The Reynolds Building

The most unusual building project of my presidency occurred when I learned of the possibility of a gift from the Donald W. Reynolds Foundation for the building of a new facility on the Harding campus. We put together a proposal for a fine arts center, including art and music, but later changed it to music and communication because the art faculty wanted to remain in their current location. The proposal was sent to the Reynolds Foundation, and they agreed to fund the project. The unusual thing about this project was that the Reynolds Foundation was the sole contributor for the project. We were required to raise twenty percent of the cost of the building for an endowment fund to be used in support of the project.

The tough decision for this project was the location of the building. We decided to build it on the south side of the campus, but had no other academic buildings there other than the Ganus Athletic Center. I remember talking to Fred Smith, chair of the Reynolds Foundation Board, as we stood in an open field knee-deep in mud where the building was to be constructed. It was a little difficult to picture what we now know as the Reynolds Building.

As part of this project, a new south entrance was designed that connected Beebe-Capps with Park Avenue.

Art and Design Building

The Reynolds Building was originally planned as a Fine Arts Center – to house the art and music departments. As this plan developed, the art faculty expressed a desire to keep their same location in the center of the campus if an addition could be completed at a later date. With that input, we decided to include the Department of Communication with the Department of Music in the Reynolds Center.

In 1999, an addition to the Art Building provided studios for faculty members and a gallery for public display. This necessitated the removal of the old Benson house, a significant historical structure that had served as the residence of Harding's second president, Dr. George S. Benson. The house had been used for many years as office space for the Art Department. This was an extremely difficult decision, but after the involvement of numerous individuals, we made the decision to raze the Benson house to make room for badly needed space. At some point in time, I became known as a president who likes to raze buildings – a dubious title.

Rhodes Field House

One of my all-time favorite building projects during my presidency was the renovation of Rhodes Field House. This facility, which had once been home to the Harding Bisons, again became the place for volleyball and men's and women's bas-

ketball. These sports had been played in the Ganus Athletic Center for many years, but the arena was so big that the noise of the crowd got lost in space. We considered many options to remedy this situation but couldn't come up with a good solution. We knew the Ganus facility was perfect for intramural play, but we had difficulty finding a solution for these intercollegiate teams.

Finally, the decision was made to remodel Rhodes Field House, which meant going back to a facility that we had left – one that would house fewer spectators than the Ganus Athletic Center.

To maximize the number of spectators who could attend, the floor was turned from east and west to north and south so that more seats could be available. Locker rooms were added, and our first game in Rhodes was against Abilene Christian University. We lost by one point, but I remember that the gym was completely full and extremely loud. The excitement and noise level have contributed greatly to camaraderie as the student body has intensified its support of our teams. Any event in Rhodes Field House is a fun experience. It is the only building on campus to which I carry a key because I have so many requests from people to see the Rhodes Field House when they visit the campus.

Pryor/England Center for Science and Engineering Building Addition

A major addition to the Joseph E. Pryor Science Center was constructed in 2004 and again in 2008 when engineering was added to the curriculum. A three-story section was added to the existing Science Building and connected to the McInteer Center with a second-floor hallway. To build this structure in this location, we had to petition the city to close that portion of Blakeney Street, making it possible to keep the science faculty in one location, a strong preference of the faculty.

In the early stages of this project, we decided to rename the entire facility the Pryor/England Center for Science and Engineering after two distinguished pro-

fessors in science. The original building was named in honor of Dr. Joseph E. Pryor, a Harding icon who had served as a professor in science and as dean of the college for many years.

Dr. Don England was also an icon on campus. He had taught chemistry all of his life and was a dedicated Christian scientist. He had worked with many of our students who had gone on to medical school and become accomplished physicians. These students loved and admired Dr. England for his rigorous study and excellent teaching. I was delighted to see this new facility named in honor of these men.

The inscription on the hallway between the McInteer Center and the Science Center, which was selected by Dr. England, is special to us. It reads "…in whom are hidden all the treasures of wisdom and knowledge" (Col. 2:3), and signifies the role of science in a Christian center for learning.

The David B. Burks American Heritage Center includes Cone Chapel and water walls with key scriptures.

The American Heritage Center

A major part of the Strategic Plan in early 2000 was the remodeling of the American Heritage Center to serve as a convention center, with added space for dining facilities for the entire campus.

Part of the plan was to build a chapel that could be used by students for weddings and by the University for other events. One of the first decisions addressed the location for the chapel, how big to make it and how elaborate it would be. Early on, the thought was to locate the chapel in the center of the campus where it would be visible to a great many people, but there was not a good location. Consideration was given to locating it on the extreme south side of the campus next to the Reynolds Center or on the north side of the campus on Race Street. Finally, we decided to add it to the front of the American Heritage Building where it would overlook the front lawn. The design is elegant and yet simple, making it the perfect venue for many special events.

Another major consideration, from a design point of view, involved the exterior of the building. The first few designs were modern and didn't seem to fit the historic, classical nature of the quadrangle. Jimmy Cone, a board member and the contractor for the project, suggested that it look more like the Administration Building. The street was closed in front of the Heritage Building to allow only pedestrian traffic. The exterior and front view of the Heritage took on a completely new appearance as the addition stretched across the entire front of the building, presenting a brand new façade for the campus quadrangle.

The lobby, designed with two grand staircases that take people up to the chapel, was created specifically to be a visitor center for people as they arrive on campus. An extension of the building was made to the north because most visitors enter the building from Market Street.

The lobby was designed to portray the mission of Harding so visitors and guests would see Harding's emphasis when they entered the building. The main focus is a globe representing world missions and statements representing the mission of the university, along with pictures depicting major events. A special feature of the lobby are water walls on each side as you enter the building from the south side. Behind the walls of water are scriptures that read, "…the Son of man did not come to be served, but to serve, and to give His life as a ransom for many" (Matt. 20:28) and "Let us fix our eyes on Jesus, the author and perfecter of our faith" (Heb. 12:2).

The globe that sits in the middle of the lobby, depicting our commitment to world missions, was purchased from a church in Houston, painted and mounted on a table that was built by Danny DeRamus. It was constructed at about ten percent of the cost of a new one from the manufacturer.

One of the interesting memories I have relative to the design of this visitor's center addition involved a trip to Nashville to look at the Opryland Hotel, which is famous for its Christmas lights. Mike Steelman, Liz Howell, Danny DeRamus and Leah and I made the trip during the Christmas season.

One of the serendipities of that trip was to have Danny DeRamus meet with the head of facilities for the hotel to learn how they did their lighting project. We learned that L.E.D. lights take very little electricity and last much longer than regular Christmas lights. We decided to upgrade the entire quadrangle by putting electricity by all of the trees so that we could light the campus for Christmas every year, one of my favorite activities for our students and the community.

<u>Harding Folklore</u>

Of course, historical things that have always been part of the quadrangle were continued. The swings are still a staple of the Harding experience. Students still refer to "three swings and a ring" on a regular basis. I know of instances where this was literally true. Students still refer to Gertie, the ghost, who occupied the dorm for Galloway Women's College that became Pattie Cobb when Harding bought the property in 1934. She reportedly moved to the Bell Tower, the old music building and still visits around the campus from time to time.

On the sidewalk across from the front of Pattie Cobb sits the old bell tower for Galloway Women's College. According to tradition at Harding, if you walk through the bell tower alone, you are destined to be single for the rest of your life. However, if you walk under it with someone of the opposite sex, your destiny lies with him or her as a marriage partner for the rest of your life.

Scientists and researchers have varying hypotheses about a tree on the southwest corner of the front lawn that has a large bulge about nine feet off the ground. No one knows where the bulge came from, but Harding students have formed their own beliefs about the tree. The story is simple – if you touch the tree, you instantly become pregnant (There is no general consensus on what happens if a male touches the tree). One look at the tree will explain how the story arose.

If you have ever visited Harding's campus around the second week of April, you will notice that the grass goes from a dull brown color to a deep green almost overnight. Because of this phenomenon, Harding is often accused of painting the grass green for Spring Sing. While this statement is not completely true, Physical Resources does fertilize the grass in early spring each year with a fertilizer that has a greenish hue.

The Thornton Center

A growing department, the College of Education shared space in the American Studies Building with the Department of English and the College of Business for many years. The College of Business moved to its new facility in 1982, and in 2004, a special addition to the American Studies Building was constructed for the College of Education. The Department of English continued to use the third floor of the American Studies Building.

Ulrey Performing Arts Center

Drama productions were hampered because of crowded space on the second floor of the Administration Building. That space was also needed for other departments, so we decided to move Performing Arts to a new location. We were able to purchase the property that had been home to Whitaker Furniture Company on the southwest corner of the campus. We razed two of the old warehouses on the property and were able to remodel and build a new front on the main structure, which was well constructed. This project provided storage at the back for Physical Resources, space for our drama productions and a beautiful addition to that area of our campus.

The front of the building was specifically designed for the Little Theater, offices, and costume and makeup areas. We chose to name the building in honor of Dr. Evan Ulrey, who served as chairman of the Department of Communication for many years. Robin Miller and Morris Ellis assisted Mike Steelman, the architect for the construction, in designing this facility. This center is one of my favorite spots on campus because of all the activities that take place there.

North Campus Entryway

In 2007, plans were made to improve the north entrance to the campus at Grand and Race avenues. People from Harding's student body in the 70s and 80s were familiar with a bus depot and gas station on the corner of Grand and Race. Apartments and businesses lined Race Street, obstructing a view of the campus from the north.

This north entrance beautification involved a number of years and the purchase of property along Race Street so that apartments and houses could be torn down, leaving a beautiful view of the campus

from Race Street. A new entry sign was built, the boulevard was upgraded at Grand Avenue and a wrought iron fence was constructed along Race Street.

Center for Health Sciences

Also in 2007, we began planning a facility for the new Pharmacy and Physician Assistant programs. This project involved a building of more than 40,000 square feet, to be ready when the first class of Pharmacy students began in 2008.

The Swaid N. Swaid Center

One of my last projects as president was the development of the second health sciences building, named the Swaid N. Swaid Center for Health Sciences. This building houses our Nursing and Communication Sciences and Disorders programs. With the addition of a graduate program in Communication Sciences and

Disorders, the facilities they were using in the Reynolds Building were inadequate. The Nursing program, which was expanding to add graduate programs, was operating in crowded conditions in the Olen Hendrix Building.

The Swaid Center is a 45,000-square-foot facility with specialized classrooms, labs and faculty offices for both programs. Located on Park Avenue next to the Farrar Center, the two buildings are connected on the second floor by a hallway. Parking is provided on the east side of the building, completing a major redevelopment of the area on the south side of Park Avenue.

Olgesby Preaching Studio

At the heart of our College of Bible and Ministry is our goal of training preachers. After years of using a variety of facilities, we decided we needed a modern studio with updated technology for this purpose. With the help of Danny Hawk, a member of the Board of Trustees from Richardson, Texas, the Waterview congregation adopted this project and contributed to its construction. We decided to name the studio in honor of Robert Olgesby, a minister who has devoted much of his life to training young preachers. He also preached for the Waterview church for many years.

Physical Therapy

Our Physical Therapy program began in 2011 in leased facilities on the south campus of White County Hospital. This lease arrangement made it possible for us  to begin and operate this program for the first three years. We then purchased the old Doctors Building next to the south campus on Main Street and renovated it into facilities for the Physical Therapy program, including a lab for gross anatomy. This building also has space for an Occupational Therapy program, which has been approved but has not yet begun.

Northwest Arkansas Professional Center

Harding began offering business and education courses in northwest Arkansas in 2005. We leased facilities for this purpose until we built our own facilities to meet the needs of this expanding program. The professional center is located on Loop 540 in Rogers, just south of the Bentonville city limits.

Mabee Business Building

The Mabee Business Building was constructed while I was dean of the College of Business. I remember the project well because it was the first building project for which I helped with the design. In 2011, a major addition to the building was completed, adding much-needed classrooms, office space and lounge areas for a growing program that had outgrown its facilities.

Interestingly, my son, Bryan, as dean of the current College of Business Administration, was the principal designer for the remodel. It had been forty years since the original construction, but I offered to help him determine the needs for the new structure. I learned quickly that he was way ahead of me in understanding the needs for this renovation.

Other Construction Projects

Space does not permit me to mention every construction project or renovation done during my twenty-six years as president. I recall two major additions to the Hammond Student Center and Bookstore; two renovations of the Olen Hendrix

Building; renovations to Cathcart, Kendall, Sears and Stephens Halls; the addition of a dining hall at Camp Tahkodah; placement of the Muncy clock in C.L. Kay Plaza; three major additions to Harding Academy; construction of Harding Place Retirement Center; building Rodgers Research Center at the Graduate School in Memphis; and the addition of the Wellness Center in the Ganus Athletic Center.

Legacy Park

Legacy Park is a comprehensive housing project that provides space for single and married student housing. The first phase of Legacy Park was completed in 2011 and contained fifteen buildings with sixty-four apartments. Phase II, which was completed in 2013, included five additional buildings with twenty-four apartments. A unique design in student housing for Harding, Legacy Park has an urban style of classical design similar to what you would find in the Northeast. This design enabled us to create a walking neighborhood environment where houses are close to the street and to each other.

This project involved razing a number of houses that had been in this area for years. We utilized the design help of Bob Chapman and Tony Sease with T.N.D. Partners in North Carolina, who worked with Mike Steelman in the execution of this new housing development.

We considered a number of names for this housing area and finally settled on Legacy Park. It was natural for us to name each house after someone who had devoted a great amount of time and effort to make Harding University possible. Those who look at Legacy Park will find the Bales House, named in honor of Dr. and Mrs. James D. Bales, a long-time professor at Harding; a house named after S.A. Bell, a long-time teacher at Harding; and a number of missionaries who have served churches for many years. There is the Berryhill House, the Burke House, the Coleman House, the Hobby House, the Lewis House, the Maddox House, the Merritt House, the Moore House, the Pryor House, the Ritchie House, the Sawyer House, the Sears House and the Tucker House. In Phase II, five additional families were honored, including Otis and Irene Gatewood, James and Sarah Hedrick, Harry and Amanda Risinger, Myrtle Rowe and J. C. and Joyce Shewmaker.

The only Starbucks in Searcy brings students and local residents to Legacy Park often.

286

Uncle Bud

A relatively new addition to campus, a statue of Dr. Kenneth Davis sits next to the lily pond in front of the Administration Building. Over the last few years, he has posed for hundreds of pictures with students who have provided hats for him to wear, built him snowmen counterparts or attempted to mimic his ever-watchful stature. Former members of his a cappella chorus pose for pictures with him when they return for visits to campus.

A Beautiful Campus

One of the joys of my time as president was the opportunity to work with so many wonderful people in designing the facilities needed for our work. I believe we are blessed with a functional and beautiful campus.

I am especially grateful to Mike Steelman for his friendship and expertise. He was a servant first, and he was committed to the mission of Harding as he assisted us in designing these buildings and renovations.

I am also grateful to Jimmy Cone and his dad, James Cone, for their work constructing many of our buildings. They provided this service in a professional way, and with the lowest bid.

I also express thanks to Danny DeRamus, who has served as director of Physical Resources since 2001. Danny has been a joy to work with and has been extremely helpful in coordinating these projects. I also express thanks to David Kelly, who has been superintendent on many of these major projects.

The Ray Muncy Clock is the centerpiece for the C.L. Kay Plaza

PART SIX

Transition

The Board of Trustees honor the Burks at a retirement reception

CHAPTER SIXTEEN
My Last Year as President

Introduction

A presidential transition is a major change for any university, especially when someone has been in that position for a number of years. Bro. Armstrong was president for the first twelve years, and a transition took place when Dr. Benson came back from China and served for twenty-nine years. I recall the significance of the major transition that took place as he stepped down in 1965 and Dr. Ganus became president. I recall vividly the comments from students and faculty members as they wondered what the future of Harding would be like under a new president. Serving as president of the student body in 1965 gave me a particularly unique vantage point from which to view this transition and hear the concerns of students and faculty.

With that background in mind, I knew that my resignation as president would be a major period of transition for Harding once again. I anticipated that the final eighteen months of my time as president would be filled with a lot of new and challenging activities and that the pace would be demanding. It turned out to be a time of unexpected emotion as well – and completing this chapter in my life ended up being one of the most difficult times for me as president.

Preparation for Resignation

I considered the possibility of retiring at the age of sixty-five and had a discussion with various board members concerning that option in 2007. The result of that discussion was a five-year agreement with the Board of Trustees that I would continue to serve until 2013 or longer. This announcement was made by the Board, and I think really helped in terms of plans for the future. With this decision made, a new five-year strategic plan was developed and put in place.

My plan was to resign when I turned seventy and, in anticipation of this resignation, I made a presentation to the Board of Trustees at a retreat setting in Branson in July 2011 concerning the nature of the job of president at Harding. My purpose in sharing this information with them was to allow all of them to be thinking in advance about the qualities needed in this position.

I have always found it interesting that people asked what kind of work I did, with a variety of preconceived ideas in their mind. In short, it is like leading a community, mainly young students, but also faculty members, alumni, parents, donors and friends. It involves real estate of more than 250 acres of land and buildings in Searcy, North Little Rock, Bentonville and Memphis, Tenn., as well as programs in six nations around the world.

The model that is used in higher education is an ancient model that comes from the Middle Ages and includes people wearing ceremonial gowns, handing out sheepskin documents, utilizing a mace and carrying out certain academic traditions.

The job entails working with more than 6,700 students, with the majority of them living in campus housing. Harding runs a fitness center, a hotel, a number of restaurants and even a bookstore. The university also sponsors performances by musicians, and we have athletic teams that compete all over the nation. We even have a retirement center.

The president is responsible for developing an annual budget of more than $113 million, with construction costs of about $12 million annually. The University also makes the largest payroll of any organization in Searcy or White County and has a police force that carries guns. The job involves working with more than 300 faculty members, who teach many subjects, and more than 1,000 employees. It also involves a pre-kindergarten through twelfth grade program at Harding Academy, with more than 700 students.

Most of the books written to guide a university president include things like pride of the place; having the right governance to deal with faculty, staff, students, donors, alumni, trustees, parents, media, city officials and neighbors – and the ability to raise funds. Stephen Trackenberg listed luck as a major factor, saying, "Great presidents have the ability to reconcile disparate situations within the institution and to change a series of flashing lights into a steady glow."[1]

I believe that most of the books I have read on the subject miss the focus of embracing the mission of the University. This has been the major topic of discussion at Board retreats. We have talked about our passion for the mission and evangelism and the desire to be the aroma of Christ. A common goal has been to make sure that academics do not outweigh spiritual development, although both are important. I believe our Board has been able to keep this focus clearly in mind as decisions were made.

My Decision to Resign

After returning to campus for the fall semester and busying myself with the normal beginning-of-the-year activities, I found myself thinking much of the time about my decision to retire. The October board meeting was just ahead of me, and I knew I needed to make a final decision. My decision time frame had been May 2013 for about five years. As the time approached to announce my decision, I was apprehensive because we were involved in numerous projects that I knew would be difficult to complete by May 2013. Another major factor weighing on the decision was my health and time with family. I felt that I was not managing stress very well at the time. I had stopped running, and I was taking work home with me. I also felt that twenty-six years was a long time for one person to be president and that Harding could be served by someone with more energy.

As I expected, Leah was very understanding but would have been supportive of my decision, regardless of the timing involved. After talking with a few friends, I finally made the decision to announce my retirement at the Homecoming board meeting.

Announcement of Decision

I submitted my resignation to Dr. John Simmons and the Board at the October 27, 2011, meeting. In the letter I stated, "I am submitting my official resignation as president of Harding University, effective at the end of the 2012-2013 academic year. This is in keeping with the timetable that I have discussed with you and the Executive Committee of the Board for a number of years. I will be 70 in May of 2013."[2]

In that letter, I said I was grateful to the Board for the opportunity to serve in this capacity for the past twenty-four and one-half years, and that it was the greatest honor of my professional life to have been asked to serve in this capacity. I wrote that I was privileged to work with wonderful students, faculty and staff members, and I especially treasured the support of the Board during this entire period of time.

I further stated that I looked forward to the next year and a half as a busy time to complete our current five-year Strategic Plan, and that I looked forward to working with our senior staff, the Board and the entire Harding community in accomplishing as much as possible during this period of time.

I indicated that I would be praying for the members of the Search Committee and the entire Board of Trustees as they went about the process of selecting the next president. I closed the letter by stating that I believe God has blessed our work at Harding, and I am confident that He will continue to do so as we make this transition and move forward.

I am grateful that the Board talked to me about becoming chancellor after my retirement as president. Dr. Ganus had talked to me personally, saying that he wanted to resign as chancellor and hoped I would be willing to serve in that capacity. I was very grateful that they were willing to give me this opportunity so I could continue my involvement with Harding.

My plan was to resign at the October meeting and allow the board to work on a procedure to make the formal announcement of my resignation at commencement in May. Doubting that the announcement could be kept confidential, the resignation was made public at the Black and Gold Banquet the day I submitted it.

Role of Trustees

The Board of Trustees quickly entered into their task of finding a new president for Harding. At the October board meeting, they discussed appointing a search committee and the procedure they would use. They agreed on a computer Web site as the primary means for members of the Harding family and others to send in names and qualifications of candidates they wished to have considered. A list of qualifications was prepared and approved by the entire board, who then invited people to submit their recommendations.

The Board met again in the summer of 2012, in a retreat setting in Branson, specifically to talk about the selection of the next president.

I talked to the Board about the presidential transition and recommended that we appoint a transition team to handle many of the responsibilities that naturally occur in this kind of change. Immediately, a communication team was appointed with Dr. Larry Long as chair, which was critical to providing a point of reference on campus for communication to take place. Included in the discussions were a support network and plans for arrival of the new president.

I also discussed with the Board the completion of the Strategic Plan for 2013-2018. Work had begun on this in the fall of 2012, beginning with the fall Pre-Session Conference. Included in the effort was an assessment of Harding and its strengths and weaknesses as viewed by the Cabinet and the Harding family. The Cabinet was also charged with producing a written report for the new president regarding future challenges. I wanted to make sure the new president would be able to influence the plan.

Final Year Activities

One of the major goals for the final year was to work effectively with the Board and transition team to provide a smooth and meaningful presidential transition. Dr. Long provided effective leadership for the campus community as he served as the liaison between the Board and many constituencies, keeping them informed as to the board's progress. Will Waldron, S.A. president, served an important role in communicating with students concerning the process. He was a member of the transition team.

I also used this last year as an opportunity to make presentations in chapel as I reflected on the events of the preceding twenty-six years. I tried to use these presentations to help students and the Harding community understand some of the challenges we face at Harding, and I was hopeful that these presentations helped to prepare the entire campus community for new leadership under a new president.

One of the objectives during this year was the construction of a new Health Sciences Building to house our Nursing and Communication Sciences and Disorders programs. This was a major project that involved all the normal kinds of planning that goes into any such construction effort. The faculty was heavily involved in creating the plans for the building, and they worked closely with the architect. Equipment had to be determined and ordered, and the building had to be built.

A primary concern involved fundraising, a major effort for this $9 million project. Construction started at the beginning of my last year and was completed in time for students when they arrived in 2013.

Another important discussion focused on a facility for Physical Therapy, which was in need of adequate facilities, including an anatomy lab. A facility was purchased south of campus, and it was renovated for their needs. This construction project was completed in time for the students to move into it in the fall of 2013.

Other construction projects underway during that year, including fundraising, were the soccer field house, a new baseball facility for batting practice, renovations to Allen Hall, construction of thirty-two new Legacy Apartments in five buildings, and building a new facility for our professional programs in Rogers, Ark.

We were also involved in planning an addition to the Science Building to include additional laboratory space because of the growing enrollment in the health sciences. A $3 million addition was planned during the spring of 2013 so that it could be built during the 2013-14 year.

A major curriculum study during this year was the consideration of new graduate degrees for the Carr College of Nursing. Work was finalized during the academic year to approve three new graduate degrees in nursing.

A feasibility study during that last year was done to explore the need for adding Occupational Therapy. The study was completed, a report was made to the Board, and they approved offering a master's degree in Occupational Therapy as soon as possible.

In addition to these academic and construction projects, we were determined to complete as many other pieces of the Five-Year Strategic Plan as possible. Wrapping up the goals to be realized for this last year was especially challenging in light of all the transition activities.

Board Announcement

The board met at its semi-annual meeting in October 2012, and made the decision, one year from the date of my announcement, as to who the next president of Harding would be. The announcement was made the following week.

On November 1, 2012, Dr. John Simmons, chairman of the Board of Trustees, announced in a meeting at 1:30 p.m. in Cone Chapel, that Dr. Bruce McLarty, vice president for spiritual life at Harding, had been named president of Harding, effec-

tive June 2013. Dr. Simmons was speaking as chairman of the Board and as chairman of the six-member Presidential Succession Process Committee that had created and executed the plan to allow the entire board to review all applications from candidates for the position.

Commenting on the McLarty's selection, Simmons said,

We are very pleased to announce that Dr. Bruce McLarty will be the next president of Harding University. The Board of Trustees had the privilege of working with an outstanding pool of applicants for what I consider to be one of the best jobs in the world. Harding's president gets to work with our faculty, staff and wonderful students who continue to choose to come to Harding for their education, spiritual growth and maturation.

Dr. McLarty is a leader, not in the mold of a typical C.E.O. or academician, but he is a servant leader with a very bright mind, a keen insight into people and the ability to communicate effectively. He brings energy and a clear vision of the mission of Harding to the table, and he will be an effective leader as our fifth president.

Just as Dr. George S. Benson was different from J.N. Armstrong, Dr. Clifton L. Ganus Jr. from Dr. Benson and Dr. David Burks from

Dr. Ganus, Dr. McLarty will be different from Dr. Burks. He will leave his unique and positive imprint on Harding just as his predecessors have done. All have served well in their time, and we are fully confident that Dr. McLarty will attain the same standard of leadership they did. He is the right man for this time.[3]

I said at that time that I had great confidence in Dr. McLarty and I believed he would be an outstanding president for Harding University. I stated that he had a very solid grasp of the spiritual mission of Harding and had written about it, helping the faculty and staff to understand this powerful mission. I further stated that he had been a valuable member of my administrative team for the past seven years. I affirmed that he had a valuable background as a pulpit minister, teacher, dean and vice president for spiritual life, all which would benefit him as he assumed this new role. I concluded by stating that I looked forward to working with him for the next seven months as he would assume the position in June. I believe he is a man of deep spiritual commitment who possesses impeccable integrity. His wife, Ann, will also be a great support for him.

While most comments from the Harding family were positive regarding his selection and Harding's mission, I was disappointed – even heartbroken – over some negative comments shared on blogs by some extremely vocal members of our family. I know we will not always agree on decisions that are made, but I have always taken the position that I would support decisions made by those in authority unless the decision violates my conscience.

I continue to pray for unity for the Harding family. I continue to love and appreciate all members of our wonderful family.

Working with Dr. McLarty

It was a pleasure to work with Dr. McLarty in an intentional way to involve him in all the decisions handled by the office of president. I tried to involve him in every decision that had a major consequence from November 1 until June 1 when he would become president. We made a number of trips together and spoke on numerous occasions to the Harding family. He went with me to the National Association of Independent Colleges and Universities meetings in Washington, D.C., and I enjoyed introducing him to friends with whom I had worked for years in this organization. He assisted with the planning of the addition to the science building, which was essentially solidified during the spring semester. We worked together to prepare the budget to be submitted to the Board in May for his first year in office. It was a very busy time for both of us.

END-OF-YEAR SPECIAL EVENTS

Chapel Service

The transition committee planned a number of events to mark the end of my time as president. The Harding family was overly kind to me, and I assure you that I would have preferred less attention, but we were grateful for the kindness ex-

Dr. Burks is surrounded by family during a special chapel service in his honor near the end of the spring semester.

pressed. The chapel service dedicated to me in May was very special. A wonderful part of the chapel service was that our grandsons, Carter, Weston and Caden, led the devotional that day. I might be a little biased, but I think they did a good job of leading us on that day. I appreciated the comments shared by Dr. Larry Long in his presentation on behalf of the faculty and administration. I also appreciated the presentation of the Bison in the lobby of the Benson, with the plaque honoring my service at Harding. I was unaware of that project from the beginning. Thanks to the donors who made this possible.

A.W.H. Luncheon

I especially appreciated the Associated Women for Harding honoring Leah for her service as First Lady. They presented a First Ladies Garden to honor Leah, Louise Ganus and Ann McLarty. Our oldest son, Bryan, spoke to A.W.H. that day on behalf of the family regarding Leah's influence during the twenty-six years. He described his mother as one who preferred to avoid the spotlight but who was willing to stand beside her husband – whose position put him in the spotlight every day.

Truly, Mom's commitment to family caused her to live in a fish-bowl for twenty-six years. To understand the view from the fishbowl, you must first understand the fishbowl, which was built in Harding Park. It had to have a big sewing room because she enjoys sewing. It had to have a garden room for flowers. Most importantly, it had to have a back yard to plant flowers and a small garden. The sunroom was full of plants, and the little shed in the back yard had a heater to keep its plants safe in the winter because – in that fishbowl was a master gardener who loves God's beautiful creation.

Mom loves her dog. I have said many times that only God and grandchildren come before this dog. I know my place. Inside the fishbowl was a woman whose love for animals brought much plea-sure and companionship.

In the fishbowl was a woman who truly loves people. Mom was a schoolteacher early in her career. She was a club sponsor for many years. Her hospitality brought many overnight guests and friends, and she hosted numerous receptions in her home. She worked closely with the Associated Women for Harding and was known for her creative and artistic flair in preparing desserts and entrees. Whether there was a reception, a church function or loss of a family member, she was always present with food she had pre-pared well.

A crucial part of Mom's life in the fishbowl was precious family time. We have been blessed to be able to raise our children in the same hometown as their grandparents.

Inside the fishbowl was a fighter who fought cancer multiple times and came out victorious.

Finally, in the fishbowl was a woman who, throughout all of her years of service, always kept God first. A woman who fears the Lord is to be praised; she not only knew God's word but lived it out as a virtuous woman.

Community Reception

I also appreciated the community reception, organized by Jim Carr and Reynie Rutledge. I appreciated the community leaders who attended. I was particularly encouraged by the attendance of Gov. Mike Beebe, who has been a friend to Harding all of these years.

S.A. Luau

I also appreciated the Student Association having a luau on the front lawn for students to honor Dr. Ganus for his service as chancellor and me for my service as president. I loved the letters presented to me from my time as S.A. president in 1964-65. I couldn't imagine that they still existed. I particularly appreciated the sentiments expressed on the cards presented to us at that time.

Last Day of Chapel

The last day of chapel was a very emotional day for me. Will Waldron described the event from his perspective –

> One memory that will be forever ingrained in my memory comes from the last day in chapel for Dr. Burks as president. Since it was the last day of the semester before finals, there were several items on the agenda. After the devotional, I officially passed off the  S.A. gavel to Tyler Gentry, who was to take my place after commencement. Then, after a few more points on the schedule and singing "The Lord Bless You and Keep You" to the seniors, Dr. Burks stood up to say his final goodbye. While both chapels were extremely emotional, the 9 a.m. chapel was particularly difficult. What I remember most is that I, standing behind him, was brought to tears to see Dr. Burks struggle to say goodbye. After he said "thank you" to all, he turned around, looked at me and we hugged. I don't think I had ever hugged Dr. Burks before, but that was all we could think to do in that moment. Neither of us had the words to say, so we simply found each other in embrace. When we let go and he turned to face the audience, and for only the second time since I'd been at Harding, I found the audience of students was giving him a resounding standing ovation. Not only that, but the students who were accustomed to leaving as soon as chapel was over stayed to applaud their president, who means so much to us all.

> As I recounted the chapel later with some of my fellow students, the general consensus was that there were no words to describe the chapel, but many found it tear-jerking.

I had not anticipated that this chapel would be so emotional. I just wanted it to be an ordinary chapel day to honor our graduating seniors. Because this was the last time I would say as president, "You are dismissed," I found this to be an unusually difficult task. I did not realize just how much my life was tied up in presiding over chapel. Making this statement for the last time – I think I will remember that moment for the rest of my life.

Board of Trustees Dinner

I still find it hard to describe the dinner given for Leah and me by the Board of Trustees. Roy Reaves, a long-time board member, made these observations –

The most powerful memory I have of David Burks as Harding University president came at the end of the Board of Trustees dinner in his honor. For the most part, the evening was light-hearted, as many of Dr. Burks' friends offered their remarks to him. Throughout the evening, several of his friends made jokes at his expense, but I don't think he would have preferred it any other way. Finally, the chairman of the Board, Dr. John Simmons, stood up to announce gifts that the board was presenting to Dr. Burks.

The first was a check that we had provided for his retirement. Dr. Burks smiled heartily and thanked us for the gift. However, the

304

Board's next gift was the truly remarkable presentation. Dr. Simmons said, "Dr. Burks, this check is not all we have to thank you tonight." He then announced that the Board was renaming the American Heritage Building in his honor. As Dr. Simmons spoke, Liz Howell presented Dr. Burks with an artist's rendering of Cone Chapel with the new name inscribed on the front. I do not recall ever seeing someone's emotions go from lighthearted joy to inexpressible gratitude so quickly. The expression on his face said all that his words were unable to say as tears streamed down his face. He turned to Leah and held her close.

He had built his presidency around furthering the mission of
Harding University – and now he was to be forever synonymous
with the building that visually represents that mission.

I appreciated the comments from the board members that evening. Leah and

I appreciated the gift presented to us, and we were overwhelmed with the naming of the Heritage building in my honor.

I was also glad that Claudette Bratcher and Cindy Hunter were honored that evening. I cannot express how valuable these two women have been to me and to Harding over these twenty-six years.

Commencement

Commencement followed the next week, and the transition committee had asked me to speak. I expressed thanks for the privilege of working with our trustees, faculty, staff, alumni, parents and college administrators, but I said in the introduction that the greatest joy of my presidency was working with the students and living out the camaraderie that was part of life at Harding University. I loved seeing them in Spring Sing, I loved seeing them on the athletic field, I loved Home-

coming musicals and I loved all kinds of activities that involved students.

In the message to the graduates, I said, "Only one thing matters because all of our efforts to be Harding are melded together in loving God, sharing Christ, living in the Spirit and reaching out to others with His love." I made reference to the late Batsell Barrett Baxter, who wrote an article several years ago, entitled "The Pow-

306

er of High Expectations."[4] In it, he made reference to John 1:42, where Andrew brought his brother, Simon, to Jesus. Simon possessed the qualities of instability and change that are seen in the biblical description of his behavior from time to time. But Jesus had high expectations for Simon. When he first met Simon, he said, "Thou art Simon, the son of John; thou shalt be called Cephas or Peter" – a new name that means "rock or stone" – a meaning that was to serve as a guiding force in his life from that point forward. We can see that he did gradually grow from an unpredictable young man into the rock that we read about in Acts and 1 Peter (his own account). Christ's high expectation helped this young man grow into a great leader.

I shared some high expectations for the graduates, and I shared four P's for success – preparation, passion, prayer and priorities. I noted that students had received marvelous preparation from a marvelous faculty and suggested that they were ready to make a difference in this world. In terms of passion, I suggested that they would really make a difference in this world if they gave their very best effort. A minimum effort is never enough. I emphasized that graduates needed to do that which they were passionate about because that is the only way they could make a difference. In terms of prayer, I talked about the influence of Jim Bill McInteer and the fact that he was a prayer warrior. In terms of priorities, I suggested that all of us need to do that which is important, not that which is seemingly urgent, that we need to be men and women of integrity and that we need to love others above ourselves. I concluded by stating that Christ expects much of us. God created us in His own image, a compliment of tremendous proportions. He gives us complete freedom to determine the destiny of our own souls. He has warmed us with countless blessings, guided us with His holy word and trusted us to make the decision of how we will spend our lives. With this great confidence placed in us by the creator of the universe, we have great responsibilities.

I concluded by stating that I eagerly look forward to hearing of the great things our graduates will accomplish in the Lord's kingdom in their lifetimes.

Mace Exchange

After the commencement exercise, a formal ceremony of transition of the Harding University mace was explained by Dr. John Simmons and Dr. Larry Long. I presented the mace to Dr. McLarty as a symbol of the transition that would take place June 1, 2013.

Key Exchange

The last letter I wrote as president was to Dr. McLarty as I wished him great success as Harding's fifth president. I moved things out of my office so it would be ready for him on June 1. I placed the letter on his desk as I left for the key exchange, which occurred in the lobby of the American Heritage Building. This also turned out to be an emotional time as I turned over the keys of the office and the University to Dr. McLarty.

But it was also a time of great joy because I had complete faith in Dr. McLarty's understanding of the mission of Harding and his love and compassion for Harding. I knew that the transition that had begun months earlier was now complete. I knew that a wonderful person had been selected, and I felt in my heart that he would succeed in taking Harding to a new level of service in the Lord's kingdom.

Dream for Harding

As I concluded my time as president, I often thought about the dream for Harding that I had presented in my inaugural address in 1987. The dream involved a deliberate effort by all of us at Harding to continue to build a great Christian university with students who would understand their role as the aroma of Christ, regardless of their choice of major. The dream stressed Christian scholarship, caring faculty members, marvelous student services and the promotion of Christian ethics in everyday living. I dreamed of an absolutely premier Christian university.

Have we succeeded in this endeavor? I will leave that for you to decide. I know the job is not finished. I know that mistakes have been made, and we have not done all that we could have done. But I am grateful to multitudes of people who have poured out their lives to help make this dream come alive for our students. I'm grateful for continued prayers on behalf of this ministry at Harding, and I request continued prayers on its behalf. This is kingdom work – Harding is needed more now than ever in our world. I pray that Harding will always be faithful in teaching God's word.

As I walked away from that emotional key exchange on that last day, my heart was filled with gratitude for all the wonderful people who made this journey such a marvelous experience.

Dr. Burks enjoys strolling across campus during any season of the year

EPILOGUE

Since my retirement, I have often been asked about my reflections on Harding from the perspective of president for twenty-six years. Why is Harding so special for so many people all over the world? Why is the Harding experience unique? I realize there are no simple answers to these questions, but part of the answer comes from the stories shared in this book. Perhaps we have all been influenced by giants in our life who were focused on serving God and others in an ordinary – yet extraordinary way.

Before I became president, I was influenced by people in my life even though I didn't recognize their influence at the time. My family, especially my dad, is at the top of the list. Brodie Crouch, our minister and friend, introduced me to Harding. Dr. Joe Pryor epitomized Harding to me when I came as a student. Dr. Benson inspired me to dream big. Dr. Billy Ray Cox and Dr. James Hedrick profoundly influenced me in my professional development. Dr. Jimmy Carr encouraged me and led by example, as did Alan Bryan. All were giants working quietly in my life, even though I was unaware of their immense influence at the time.

I was humbled by the opportunity to serve as president and amazed at the way God worked in the process before and after the decision was made. I was grateful for the support of the Board as they empowered me while I was president. I was especially glad to get to know these men and women on a personal level.

During my first year, James Cone mentored me, which allowed me to assume responsibilities that were greater than I thought I could bear. Dr. Ganus was a rock for the institution. Lott Tucker provided daily help for me as to what I was expected to do as president and was invaluable to me as a friend. Our faculty and staff eagerly assisted with "Our Dream for the Future," which I called strategic planning. I believe the sense of camaraderie was already in place even though I hardly knew how to spell it, let alone recognize its existence.

Harding's unique mission was the center point of the strategic plan. Our goal was to create an absolutely first-rate Christian university. We were all about integrating faith, learning and living, and we were all serious about the message behind the words. I spoke more often on Harding's mission than any other topic while I was president. I loved sharing the message, "We are, at our core, a Christian university, deeply connected with churches of Christ." The response of the Harding family in our efforts to communicate our reaffirmation of this mission over many years was very strong.

At the heart of our unique mission was our effort to integrate faith into the fabric of everything that takes place at Harding. I was influenced by the preaching of Jimmy Allen, Neale Pryor, Monte Cox and others. I was influenced by student giants like B. Chris Simpson, Nathan Mellor, Steve Cloer, Justin Sims, Taylor Payne and others who led campaigns and worked with God to transform lives.

As we sought to integrate faith into the fabric of our learning, we were influenced by giants like Dr. Neale Pryor, Dr. Don England, Dr. Dean Priest, Dr. Betty Watson, Pat Rice and so many others who shared their expertise and their faith with students. God was always the center of our curriculum, and we have been blessed with colleagues who came and lived out this mission in a beautiful way.

I became a believer in international education, and it became an important part of the academic curriculum as students were able to experience other cultures as part of the learning environment. Led by giants like Dr. Don Shackelford, Dr. Jeff Hopper, Janice Bingham and many others, students' lives have literally been transformed by this experience as they traveled and studied at sites all over the world.

I was inspired by the international speakers who spoke on our campus as a regular part of our American Studies Program. What a blessing to host national leaders like Margaret Thatcher, Mikhail Gorbachev, George H. W. Bush, Sam Walton, Condoleezza Rice and so many others.

I was grateful for new academic programs that were designed and instituted, always taught from the perspective of a Christian worldview. I could see God's hand in the development of our Physician Assistant, Pharmacy and Physical Therapy programs. I was especially pleased to see new programs added in the Health Sciences because of their wonderful fit with our mission of serving others. Giants like Henry and Grace Farrar led the way by devoting their lives in service to others.

I look forward to seeing who follows in their footsteps in the years to come.

I watched as our students became giants by leading the student body in providing relief efforts in Arkansas and beyond as disasters occurred. Students like Jimmy Huff, Charlie Walker, Bryan Clifton and Will Waldron led the student body as they demonstrated to us what service is all about.

I was amazed by our student athletes who competed so well on a national stage. These students were led by Christian coaches like Ronnie Huckeba, Jeff Morgan and others. Student athletes like Weston Jamison, Kristen Celsor and Mollie Arnold performed at exceptional levels, and we rejoiced with them and loved cheering for them.

We marveled at student activities and productions as we witnessed camaraderie in action in Spring Sing, theater productions, musicals, social club activities, professional clubs, Quiz Bowl competition and so many other events.

As a result of our unique mission and the acceptance of it by a growing number of people, God blessed us with growth so that more students were able to be influenced by their own Harding experience.

Harding was blessed by generous people who believed in our mission. Giants like Bob and Sandy Brackett, May Keller, Jack Stephens and so many others allowed us to provide an affordable education for more and more students. Because of their investments, Harding enjoys a beautiful and functional campus, designed to meet their needs.

The influence of trustees was ever present, never more so than at times of transition. Where would Harding be without the influence of these largely invisible, unsung heroes of Harding? These men and women love Harding and bear a heavy responsibility for setting policy for the institution. I am thankful for spiritual giants like Paul Carter, Jim Bill McInteer, John Simmons, Russ Burcham, Pat Bell and Don Shores.

I believe all of us who have shared the Harding experience have been influenced by giants. One of the giants in my life has been Dr. Carl Mitchell. He taught me to read the Bible on a regular basis, and he encouraged me at critical times when tough decisions had to be made. He encouraged me to travel internationally. He and his wife, Frankie, were good friends, and Jesus Christ permeated every part of their lives. I am grateful for their friendship.

Family has played a key role in my life. Leah has been a special blessing. Our family has been blessed to live in Searcy and to be able to share many activities together. The most recent celebration was the marriage of our oldest granddaughter, Emily Ann Burks, to Chris Meyer. The wedding was on the front lawn with the reception in Cone Chapel overlooking the quad. What a celebration for our families as prayers were shared by the Burks and Meyer families!

Members of the Harding family – students, faculty, staff, parents, donors, community members and friends – are all special because they love God with all of their heart, mind, body and spirit. I believe they love Christ and His church. They know how to love and how to spread love. These are the giants who make up the Harding community, and their fellowship is sweet.

So why is the Harding experience unique? The answer lies in the people. Harding University would not be who it is without the godly people who seek to follow His will. For several years of my presidency, I called this camaraderie or "high spirited fellowship."

In recent years, I have called this fellowship, which we enjoy at Harding – a foretaste of heaven itself. Camaraderie is really the process of developing lasting, eternal, forever relationships. And as I have said often in chapel, let's all meet on the northeast corner of heaven when the roll is called up yonder.

Leah Burks and Ann McLarty share the moment with their husbands as the president's office keys are passed from Dr. Burks to Dr. McLarty the afternoon before Dr. McLarty moves in to the president's office in the David Burks American Heritage Center.

Harding Academy provides Christian education for kids of all ages

APPENDIX A

Harding Academy

Introduction

I love Harding Academy. It is a wonderful Christian Academy, with its unique spirit and traditions. While this book addresses my leadership in higher education at Harding University, my responsibilities as president included oversight of the work at Harding Academy. I loved working with the faculty and staff and the marvelous learning experience they provided their students.

Wildcat Spirit

At Harding University, everything is black and gold. At Harding Academy, everything is red and white. At Harding University, camaraderie rules the day. At Harding Academy, Wildcat spirit represents the essence.

Will Frances was one of those Wildcats – and in fact, had been a Wildcat since pre-school when he graduated in 2013. He is quoted in the yearbook in his senior year – "Harding [Academy] is a place like no other. The influence of my teachers, coaches and friends has made me a better man of God and has prepared me for the rest of my life."

Will was active in many organizations, but he was particularly gifted in athletics. The football team, basketball team and baseball team his senior year won state championships. Will was the most valuable player in football and basketball. Since graduation, he has continued his education on a basketball scholarship at Harding University. His parting advice to students was, "The quicker you make Jesus Christ your number one priority in your life, the more joy and peace you will have each and every day." Will Francis was a great example of the Wildcat spirit.

The Wildcat spirit can be seen on the football field, in the gym, in the class-room, when the chorus sings and on numerous mission trips. It is pervasive to the Academy and to all activities at the Academy. It began with teachers like Ed Higginbotham, Katherine Ritchie, Bill Diles, Lois Lawson, Bill Barden, Randy Lambeth, Treva Pryor and a host of other people who were the role models for these young Wildcats. This, indeed, is a special place that we call Harding Academy.

Ed Higginbotham

Coach Ed Higginbotham was superintendent when I became president in 1987. Harding Academy enrolled 428 students in kindergarten through twelfth grades, with thirty-six faculty members, twenty-six of these being fulltime. Harding Academy graduated fifty-three seniors in 1988. Carla Olree and Jill Smith were honor graduates.

After four years, in May of 1991, Coach Ed decided to step down as superintendent and left me with the important decision of selecting a new individual to lead the Academy. Coach Ed had served Harding Academy for thirty-one years. He came to the Academy in 1960 as a teacher of Bible and American History and as a coach in football and basketball. I remember the feelings of surprise and sadness that flowed through the halls when they received the news of his resignation. He stated in the *Wildcat News* in May of 1991, "I think this is the best school in the world, and I want my grandchildren to attend here." He assumed a position at the University after stepping down at the Academy.

He reflected on his experience there –

The time is late August 1960, my first year as teacher/coach at Harding Academy and the first day of school. The place is the old Harding Academy building – the gray, cinder-block building that stands where the Mabee Business Building will one day stand. First period class has just been dismissed, and everyone is walking down the hall toward the auditorium for chapel. I fall in beside Ted Lloyd, talking to him as we walk. He ignores me – and as I continue to talk, he whispers, "Shhh; we don't talk on the way to chapel." That's when I realized that I was the only one in the hall who was talking.

318

*I later learned that when the bell sounds to end first period
class, students and faculty leave their books and materials on their
desks and proceed quietly to chapel – no talking, no laughing, no
locker doors slamming – no noise. Everyone moves quietly to his/
her chapel seat and prepares to worship. This is a beautiful thing
to see every morning; it is especially impressive to visitors, who
usually marvel at the self-discipline of the students. This is one of
my favorite memories of Harding Academy, and it is a tradition that
I hope is carried into the future.*

Randy Lambeth

The Academy was fortunate to have an individual serving as elementary
principal and director of Camp Tahkodah who could step up and become the new
superintendent. Randy Lambeth was selected for this position in late May of 1991.
He had demonstrated a real love for the Academy and its mission. In a statement of
philosophy given to me in May 1991, Randy said,

> *The concept of the Christian academy is a very important con-
> cept. It is the idea of putting a sound educational experience in the
> setting of the Christian environment. The moment that other parts of
> the program overshadow the Christian environment and direction,
> we need to close the doors. For this reason, we want to keep many
> of the traditions and guiding principles at the forefront as we look at
> ways to strengthen the support programs.*

During his tenure as superintendent, the Strategic Plan called for improving
faculty salaries to bring them up to a par with other Christian academies and public
schools in the surrounding area. Salaries were increased at a higher rate during this
time at the Academy than at the University to help achieve this goal.

In 1992, students went to New York City to sing at Carnegie Hall the first
time, and they have continued this tradition to the present. A significant improvement for the Academy was the establishment of the Early Learning Center in 1994.
Six teachers were hired and an addition to the building was put in place at a cost

of $200,000 to make possible a pre-school program. In 1995, for the first time, two kindergarten classes were offered.

Construction of a new gymnasium was completed and named in honor of long-time supporter, Bill Harris. This allowed the Academy to have their own gym, which helped alleviate practice conflicts with the University and gave them a place of their own for basketball games.

During the 1996-97 year, a decision was made by the University in conjunction with the Academy to raise tuition discounts from fifty percent to seventy-five percent for faculty and staff members who had children attending the Academy. This significant change was made to assist faculty and staff members financially with the option to enroll their children in the Academy.

In 1997, long-time head football coach Bill Barden made the decision to step down after more than 200 victories. Coach Barden had won three state championships and was literally a legend in Arkansas high school football coaching circles. In my judgment, he had a tremendous influence on the Academy and in the lives of the young men who played for him. I will always be indebted to him for his positive spiritual influence on so many students, including our two sons, Bryan and Stephen.

I noted in the Report to the President in 1997 the following statement, "We have made six trips to the church building in the last month to baptize students, plus several have responded at meetings and camp." That sentence seems like an unusual statement, but really it is at the heart of the work at Harding Academy. You can find these statements in all of the annual reports.

<u>Mark Benton</u>

In 1999, Randy Lambeth resigned to move to the University to pursue a career in athletic training, and Mark Benton was selected to become the new superintendent. Mark had served as the high school principal and as a coach. One of the first changes that Mr. Benton made was the establishment of an everyday chapel for elementary students.

In the 2001 Report to the President, the statement was made that more than thirty students were baptized and 135 students requested prayers during the year.

That particular year began with an area-wide youth retreat on the Academy campus, which focused on prayer.

Because of enrollment growth, two portable buildings for classrooms were added on the elementary side in 2001. Harding Academy athletic teams continued to do well, reaching the state level in competition almost every year. In 2003, they were state champions in football and conference champions in basketball.

The Academy continued to do well academically. The average A.C.T. score in 2004 was 24.1, while the state average was 20.4. The unique part about this average score is the fact that all Academy students take the test, which is not true in all schools.

Spiritual values continued to be emphasized during this entire time under Mark's leadership, and in 2006, twenty-two students went to Mexico for a spring break trip, and eighteen students went to Cancun. In 2007, elementary students adopted the Village of Hope in Ghana, West Africa, and the high school sent forty percent of the entire student body on mission trips.

James Simmons

In 2009, after the resignation of Mark Benton, James Simmons was selected as the new superintendent. James had previously served as an adjunct professor at the University for the College of Education and had been a superintendent in Conway Public Schools.

In 2010, a major addition for Harding Academy was made on the high school side that included renovation of the auditorium, enlarging the cafeteria, a new elementary art room and the addition of eight classrooms on the high school side next to Harris Gym. Much of the fundraising work had been done for this during the preceding two years. The auditorium was named in honor of long-time high school principal, Bill Diles, and his wife, Billie.

As part of the academic emphasis at the Academy, a number of junior and senior students were encouraged to take dual credit classes at the University, and forty-three students took ninety-nine classes during the 2012-13 academic year. Mandarin Chinese was offered for the first time at the Academy in 2012. The rookie year for Harding Academy's robotic team was also 2012, with Brian Jones as coach. They won Rookie All-Star that year and a trip to the world competition.

In 2012-13, enrollment at the Academy reached 684 students, with a faculty and staff of seventy people. The average A.C.T. score for students that year was 24.9. Teams won state championships in football, boys' basketball, baseball and girls' track, proving it an exceptional school for athletic competition as well.

Record of Success

The most recent accreditation report for Harding Academy came in the spring of 2011 when the nine-member team of professional educators from public and private school districts in four states reviewed Harding Academy, representing NCA CASI, AdvancED, the Arkansas Non-Public Accrediting Association and the National Christian School Association. During the visit, members of the team interviewed administrators, teachers, support staff, parents, students and University board members. They also interviewed school stakeholders and observed classrooms and documents related to student performance data. Their report noted that Harding Academy has a shared stakeholder purpose and that the school community embraces and lives its mission as a faith-based, close-knit family committed to a strong Christian education and a nurturing Christ-centered atmosphere. It concluded that Harding has a strong partnership with the University. The Academy was commended for promoting a spiritual, academic, social and physical climate that incorporates the components of the school's mission throughout the school community.

During the past three years, ninety-four percent of Harding Academy graduates have moved directly into a four-year college, with eighty-two percent choosing to attend Harding University. The record of service from these graduates at Harding University, as well as in their work in the community, is exemplary.

United Front

One of the items mentioned by the accreditation review team that was here in 2011 was the strong relationship of the Academy with the University. A reference was made to students taking dual credit classes and sharing use of athletic fields, and to cooperation between the Academy and the University in general. I believe this is an important evaluation because it represents one of the real strengths of Harding Academy. Harding Academy is important for the University, and the University is important for the Academy.

There is a tendency in some parts of the country to separate the university setting from an academy setting and to create a separate administrative structure for each. This has been done in many cities with limited success. Searcy is a small community, and the overlapping of parents and students between the University and the Academy is such that creating a separate structure for each would be nearly impossible. I believe we have the best of both worlds by having a close communication and tie between the Academy and the University.

The seventy-five percent discount, which is offered to faculty and staff members of the University so their children can attend the Academy, makes it possible for children to participate in this special experience. The facilities make it more efficient to operate both programs. The opportunity to share information at a collegiate level is an important part of the growth process. While there will always be a significant difference between a high school curriculum and a university curriculum, there is commonality in terms of the basic mission, vision and purposes of these institutions.

Whether students are in a pre-kindergarten program, an elementary program, a secondary program, an undergraduate program or an advanced doctoral or professional degree program, our purpose is essentially the same – to make it possible for students to see the value of following Jesus Christ in everything they do. I believe our united front in working together between the University and the Academy is a significant strength for us. The Academy is indeed a very special place, and so is the University. Together, they are stronger than they would be separately.

I am grateful to the many teachers who have sacrificed to make Harding Academy possible. I am grateful to Coach Ed, Bill Diles, Bill Barden, Randy Lambeth, James Simmons, Craig Jones and a host of other individuals who have made Harding Academy such a positive experience. They are the individuals who, in working with our students, have created the Wildcat spirit. Check out the Academy – you will feel the Wildcat spirit.

APPENDIX B

The Mission of Harding University

The following statement of Mission was adopted by the Harding University Board of Trustees in May 2008 and reaffirmed in May 2011.

Harding University was founded in 1924 upon spiritual convictions. We are, at our core, a Christian university. The character, example and concerns of Jesus Christ are the standards that shape us and chart the course for our future. Because of this, an all-encompassing love for God and a corresponding love for people are at the heart of who we are.

We are committed to retaining the Christian identity of Harding University. Realizing that there is a powerful, almost overwhelming tendency for Christian institutions to drift toward secularism, we recommit ourselves at this time to the distinctive practices that have always been central to Harding's Christian mission: required Bible classes, daily chapel and a lofty code of behavior for the board, administration, faculty and students.

For many years it has been our motto that Harding University integrates and celebrates "faith, learning and living." The Christian worldview is to be at the core of every academic discipline and every extracurricular activity on campus. Every professor who stands in front of a class, every coach who stands in front of a team and every director who stands in front of a cast or a chorus is to speak and lead as a man or woman of God. They are to confess, both in words and actions, that God created the world, that He redeems us through the blood of His Son Jesus, that He fills his children with His Holy Spirit and that He calls us to be holy as He is holy. Such core themes will be emphasized in chapel services, in faculty meetings and throughout the University.

The gospel of John states that "the Word became flesh and lived for a while among us. We have seen His glory, the glory of the one and only Son who came from the Father, full of grace and truth" (John 1:14). Grace and truth were perfectly blended in Jesus. He spoke truth but always in a gracious way. He extended His hand in grace but never betrayed the truth in doing so. However, Christians constantly struggle to demonstrate that same sacred balance. Gracious people are easily tempted to compromise truth, and truth-seeking people often communicate ungraciousness. Recognizing this challenge, we are determined to be a people who are "full of grace and truth," sacrificing neither in the pursuit of both. Cheap grace and harsh truth are two extremes we will seek to avoid. Our hope is that when people think of Harding University, they will think of both grace and truth.

Another important aspect of our institutional identity is our belief in the Bible as the fully inspired and authoritative word of God. We hold it to be "God-breathed" and the basis of our teaching and life. The Bible is central to our goal of spiritual formation in the life of everyone at Harding. Consequently, it is our goal that every graduating senior leave our university with a greater level of confidence in Scripture than they had when they first arrived on campus.

Harding University has always been a leader in world missions. Nearly one-third of the missionaries who have gone out from churches of Christ have graduated from Harding. We believe that, at this critical point in history, it is important that we renew our commitment to participate fully in the mission of God, both at home and abroad. While the pluralism of our postmodern culture denies the need to preach the gospel, we continue to believe that salvation is found only in Jesus Christ and that Christians are to "go and make disciples of all nations" (Matthew 28:19).

Harding has always been deeply connected with churches of Christ, and we reaffirm this connection. Our goal will be to continue to hire only members of churches of Christ as faculty and administrators. Though we live in a time of significant confusion over our brotherhood's identity, we are determined that Harding University will become captive to neither a rigid legalism on the right nor a formless liberalism on the left. "With gentleness and respect" (1 Peter 3:16) we affirm on this occasion such distinctive convictions of the mainstream churches of Christ as baptism for the remission of sins, a cappella music in worship and male spiritual leadership.

While we maintain our close ties with the churches of Christ, we make clear that Harding opens her arms to all. Those who do not share all of our convictions are always welcome, and we will work hard to see that they are always treated with kindness, fairness and respect.

This Statement of Mission is presented, and we offer it to God with the words of our Lord, Jesus: "Father, not [our] will, but yours be done" (Luke 22:42).

APPENDIX C

American Studies Institute
Lecture Series History

1987-2013

Feb. 26, 1987	Gene Stallings	April 25, 1991	Khalil Jahshan
Oct. 20, 1987	Zig Ziglar	Sept. 26, 1991	Benazir Bhutto
Feb. 9, 1988	Thomas Sowell	Oct. 8, 1991	Dr. Tony Alessandra
Feb. 16, 1988	Ken Blanchard	Nov. 14, 1991	Eugene McCarthy
April 19, 1988	John Naisbitt		James Watt
Sept. 15, 1988	Og Mandino	Dec. 10, 1991	Alexander Akhtyrsky
Sept. 19, 1988	William Bennett	Feb. 27, 1992	Dr. Alan Keyes
Oct. 7, 1988	Dr. Kenneth Cooper	March 24, 1992	Barbara Sanfilippo
Nov. 29, 1988	Jack Shewmaker	April 21, 1992	Admiral Stansfield Turner
Feb. 6, 1989	Fran Tarkington	Oct. 8, 1992	Robert D. Novak
Feb. 24, 1989	Philip B. Crosby		Bob Beckel
March 28, 1989	David Eisenhower	Nov. 19, 1992	Jim Cathcart
April 13, 1989	Robert Bork	Feb. 4, 1993	Paul Craig Roberts
Sept. 28, 1989	Dr. Dennis Waitley	Feb. 12, 1993	Sidney Moncrief
Oct. 12, 1989	Frank Carlucci	Feb. 25, 1993	Gerald W. Ebker
Oct. 23, 1989	John Akers	March 25, 1993	Cal Thomas
Nov. 6, 1989	Tommy Robinson	April 15, 1993	Brian Bex
Feb. 20, 1990	Dr. John Lee	April 29, 1993	Jim Burnett
March 22, 1990	Ken Adelman	Sept. 7, 1993	George R. Walther
April 2, 1990	Ken Hatfield	Sept. 21, 1993	Michael Medved
April 26, 1990	Edmin Meese III	Nov. 4, 1993	Dick Cheney
Sept. 4, 1990	Brian Tracy	Feb. 8, 1994	James Humes
Sept. 24, 1990	Howard Baker Jr.	March 24, 1994	Fred Barnes
Oct. 15, 1990	Admiral William Crowe	April 14, 1994	Dan Quayle
Oct. 30, 1990	Robert Jones, M.D.	Sept. 20, 1994	Rob Bremer
Nov. 29, 1990	Dr. Bill Cox	Oct. 13, 1994	Dr. George Lebo
Feb. 26, 1991	Dith Pran	Nov. 8, 1994	Malcolm Forbes Jr.
March 21, 1991	Harvey MacKay	Feb. 7, 1995	Count Hubert de Germiny
April 2, 1991	William Buckley Jr.	April 28, 1995	Lady Margaret Thatcher

Sept. 19, 1995	Jack Kahl	Sept. 20, 2005	Gracia Burnham
Oct. 12, 1995	John H. Sununu	Nov. 3, 2005	Scott Waddle
Jan. 25, 1996	Ron Townsend	Feb. 14, 2006	Jose Maria Aznar
Feb. 29, 1996	Lynne Cheney	April 27, 2006	Zell Miller
April 25, 1996	Brian Mulroney	Sept. 21, 2006	Sean Hannity
Sept. 19, 1996	Captain Scott O'Grady	Nov. 9, 2006	Don Soderquist
Oct. 15, 1996	Congressman Tim Hutchinson	Feb. 27, 2007	Janice Rogers Brown
Jan. 30, 1997	Governor Mike Huckabee	March 20, 2007	Dr. Inonge Mbikusita-Lewanika
Feb. 25, 1997	Gary L. Baur		
April 24, 1997	George Bush	April 26, 2007	Vicente Fox
Sept. 25, 1997	Armstrong Williams	Sept. 11, 2007	LTC Steve Russell
Feb. 5, 1998	Linda Chavez	Sept. 27, 2007	Levy Mwanawasa
March 3, 1998	Bobby Bowden	Nov. 8, 2007	Herman Cain
April 16, 1998	Lamar Alexander	Feb. 12, 2008	David Barton
Oct. 15, 1998	Mikhail Gorbachev	March 13, 2008	Fred Gray
March 25, 1999	John Major	April 24, 2008	Steve Forbes
April 22, 1999	Dr. James Dobson	Sept. 23, 2008	Dinesh D'Souza
Sept. 7, 1999	Rep. Asa Hutchinson	Nov. 13, 2008	Truett Cathy
Oct. 7, 1999	Heather Whitestone McCallum	Feb. 10, 2009	Ben Stein
Nov. 9, 1999	Dr. Leland R. Kaiser	Sept. 17, 2009	Nonie Darwish
Feb. 8, 2000	Governor Frank Keating	Nov. 12, 2009	Cynthia Cooper
March 7, 2000	Lech Walesa	Feb. 16, 2010	Laura Ingraham
Oct. 24, 2000	Colin Powell	April 22, 2010	George W. Bush
Feb. 13, 2001	Houston Nutt	Sept. 7, 2010	General Richard Myers
April 19, 2001	Judge Kenneth W. Starr	Oct. 5, 2010	Bob Beckel & Cal Thomas
Oct. 30, 2001	Randall Mott	Feb. 17, 2011	Tommy Tuberville
Jan. 22, 2002	General Wesley K. Clark	April 7, 2011	Steve Forbes
April 11, 2002	Barbara Bush	Oct. 6, 2011	Richard Picciotto
Sept. 12, 2002	Walter E. Williams	Nov. 10, 2011	Paul Sperry
Nov. 14, 2002	Dinesh D'Souza	Feb. 2, 2012	Dr. Victor D. Hanson
March 6, 2003	Khalil E. Jahshan	April 19, 2012	Dr. Condoleezza Rice
April 3, 2003	William J. Bennett	Sept. 20, 2012	Star Parker
Sept. 23, 2003	Asa Hutchinson	Oct.16, 2012	Karl Rove
Nov. 17, 2003	Jim Ryun	Feb. 7, 2013	Stephen Moore
Feb. 5, 2004	Deena Burnett	March 5, 2013	Mike Beebe
April 22, 2004	General Tommy Franks	April 25, 2013	Bill Simon
Sept. 21, 2004	David Barton		
Oct. 26, 2004	Michael Medved		
Feb. 24, 2005	J.C. Watts		
April 21, 2005	John Ashcroft		
Sept. 8, 2005	Cheri Pierson Yecke		

APPENDIX D

Fall Headcount Enrollment

1987-2013

Fall	Undergraduate	Graduate	Grand Total
2012	4390	2425	6815
2011	4340	2815	7155
2010	4201	2609	6810
2009	4098	2515	6613
2008	4188	2322	6510
2007	4154	2178	6332
2006	4048	2060	6108
2005	4136	1839	5975
2004	4067	1535	5602
2003	4074	1280	5354
2002	4104	1172	5276
2001	4008	1005	5013
2000	3828	837	4665
1999	3710	740	4450
1998	3631	689	4320
1997	3505	635	4140
1996	3550	537	4087
1995	3514	557	4071
1994	3455	564	4019
1993	3365	393	3758
1992	3248	433	3681
1991	3160	411	3571
1990	3195	360	3484
1989	3154	289	3443
1988	3080	302	3382
1987	2709	288	2997

ENDNOTES

Chapter 1

1. Craig Hlavaty, "47 Years Later, Whitman's Tower Shooting Still a Haunting Memory for Texans," *Houston Chronicle*, August 1, 2013, http://blog.chron.com/thetexican/2013/08/47-years-later-whitmans-tower-shooting-still-a-haunting-memory-for-texans/#14558101=0 (accessed June 2, 2014). Some tallies indicate 15 were killed, but they do not account for a man who died from his injuries later and an unborn child.

2. J. Stanley Marshall, *The Tumultuous Sixties: Campus Unrest and Student Life at a Southern University* (Tallahassee: Sentry Press, 2006).

3. David B. Burks, *The Christian Alternative for Business* (Dallas: Gospel Teachers Publications, 1978).

Chapter 2

1. David Burks, "Integrating Faith and Learning" (Inaugural address made at Harding University, Searcy, AR, September 18, 1987).

2. Nancy Austin and Tom Peters, *A Passion for Excellence: The Leadership Difference* (New York: Random House, 1985).

3. Alice Ann Kellar, "Leah Burks: From 'Country Girl' to First Lady," *Harding University Bulletin*, October 1987.

4. Russell P. Kropp, letter to author, November 12, 1987.

5. George Tipps, letter to author, November 10, 1987.

6. David Burks, "Harding University Strategic Planning Report" (report presented to the Harding University Board of Trustees, Searcy, AR, November 1987).

Chapter 3

1. Harding University, *Harding University Catalog* (Searcy, Harding Press, 2014), under "Harding University: Our History," http://harding.catalog.acalog.com/content.php?catoid=23&navoid=1492 (accessed June 2, 2014).

2. David Burks, ed., *Against the Grain: The Mission of Harding University* (Searcy: Harding University, 1998), 20.

3. Ibid., 24.

4. L. C. Sears, *For Freedom: The Biography of John Nelson Armstrong* (Austin: Sweet Publishing Company, 1969).

5. Ibid., 115.

6. Ibid., 116.

7. Harding University, *Harding University Catalog* (Searcy, Harding Press, 1990).

8. Burks, *Against the Grain*.

9. David Burks, From the President, *Harding Magazine*, Winter 2000.

10. David Burks, "Harding University 2007-2008 Strategic Planning Report" (report presented to the Harding University Board of Trustees, Searcy, AR, 2008).

11. Bruce D. McLarty, *Embracing the Mission* (Searcy, Harding Press, 2010).

12. David Burks, "Statement from the President Regarding a Controversial Web Site" (announcement in Harding University chapel, Searcy, AR, March 3, 2011).

Chapter 4

1. 2 Cor. 2:14-6:1 (New International Version).

2. Prentice Meador, "Near to the Heart of God when I Grieve" (keynote lecture at Harding University annual Bible lectureship, Searcy, AR, October 1, 2007).

3. Bruce McLarty, "2013 Report of the President" (report presented to the Harding University Board of Trustees, Searcy, AR, October 2013), 24.

4. Alice Ann Kellar, "The Uganda Team," *Harding Magazine*, Fall 1995.

5. Bruce McLarty, "2013 Report of the President," 23.

6. David Burks, From the President, *Harding Magazine*, Spring 2006.

Chapter 5

1. Harding University, <u>Neale Pryor.</u>

2. Harding University, <u>Howard Wright.</u>

3. Harding University, <u>Mike Huckabee.</u>

Chapter 6

1. David Burks, "The Development of Model Faculty Recruitment and Retention Programs for Selected Senior Colleges Supported by Churches of Christ" (Ph.D. dissertation, Florida State University, 1974).

2. Howard Norton, letter to the author, April 7, 2014.

3. Neale Pryor, "Passing the Torch," *Harding Magazine*, Winter 2000.

Chapter 7

1. Jeff Hopper, letter to author, January 5, 2014.

2. Tom Howard, "Harding on the Aegean," *Harding Magazine*, Spring 1995.

3. Paul Haynie and Kayla Haynie, "A Taste of Merry Olde England," *Harding Magazine*, Spring 1996.

4. Bill Richardson, "Chile has it All," *Harding Magazine*, Winter 2003.

Chapter 8

1. Phillip Tucker, "Good Show, Iron Lady," *Harding Magazine*, Summer 1995.

2. Jamie Martin, "An Obligation to Lead," *Harding Magazine*, Summer 1997.

3. Ibid.

4. Ronald Reagan, *An American Life: The Autobiography* (New York: Simon and Schuster, 1990), 683.

5. David Burks, From the President, *Harding Magazine*, Winter 1999.

6. Condoleezza Rice, *Extraordinary, Ordinary People: A Memoir of Family* (New York: Crown Archetype, 2010).

7. Phillip Tucker, "Dan Quayle Flies High at Harding," *Harding Magazine*, Summer 1994.

8. Nicky Boyd, letter to the author, February 10, 2014.

Chapter 9

1. Larry Long, letter to the author, January 29, 2014.

2. David Burks, "Report of the President" (annual report presented to the Harding University Board of Trustees, Searcy, AR, October 1987-2013).

3. Bill Richardson, letter to the author, May 10, 2014.

4. David Burks, "Report of the President" (annual report presented to the Harding University Board of Trustees, Searcy, AR, October 2001-2013).

5. Evertt Huffard, letter to the author, June 10, 2014.

6. Tony Finley, letter to the author, June 5, 2014.

7. Caitlin Anderson, "A Shining Example of Hope: Remembering PA Student Lauren Bump," *PA Professional*, April 2014, http://www.nxtbook.com/nxtbooks/aapa/pa-professional_201404/index.php?startid=1#/33/OnePage (accessed July 7, 2014).

8. Julie Hixson-Wallace, letter to the author, June 1, 2014.

9. Ibid.

10. Mike McGalliard, letter to the author, May 10, 2014.

Chapter 10

1. David Burks, "1992 Report of the President" (report presented to the Harding University Board of Trustees, Searcy, AR, October 1992).

2. Mike Chalenburg, letter to the author, June 10, 2014.

3. Keith Cronk, letter to the author, June 20, 2014.

Chapter 11

1. Jimmy Huff, letter to the author, June 2014.

2. Michael Campbell, letter to the author, June 2014.

3. Steve Cloer, letter to the author, May 2014.

4. Editorial, *Arkansas Gazette*, July 22, 1990.

5. Charlie Walker, letter to the author, April 2014.

6. Ibid.

7. Terry Davis, letter to the author, May 2014.

8. Bryan Clifton, letter to the author, April 2014.

9. Jim Gowen, letter to the author, May 2014.

10. Wanise Lemmons, letter to the author, May 2014.

11. Phillip Tucker, "A Flood of Help," *Harding Magazine*, Winter 1994.

Chapter 12

1. Ronnie Huckeba, letter to the author, February 5, 2014.

2. Ibid.

3. Jeff Morgan, letter to the author, April 11, 2014.

4. Ibid.

5. Ibid.

6. "A Fitting End for a Confrontation at Harding," *Log Cabin Democrat*, January 18, 2006, http://thecabin.net/stories/011806/spo_0118060027.shtml (accessed July 29, 2014).

7. Kristen Celsor Johnson, "Hashtag Right Now," Facebook Note, posted March 15, 2014, https://www.facebook.com/notes/kristen-celsor/hashtag-right-now/766395350045734 (accessed July 29, 2014).

8. Meredith Fear, letter to the author, April 14, 2014.

9. Ibid.

10. Ibid.

11. Ibid.

12. Steve Guymon, letter to the author, April 7, 2014.

13. Greg Harris, letter to the author, July 7, 2014.

14. David Elliot, letter to the author, April 10, 2014.

15. Pat McGaha, letter to the author, May 30, 2014.

16. Ibid.

Chapter 13

1. Stephen Joel Trachtenberg and Tansy Howard Blumer, *Big Man on Campus: A University President Speaks out on Higher Education* (New York: Simon & Schuster, 2008).

2. Flavil Yeakley, memo to the author, November 2008.

3. Glenn Dillard, email to the author, January 21, 2014.

4. Ibid.

5. Ibid.

6. Ibid.

7. Ibid.

8. Scott Hannigan, letter to the author, Feb. 10, 2014.

Chapter 14

1. Matt. 6:19.

2. Matt. 6:33.

3. Mark 10:23.

4. Mark 10:29-30

5. Douglas M. Lawson, *Give to Live: How Giving Can Change Your Life* (La Jolla, California: ATLI, 1991), 130.

6. Ibid., 89.

7. Harding University, "Library Receives $1.6 Million Gift," *Harding University Bulletin*, April 1987.

8. Mike Williams, letter to the author, July 23, 2014.

Chapter 15

[No footnotes / endnotes]

Chapter 16

1. Trachtenberg, *Big Man on Campus*, 257.

2. David Burks, letter to the Harding University Board of Trustees, October 27, 2011.

3. Harding University, "Harding University Selects New President," November 1, 2012, http://www.harding.edu/president.html (accessed July 23, 2014).

4. Batsell Barrett Baxter, "Power of High Expectations," *Alternative*, April 1, 1982, 3.

Chapter 5 iTunes References

Harding University, "Singing – September 18 2009," iTunes, MPEG-4 Video File, https://itunes.apple.com/us/podcast/singing-september-18-2009/id448942491?i=122399896&mt=2 (accessed June 4, 2014).

Harding University, "Feb 22, Devo – Jim Bill McInteer," iTunes, MPEG-4 Video File, https://itunes.apple.com/us/podcast/feb-22-devo-jim-bill-mcinteer/ Harding University, "Struggles of the Faith with Gene Stallings, March 19, 2012," iTunes, MPEG-4 Video File, https://itunes.apple.com/us/podcast/struggles-faith-gene-stallings/id494395313?i=111821573&mt=2 (accessed June 4, 2014).

Harding University, "'Chicken Biscuit' with B. Chris Simpson, September 5, 2012," iTunes, MPEG-4 Video File, https://itunes.apple.com/us/podcast/chicken-biscuit-b.chris-simpson/id555004794?i=120265745&mt=2 (accessed June 4, 2014)

Harding University, "Student Lecture Series with Clay Smith, January 28, 2013," iTunes, MPEG-4 Video File, https://itunes.apple.com/us/podcast/student-lecture-series-clay/id596119507?i=130972057&mt=2 (accessed June 4, 2014).

Harding University, "A Conversation with Jim Bill McInteer About Harding, February 25, 2012", iTunes, MPEG-4 Video File, https://itunes.apple.com/us/podcast/conversation-jim-bill-mcinteer/id448942969?i=122400612&mt=2 (accessed June 4, 2014). Also see the four subsequent videos in the Spring 2009 – Harding University Chapel iTunes collection.

Harding University, "Willie Robertson, November 28, 2012," iTunes, MPEG-4 Video File, https://itunes.apple.com/us/podcast/willie-robertson-november/id555004794?i=125389009&mt=2 (accessed June 4, 2014).

Harding University, "The Christian Worldview with Monte Cox, October 7, 2011," iTunes, MPEG-4 Video File, https://itunes.apple.com/us/podcast/christian-worldview-monte/id460071442?i=100938251&mt=2 (accessed June 4, 2014).

Harding University, "Goals for New Year – Dr. David Burks, January 19, 2011," iTunes, MPEG-4 Video File, https://itunes.apple.com/us/podcast/goals-for-new-year-dr.-david/id448941146?i=95483612&mt=2 (accessed June 4, 2014); Harding University, "Belles and Beaux, April 11, 2013," iTunes, MPEG-4 Video

File, https://itunes.apple.com/us/podcast/belles-and-beaux-april-11-2013/id596119507?i=149714887&mt=2 (accessed June 4, 2014).

Google, "Dr. David Burks' (alleged) Freudian Slip-Up," YouTube, http://youtu.be/eAtGsjLtjW8 (accessed July 31, 2014).

BIBLIOGRAPHY

Austin, Nancy, and Tom Peters. *A Passion for Excellence: The Leadership Difference*. New York: Random House, 1985.

Burks, David, ed. *Against the Grain: The Mission of Harding University*. Searcy: Harding University, 1998.

Burks, David. *The Christian Alternative for Business*. Dallas: Gospel Teachers Publications, 1978.

Lawson, Douglas M. *Give to Live: How Giving Can Change Your Life*. La Jolla, California: ATLI, 1991.

Marshall, J. Stanley. *The Tumultuous Sixties: Campus Unrest and Student Life at a Southern University*. Tallahassee: Sentry Press, 2006.

Reagan, Ronald. *An American Life: The Autobiography*. New York: Simon and Schuster, 1990.

Rice, Condoleezza. *Extraordinary, Ordinary People: A Memoir of Family*. New York: Crown Archetype, 2010.

Sears, L. C. *For Freedom: The Biography of John Nelson Armstrong*. Austin: Sweet Publishing Company, 1969.

Trachtenberg, Stephen Joel and Tansy Howard Blumer. *Big Man on Campus: A University President Speaks out on Higher Education*. New York: Simon & Schuster, 2005.

NAME INDEX

340

Burks family, with David's sister, Karen, on a cruise – David & Leah

Bryan and Laura with their children – Emily & Chris' wedding

Stephen & Jeanne with their children – Marriage of David's dad & Maurice

Unveiling of the presidential portrait of David B. Burks